What Price Hollywood?

What Price Hollywood?

Gender and Sex in the Films of George Cukor

Elyce Rae Helford

UNIVERSITY PRESS OF KENTUCKY

Scholarly publisher for the Commonwealth,
serving Bellarmine University, Berea College, Centre College of Kentucky, Eastern Kentucky University, The Filson Historical Society, Georgetown College, Kentucky Historical Society, Kentucky State University, Morehead State University, Murray State University, Northern Kentucky University, Spalding University, Transylvania University, University of Kentucky, University of Louisville, University of Pikeville, and Western Kentucky University.

Editorial and Sales Offices: The University Press of Kentucky
663 South Limestone Street, Lexington, Kentucky 40508-4008
www.kentuckypress.com

Library of Congress Cataloging-in-Publication Data

Names: Helford, Elyce Rae, 1962– author.
Title: What price Hollywood? : gender and sex in the films of George Cukor / Elyce Rae Helford.
Description: Lexington : The University Press of Kentucky, 2020. | Includes bibliographical references and index.
Identifiers: LCCN 2020004184 | ISBN 9780813179292 (hardcover) | ISBN 9780813179315 (pdf) | ISBN 9780813179322 (epub)
Subjects: LCSH: Cukor, George, 1899–1983—Criticism and interpretation. | Sex in motion pictures. | Sex role in motion pictures.
Classification: LCC PN1998.3.C8 H45 2020 | DDC 791.430233092—dc23
LC record available at https://lccn.loc.gov/2020004184
ISBN 978-0-8131-9702-9 (pbk. : alk. paper)

This book is printed on acid-free paper meeting the requirements of the American National Standard for Permanence in Paper for Printed Library Materials.

Manufactured in the United States of America.

Member of the Association of University Presses

Heaven knows, everyone has his limitations. But why make them any narrower than they are?

George Cukor

Contents

Introduction

In 2015, as I was drafting this book, I was surprised and delighted to see the publication of Murray Pomerance and R. Barton Palmer's edited collection, *George Cukor: Hollywood Master.* I cheered the new volume on this inadequately studied director, even as I feared my own book would be made redundant. Instead, as I read, I found engaging new perspectives, reinforcement of some of my own thoughts, and encouragement to continue my project. Cukor's work deserves far more than scholarly critics have given it to date. I say this neither to celebrate the director as some exceptional auteur deserving praise nor, by contrast, to applaud his prolific output. Instead, through consideration of Cukor's work within its era and today, we can learn much about American popular culture, the Hollywood film industry, multifaceted social issues, and ourselves as viewers, critics, and/or fans.

Scholarly books on Hollywood director George Cukor have, apart from the Pomerance and Palmer collection, largely consisted of biographies and filmographies that offer limited sustained close work with specific films. Reasoning for this often involves Cukor's seeming enjoyment in proclaiming that he was not an auteur.[1] He did not write scripts, emphasize a sustained visual style, or address a group of unified themes. He worked in multiple genres, with the notable exception of the crime picture. Cukor claimed he had little taste for filmic violence, but labels such as "woman's director" and "actor's director" certainly had an impact on his options. Given that the majority of the films he directed are centered in and at the edges of genres such as drawing-room comedy, melodrama, and romantic comedy, we may not find it surprising that gender and sexuality are central to his films. Because Cukor's output blossomed during the height of the Hollywood studio system, we should similarly not be surprised that issues of class and ethnicity also inflect the content, form, and style of his pictures. Beyond such issues as genre and social context, we can perhaps best understand Cukor's oeuvre as a collective portrait of the options and limitations faced by a gay second-generation Jewish American man determined to survive and thrive in the Hollywood system.

The son of middle-class Hungarian-Jewish immigrants, Cukor became fascinated with the theater before moving to Hollywood to become a speech coach in the early days of the sound era. Before he died in 1983, he had become the noted director of nearly fifty films over a fifty-year period (1931–1981). He found steady success, through Hollywood's golden age and somewhat beyond, including a Best Director Oscar in 1964 for *My Fair Lady.* Cukor was often called an "actor's director" because he labored intimately to get his stars to deliver superlative performances, from those of James Stewart to Judy Holliday and from Spencer Tracy to Judy Garland. Cukor was also the go-to director for adapting Broadway plays, such as *The Women* (1939) and *Born Yesterday* (1950). His remakes of older or foreign films, including *A Woman's Face* (1942), *Gaslight* (1944), and *Rich and Famous* (1981), have long been praised as well.

In fact, despite the limited number of official accolades presented to the prolific Cukor, he has been lauded heartily by those who have devoted books to him. To Emanuel Levy, Cukor is the "Master of Elegance," for example, and to Pomerance and Palmer, he is more generally a "Hollywood Master."[2] The latter scholars argue, "Cukor was much more than a man of the theater who happened to spend most of his career making films. His accomplishments as a filmmaker deserve more than the only occasional and spotty appreciation they have hitherto received from academic film critics."[3] I share this assessment, and the following pages are an effort to add new depth to studies of the work of Cukor, in this case with a particular investment in issues of gender and sexuality.

Most directly relevant to my interests is a second label applied to Cukor in his own time: "woman's director." On the positive side, this identifier points to his successful work on pictures with strong female leads and his ability to handle "difficult" (i.e., determined, independent) actresses, from Katharine Hepburn to Marilyn Monroe. Equally, however, "woman's director" was and is a homophobic slur. It branded Cukor in his time as suited only to female-centered genres, such as the woman's film (melodrama) and romantic comedy.

Sophia Loren in a platinum wig to play a heartthrob of the Old West in the comic *Heller in Pink Tights* (1960), between scenes with "woman's director" George Cukor.

The impact of this verdict is well exemplified by two formative experiences in Cukor's early directing career. First, in Cukor's *Sylvia Scarlett* (1935), Katharine Hepburn performs much of the movie in drag as "Sylvester." Our protagonist adventures in petty crime and traveling performance until s/he falls for a bohemian artist who claims to experience a "queer feeling" in Sylvester's company. The film was an overtly campy romp with poignant notes, but it was a failure with critics and at the box office. Producer Pandro S. Berman directly attacked Cukor for the terrible final product and was determined never to work with him again. This immediately led Cukor to rethink his position. He became determined to rein in impulses to take risks in filmmaking, particularly related to gender and sexuality in content. He would adhere to the formula of classic Hollywood (including its heteronormativity and homophobia) more strictly from then on, preferring the comforts of stability and security to the dangerous pleasures of challenge and controversy. Above all, he wanted to be a Hollywood success story.

Nevertheless, even relatively tame productions proved complex, as Cukor learned when he experienced a worse tragedy while directing another picture that featured a Scarlett: *Gone with the Wind* (1939). Cukor was well into shooting the picture when he was taken off the assignment, allegedly because Clark Gable felt Cukor was weakening the picture by giving too much attention to Vivien Leigh. Victor Fleming—director of many an action picture—was brought in to replace Cukor. Then, with several of Cukor's filmed scenes making it into the final cut (such as Scarlett dancing in her widow's garb), Fleming won the 1939 Academy Award for Best Direction of a Motion Picture. Being so unceremoniously removed from this major, award-winning picture was deeply humiliating to Cukor; the painful lesson, like the poor response to *Sylvia Scarlett,* stayed with him for the rest of his career. Together, these examples illustrate well how the sexism and homophobia of Hollywood validated the "woman's director" tag that also stuck to him throughout his years.

Despite such gendered attacks on his directing ability, however, Cukor did go on to achieve great success. If he was pigeonholed, he was appreciated within that narrow sphere. Moreover, even if he had to temper his tone and yield to some Hollywood demands, he could—and would—continue to explore gender and sexuality in diverse and compelling ways across his works. He would celebrate powerful actresses, decry hypermasculine norms, bend genre, and dabble in camp more than a few times. He would even turn the system back on itself through Hollywood cautionary tales, genre blending, and reversals of gender expectations. With such approaches in mind, this book posits that through investigation of form, method, style, and content within Cukor's films we can learn a great deal about Hollywood history and gender/sexual politics. We can also explore how related social and identity issues such as ethnicity and class inflect presentations and considerations of gender and sexuality. In addition, we can interrogate our own pleasures and practices as contemporary viewers, scholars, and/or fans.

Presuming that my reasoning for exploring gender and sexuality in Cukor's films persuades, next I must explain my method. This book's approach involves close readings of small clusters of Cukor films through a queered, intersectional feminist lens. This means chapters are best understood as critical case studies, sometimes overlapping in work with several key films in differing contexts. For each chapter, I take what I consider the most appropriate critical or theoretical perspective for the subject matter. Chapters range widely in terms of focus and reading strategies, but all attend to gender-related patterns I find in Cukor films—both within and across eras.

I also engage with biography as relevant. For example, the roles of class and ethnicity in Cukor's life and work are mentioned but not addressed in a sustained manner in Cukor studies. These issues, I find, are important to the study of Cukor films, combined with gender and sexuality. Cukor is racially identifiable as what had only been relatively recently coined as "white" in America, as well as "male" and "gay," but he was also of middle-class Hungarian Jewish heritage. Although he rarely spoke of his religion or class background—feeling they were private matters—others did. When he was younger, he faced antisemitism in New York, but this was less true in Hollywood, with predominantly Jewish moguls running the studios. Although his parents came over at the turn of the century—as did 2.5 million Eastern European Jews—Cukor was second-generation and considered himself assimilated, unlike the immigrant Jews who created Hollywood. Unlike Samuel Goldwyn (born Schmuel Gelbfisz), for instance, he was Germanic not Slavic, and his family did not struggle for survival. Cukor was ambitious, but not clawing and impatient like Goldwyn, who fought his way up from glove salesman into film production with Jesse Lasky and Cecil B. DeMille.[4] Cukor did not tend to fraternize with these Eastern European Jews. He saw them as coarse and uncouth—even though biographies show that Cukor himself could swear and tell a crass joke with the worst of them.

In addition, Cukor felt the pressure to fit in among Hollywood's beautiful elite, decrying his chubbiness, near-sightedness that necessitated glasses, and bookish appearance.[5] "*Ugly* is the word that frequently cropped up, unprompted" from friends, and Cukor nicknamed himself "the little ogre" in youth.[6] That Cukor and producer David O. Selznick were often mistaken for one another, despite the latter being five inches taller than Cukor and not as stout, can be seen as adding a Jewish element to his self-doubt over looks.[7] Patrick McGilligan laments this tendency, one that let up only in his late years, when he was slimmer and less concerned about flamboyancy. "For too many years," McGilligan declares, Cukor decried his looks and "suffered needlessly from looking more Jewish (in his own eyes) than he really was."[8]

To make up for his inadequate appearance within the Hollywood context and among the young gay actors with whom he had fleeting and primarily sexual rather than emotional affairs, Cukor indulged in such pretensions as "frequent changes of clothing, regular manicures, the habitual application of perfumes and ointments, [and] calculated cleanliness."[9] In addition, he had affectations of class. Cukor favored elegant dinner parties with well-spoken elite friends over the wild revelries of Cole Porter and his naked pool parties for young gay men across town. Cukor admired the wealthy, and he tended toward British and European style. He loved the Swedish and was an overt Anglophile; he treasured the company of English Hollywood royalty, such as Laurence Olivier and Vivien Leigh, and used British spelling and salutations in his personal correspondence.[10]

As several chapters within the book reveal, Cukor's background and preferences bear directly on choices he made as a director. Furthermore, they inflect his consideration and presentation of gender and sexuality, sometimes in openly contradictory fashion, from Cinderella stories that celebrate wealth and beauty to tragicomic renderings of alcoholics in Hollywood and from joyful portrayals of defiant women to conflicted depictions of crass "ethnic" females.

To begin my inquiries, I focus on white, privileged women—the most obvious and frequently represented subject within Cukor films and criticism. Rather than an overview of his work with major female stars or his representations of upper-class white feminine norms, chapter 1 offers an exploration of women's friendships. Such a focus allows me to attend to both the expected emphasis on heteronormative romance as well as the bonds between women that are more tangential to the classic Hollywood film. I offer close readings centered primarily on character and narrative in *Girls About Town* (1931), *Our Betters* (1932), *The Women* (1939), and *Rich and Famous* (1981), thus studying representations of female friendship from the beginning to the end of Cukor's career. The chapter concludes with a coda on *The Chapman Report* (1962), a film about women's sex lives that forecloses almost entirely the possibility of friendship between women.

Chapter 2 shifts focus from content to production context as it explores methods and impacts of collaboration between Cukor and Katharine Hepburn. The ten films the duo made together span much of Cukor's career, but the chapter centers on three key pictures: *The Philadelphia Story* (1940), *Adam's Rib* (1949), and *Love Among the Ruins* (1975). Examined together, this trio of films illustrates the professional bond between director and actor, focusing in particular on how the Cukor/Hepburn alliance utilized a feminist understanding of audience reception, where gendered chastisement of the characters Hepburn plays allows for celebration of her iconoclastic stature as a female Hollywood star.

Chapter 3 addresses the subject of tone and genre and their impact on gender within the course of a highly productive decade in Cukor's career. *The Women* (1939), *Susan and God* (1940), and *Edward, My Son* (1949) are all films based on plays originally written as satire or parody. They become more complicated productions when adapted for film and directed by "actor's director" Cukor. By emphasizing earnest and dramatic, heavily gender-normative portrayals, the director shifts both the tone and the impact of the satirical films. In *The Women,* the serious, sympathetic central character detracts from the biting social critique of wealthy, catty wives. *Susan and God* suffers even more jarring shifts—particularly from romantic comedy to melodrama—and holds the wife character to account for the confines of conventional marriage, excising any potential social critique. Finally, *Edward, My Son,* one of Cukor's major and more interesting failures, yields its satirical edge to the questionable casting and directing of its hypermasculine lead.

The next two chapters interrogate masculinity, first through analysis of the figure of the male alcoholic in multiple Cukor films, and then through study of a gender countertype based on the East European Jewish ideal of the gentle, creative man. Hollywood in general and

Cukor's films in particular feature many a drunk. These include female characters—for example, aging model Mary Ashton (Ann Dvorak) in *A Life of Her Own* (1950) and the mother figures of *Rockabye* (1932), *Zaza* (1938), and *Edward, My Son* (1948)—but Cukor's most developed alcoholics are white men of privileged class who are portrayed as failing to live up to gendered social expectations. I begin chapter 4 with an emphasis on how the cause and effects of alcoholism in male characters are downplayed in romantic comedies, through close readings of *Susan and God* (1940) and *The Philadelphia Story* (1940). I then consider the specific figure of the Hollywood alcoholic through actor and director characters in *What Price Hollywood?* (1932), *Dinner at Eight* (1933), and *A Star Is Born* (1954). These performances show the cost of success for male celebrities and the impact of social demands on the individual. Maintaining youthfulness, audience favor, and masculine virility depletes the men in these films, and their experience of failure following high accomplishment leads to them desperation and self-destruction.

Chapter 5 illustrates an alternative to the hypermale ego by attending to more sensitive, creative male characters within Cukor's oeuvre through the concept of *Edelkayt*, as discussed in the work of Daniel Boyarin. The chapter begins with a transition into the subject through focus on one final alcoholic, Ned Seton in *Holiday* (1938). The tragic fate of the character exemplifies the importance of challenging hypermasculine norms by exploring alternatives that can offer a potential queer feminist countertype. To explore this figure, I discuss Cukor's own identity within Hollywood alongside several of his most complex masculine characters: Macaulay "Mike" Connor in *The Philadelphia Story* (1940) and Paul Verrall in *Born Yesterday* (1950).

The next pair of chapters explore the concept of gender performativity and issue of queerness in Cukor films and audience reception. Chapter 6 attends to a seemingly disparate trio of films, the romantic adventure *Sylvia Scarlett* (1935), the theatrical Western *Heller in Pink Tights* (1950), and the melodrama-with-music *A Star Is Born* (1954). In each film, the female protagonist appears in drag. While drag is used for a different purpose and with a different impact in each film, all three illustrate the concept of gender-as-performance as it bends but does not break classic Hollywood cinematic traditions. Chapter 7 shifts from genderqueer imagery to queer reading strategies through study of transgressive moments in Cukor's three musical comedies: *Les Girls* (1957), *Let's Make*

Love (1960), and *My Fair Lady* (1964). In each, I enact close work with queer conceptualizations of the Hollywood musical, centering on specific scenes that disrupt the heteronormative flow of the narratives.

The final chapters of the book build on areas of consideration in the previous chapters to provide a more fully intersectional approach, directly attentive to issues of ethnicity, race, and nation. In chapter 8, I explore Cukor's wartime and postwar handling of noir style and content in *A Woman's Face* (1941), *Keeper of the Flame* (1942), *Gaslight* (1944), and *A Double Life* (1947). Through focus on subjects from fascism to blackface, the chapter explores the intersection of gender, race, and national anxiety central to World War II–era Hollywood aesthetics.

Finally, in chapter 9, I turn to the subject of gender and ethnic assimilation in Cukor's films during the 1950s, the last years in which the director would find regular work. Within a communist-baiting era heading into the long Cold War, Hollywood films of the 1950s suppressed, but nonetheless (or necessarily) addressed, familiar fears in new ways, from attention to a postwar version of melting-pot politics to modernized versions of gender roles for "ethnic" women. I consider these subjects across Cukor's most successful films of the decade, including two urban romantic comedies, an Indian epic, and an Italian immigrant melodrama in a western setting: *Born Yesterday* (1950), *It Should Happen to You* (1952), *Bhowani Junction* (1956), and *Wild Is the Wind* (1957).

Together, these chapters and the more than twenty-five films they explore through a variety of critical lenses and contexts help us to interrogate the limitations and the potentialities of Hollywood film. They also, I hope, reflect the pleasure of feminist and queer critical endeavors in Hollywood film studies.

1

The Woman's Director and Women's Friendships

While George Cukor is known for his focus on female characters and work with major and sometimes "difficult" female stars, he is less known for his interrogation of women's friendships. Regardless of genre, heteronormative romance is central to most Cukor films, as it is for much of classical Hollywood cinema. This is true even when the film's content is at odds with its description. The trailer for *The Women* (1939), for example, describes a film that features over one hundred women and not a single man as "all about men!" This is the heteronormative imperative writ large, but although the women of *The Women* are obsessed with men, they have strong bonds with other women, too. Whether devoted or divisive, the intensity of female relationships in *The Women* cannot be denied.

The importance of female friendships within Hollywood cinema is explained well by Karen Hollinger, who argues, "Because these films have the potential to affect their female audience so strongly, it is particularly important that we analyze closely both their modes of production and the response they attempt to elicit from their female viewers."[1] She begins her book-length study of female friendships in late twentieth-century Hollywood cinema by providing a historical overview of the origins of the contemporary female friendship film in the 1930s and 1940s woman's film. Here, Hollinger asserts, "The issues filmmakers deemed important to women . . . involved romance and domesticity, not female friendship."[2] I share with Hollinger the concern that early sound films, whether masochistic, conciliatory, or, in rare examples, resistant to social norms of female behavior, center almost exclusively on the lives of white heterosexual women of privileged class, depicting what Hollywood banked on being their central emotional concerns and pleasures. When friendships are presented in such films, they are constructed in relation to and almost always subordinated to heterosexual romance. We see within these friendships what Hollinger describes as "conflict between 'good' passive and 'bad' aggressive femininity" and "jealousy, envy, and competition for men." She thus concludes that the "primary legacy of these films seems to be a typically patriarchal championing of female devotion to husband and family."[3]

Nonetheless, diverse feminist approaches to Hollywood cinema—from Molly Haskell's 1974 study of images in *From Reverence to Rape: The Treatment of Women in the Movies* to Jackie Stacey's 1994 exploration of viewer/star identifications in *Star Gazing: Hollywood Cinema and Female Spectatorship*—illustrate scholars' awareness that prescriptive norms are not absolutes and that there may be within classic films or their audiences' responses a more complex presentation of women's lives and experiences.[4]

One issue many critical approaches contend with is an essentialism that champions a narrow range of feminine traits rather than considering the social construction of gender within an unequal cultural system. Feminist psychoanalytic approaches attempt to address this issue, as in Laura Mulvey's "Visual Pleasure and Narrative Pleasure" and extended in Mary Ann Doane's *The Desire to Desire: The Woman's Film of the 1940s*.[5] Their methods highlight film production and style rather than content (images) or viewer response, including such elements as the positioning of character and spectator before the patriarchal gaze of the camera, the (white) male director, and/or the film's male characters. Such emphasis redresses the limits of images of women criticism in particular, including that of Hollinger. Of course, there are limits to such methods as well, including ahistoricity, proposed cultural universality, and sexism in the theories of Sigmund Freud.

Whether or not female viewers absorb or resist the gender and sexual (as well as race and class) hegemony of Hollywood's presentation and reception of the construction of "woman," the films themselves are worthy of study as they articulate cultural tensions both within specific eras and within Hollywood representation. It is ostensibly true that "most of the women's films of the 1930s and 1940s that deal with female bonding end up centering on male-female relationships and reaffirming the female protagonists' dedication to men," thus denigrating female friendships and career ambitions, for example.[6] But is this all there is to say about this enormous group of films? We learn much by considering precisely *how* these films accomplish their conservative ends while entertaining and engaging certain female (and sometimes certain male) audiences. Indeed, between their opening moments and their happily-ever-afters, there are films that subvert some norms, even when they adhere to others.

Within this context, this chapter asks how Cukor's films address the subject of female friendship. A productive path is to explore the ways in which Cukor's films both adhere to and challenge traditional representations of white, privileged-class female friendship across the fifty years of his filmmaking career. With this goal in mind, the following pages provide comparative study of the central elements of four films that directly address the subject of female friendship: three from the 1930s—*Girls About Town* (1931), *Our Betters* (1933), *The Women* (1939)—and Cukor's final film, *Rich and Famous* (1981), a remake of the woman's film *Old Acquaintance* (1943). This focus necessarily means I devote a great deal of attention in this chapter to content rather than form (beyond genre). Once the characters, plots, and themes of the films under consideration are established, however, I do attend to such issues as the male and queer gaze as they inflect content and representation.

The two earliest films this chapter considers, though technically pre-Code, are Code-influenced productions, comedies about women whose business is men—or, more precisely, getting financial support from men without sexual entanglements. In *Girls About Town,* Wanda Howard (Kay Francis) and Marie Bailey (Lilyan Tashman), the former brunette and the latter blonde, are roommates who earn $500 a night in Depression-era New York, serving as flirtatious escorts for businessmen, aided by a procurer and friend, Jerry Chase (Alan Dinehart). The two share a happy upper-class domestic life, including overtones of intimacy in shared breakfasts in Marie's bed, brought by their doting African American maid and occasional accomplice, Hattie (Louise Beavers). They even exchange partners when they don't like their "dates," although this brings potential discord when Wanda comes to seek a way out of their lifestyle and into marriage while Marie does not. Yet tension never arises between the women. Marie supports Wanda's choice of dull, midwestern Jim Baker (Joel McCrea) so much that she auctions off her own fineries to get the money needed to get Wanda a divorce from her estranged husband (Anderson Lawler). In the end, although female friendship is represented as temporary (until marriage), it is also shown to be true and intimate.

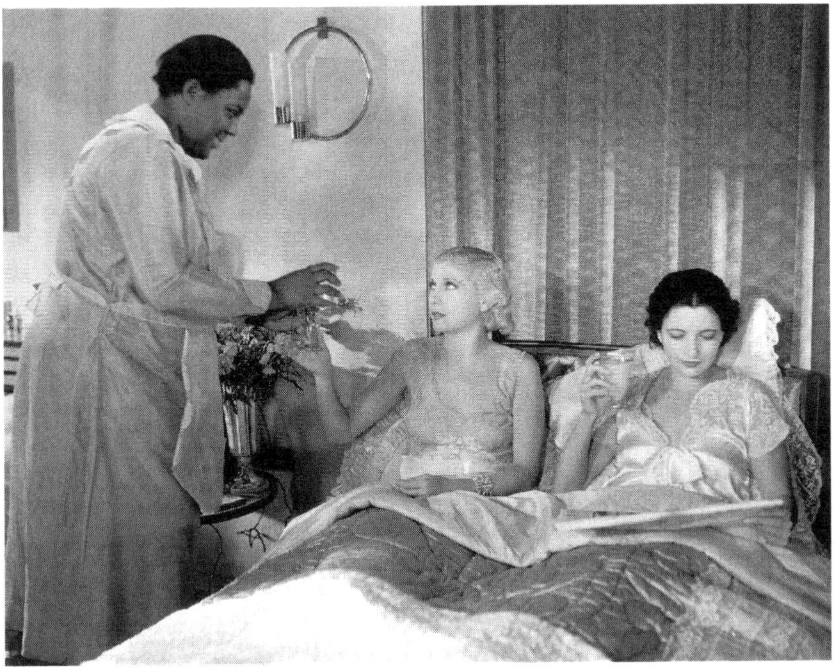

Bedsharing shows the closeness of Wanda (Kay Francis) and Marie (Lilyan Tashman) in *Girls About Town* (1931), shown here with maid Hattie (Louise Beavers). (Photofest)

Such sympathetic focus on gold-digging escorts would not last long into the 1930s, just as it does not last through the ending of the film, which makes *Girls About Town* an important touchstone for Cukor's later films dealing with female friendship.

Released only two years later, *Our Betters* differs significantly from *Girls About Town*. The film is an occasionally dramatic comedy of manners based on a play by Cukor's lifelong friend M. Somerset Maugham. The theme of female friendship threatened by male–female romantic entanglements is heightened through the multiple pairings in this ensemble piece; however, as in *Girls About Town*, female–female bonds are shown to be resilient and durable, particularly for the protagonist, Lady Pearl Grayston (Constance Bennett). The picture's ostensible subject, wealthy American women who married into the British aristocracy in the early part of the twentieth century, limited its appeal upon release and continues to restrict its interest for audiences and critics today. Nonetheless, *Our Betters* is notable for its scathing critique of upper-class interpersonal relationships and the deft touch of Cukor, who, argues Emanuel Levy, "softened Maugham's harsh attitude toward women" and set an affectionate tone that he would use again in *The Women* and, arguably, in his final film, *Rich and Famous*.[7]

Our Betters blends biting comedy with touches of melodrama. Unlike the earlier and latter films on which this chapter focuses, however, *Our Betters* is not centrally about female friendship. Protagonist Pearl is a wealthy American who comes to England to marry Lord George Grayston (Alan Mowbray), only to discover on her wedding day that his lordship only married her for her money. Moreover, he has no intention of stopping the love affair in which he was involved before their marriage. Pearl is at first naive and bereft, but a quick cut takes us past her mourning to the ultimate result of this catastrophe: strength of will sees Pearl become a wildly popular and frequently scandalous hostess for the disenchanted wealthy set. Like *Girls About Town,* friendship is at least partly centered in a shared pursuit of money. Missing is the gentle intimacy between women, replaced by a consideration of how competition displaces closeness—an issue also central to *The Women,* as we shall see.

The film takes place over the course of a weekend gathering at Pearl's luxurious home, featuring her closest companions. These include a somber princess (Phoebe Foster), estranged from the neglectful husband she still loves; crass American Arthur Fenwick (Minor Watson), who supports Pearl in the lifestyle she desires; and a monocled American sponger (Grant Mitchell), who feigns an upper-class British demeanor to attain the gossip he trades in. Most important to the subject of female friendship, there are also Pearl's innocent younger sister Bessie (Anita Louise), who has recently come to visit, and Pearl's closest friend the Duchess (Violet Kemble-Cooper), a wealthy widow who goes by the nickname of "Minnie" and attends the weekend gathering with her cherished Latin lover, gigolo Pepi D'Costa (Gilbert Roland).

Like *Girls About Town*'s Marie, Pearl is presented as self-confident and cynical. Pearl's most defining feature, key to her relationships with both women and men, is the tough shell she has grown by experience, built early on the poor advice given to her by her mother, which led her to marry a man who neglects her and quickly spends most of her fortune. We see this in her emphasis on superficiality, in a tendency to pose, to create formal entrances at every opportunity, and to wave about a long cigarette holder. Unlike Marie, who is self-absorbed but not selfish, Pearl is deeply cynical, which leads her to see friends, lovers, and financial backers as all of a kind. Her perspective is interestingly similar to maid Hattie's in *Girls About Town,* who says of men, "They's all alike; I don't care what color they is." Pearl yields to the demands of her surroundings, and the best way to support herself is through a "career" as an in-demand hostess. For Hattie, by contrast, the only route to financial stability is as a domestic.

The central conflict of *Our Betters* is less sentimental and even more raucous than that of *Girls About Town.* Pearl agrees to a tryst in the gazebo as part of an affair she is casually carrying on with Minnie's lover Pepi. She is not in love with him. Her motives seem more centered in ennui than desire or loneliness, and competition with Minnie rules out the kind of affection there is between Marie and Wanda. Certainly, Pearl has and wants no sexual relationship with her benefactor Arthur, and she harbors only ill-will toward her putative husband. Pursued and flattered by Pepi, she simply decides to yield, perhaps drawn to the excitement of risk-taking, showing her life to be even emptier than that of Marie and Wanda and illustrating the difference between romantic comedy and Maugham's comedy of manners. Interestingly, however, the resulting discovery has a greater impact on Pearl's relationship with women than men. She easily talks Arthur around to forgiveness and continued financial support, for example, knowing that "Men are trivial, foolish creatures. Kind hearts but no heads. And they're so vain, poor dears, they're so vain." The camera reinforces this emphasis by keeping Pearl and Pepi's lovemaking entirely off-screen. Whenever we see the two together in the film, Pearl is rebuffing Pepi's advances—at times because he clings, but at other times to maintain her image. Pearl's relationships with Bessie and Minnie are revealed to be her greater concerns despite her indiscretion, and they require quite different handling but for somewhat similar reasons. Above all, Pearl must be able to continue in her lifestyle, which requires protection of her self-image as well as her reputation, and she knows women are most likely to do her damage. Yet cynicism does yield to sentiment at times.

Pearl has shown Bessie the best of London life, excitement and spectacle beyond her wildest dreams for a girl who, like Pearl, hails from small town USA. She actively guides Bessie toward a more successful version of her own life, encouraging her to reject her former all-American middle-class beau, Fleming Harvey (Charles Starrett), and marry Lord Harry

Bleane (Hugh Sinclair), who claims to love her though Bessie does not return his ardor. Nor, however, does Bessie seem to love Fleming as she once did, having been dazzled by the wealth and splendor to which she has been led. The sisterly camaraderie and the dreamlike illusion of wealthy life in London become nightmare when Bessie learns of Pearl's "indiscretion" with Pepi. "You fill me with shame and disgust," Bessie snaps, assuming Pearl need not take any more money from Arthur, whom she treats so cruelly. Pearl displays anger for the first time in the film, stating plainly that her husband, Lord Grayston, spent most of her money early in their estranged marriage. Then she explains the facts of her world to innocent, judgmental Bessie, her voice rising to a fevered pitch by the end of her speech: "I've made myself the fashion. I've got power. I've got influence. But everything I've got—my success, my reputation, my notoriety—I've bought it, bought it, bought it!" From this uncharacteristic fury that shows how troubled she is by Bessie's attack, Pearl quickly shifts back to the role of older sister and mentor, advising Bessie to be "philosophical"—about love, marriage, and even the tryst with Pepi. Bessie cannot muster the slightest sympathy. She calls Pearl "cheap and common and sordid" before storming off, intending never to see her sister again.

The value of Bessie's affection appears clearly in Pearl's response. She cannot immediately return to her posture of elegant aloofness. As Bessie departs, the camera lingers on Pearl, who faces away from her sister but toward the viewer. She closes her eyes and drops her head, clenches a fist around her ever-present cigarette, and then tightens her face against tears. This reaction is unique in the film, diverging from the biting comic tone to melodrama, continued in Pearl's next step, which is asking Lord Bleane to break off his engagement to Bessie. "I've hardened," says Pearl, a tremor of both regret and shame in her voice as well as her posture as she wipes away a tear. Bitterness and self-recrimination that are no part of *Girls About Town* simmer in *Our Betters* and loom even larger in Cukor's later woman's films.

Coming up short of wandering too far into a depiction of self-loathing that would champion Bessie's conventionality over Pearl's modern if cynical coping strategies, the film regains its comedic footing without giving way to romance as it shifts to what Pearl is going to do about Minnie. If Bessie's judgment causes Pearl some self-doubt, she quickly recovers. She does what she can to ensure her sister will be happy in traditional domesticity, but she rejects it for herself. Instead, she focuses on reputation and social connections, central to her world and worldview. Her wit and Bennett's confident performance shifts potential pity to admiration—or at least comedic pleasure. "I never mind scandal," Pearl declares, "but I don't expose myself to ridicule if I can help it." In short, she must keep Minnie and Pepi from leaving before the weekend is over. Accomplishing this would cause any attempt at gossip to fall flat. This endeavor drives the film to its conclusion, with Bessie and her concerns removed from the action.

Pearl has already done exactly the opposite of what viewers might expect, thwarting sexism in her moment of shame before Bessie. She sleeps in late and says nothing about the affair with Pepi, while she ensures behind the scenes that there is no car to take the Duchess to the train station. Minnie will have to suffer the humiliation of the donkey cart if she wants to leave. Her friend is determined, however, so Pearl must go further. Rather than showing the slightest sign of contrition, she insists that Minnie speak to her if she wants the cart for her escape. When Minnie acquiesces, Pearl accuses her of "not playing the game" the previous day by getting Arthur to discover Pearl and Pepi in the gazebo once she knew what was going on. To forge a reunion with Minnie, she then shifts from accusation to invitation to the dinner party she is giving that night for even greater members of London nobility. She knows Minnie is as much a social climber as she. However, when this does not produce the desired result, Pearl at last addresses the subject of Pepi, posing him as a man who has come between them. She makes clear that Pepi means nothing to her, and then claims she is actually working on getting Pepi a job, something Minnie has long sought for her philandering beau. Finally, Pearl scrambles to finagle a deciding coup to woo Minnie back: she invites the talk of their social set to her home, dancing instructor Ernest (Tyrell Davis). This coiffed and made-up dandy is vital to the scene, which illustrates Pearl's skills and status as it displaces Pepi with a desexualized pansy figure. In the final moments of the film, Ernest gives Minnie a farcical tango lesson that mimics intimacy while Pearl and Pepi look on indulgently . . . and then suggestively at one another.

In all the maneuvering Pearl must do to return everything to rights for the film's happy ending, the most significant feature is the difference between the film's romantic reunions and the female friendships. Once she receives the letter ending their engagement from Lord Bleane, Bessie

Pearl (Constance Bennett) plays the victim with Minnie (Violet Kemble-Cooper) in *Our Betters* (1933), but their friendship is central to the film. (Photofest)

quickly reconciles with the affable Fleming and plans to return immediately to America. Not love but heteronormativity governs her ultimate actions. Meanwhile, Minnie not only forgives Pepi, but the gigolo deftly blackmails her into marriage, to include a new car and a shared bankbook. And Pearl, playing martyr, manages to make Arthur more sympathetic to her than ever while potentially enabling a continued liaison with Pepi. All of this is done in relatively perfunctory style, evoking far less emotion than the severing of affections between Pearl and Bessie. Moreover, regaining Minnie's friendship is the task that requires the most effort and finesse, and their reunion caps the film. As Cukor critic Carlos Clarens concludes, "Much of the delight in this cruel, brittle comedy derives from the suggestion that, behind all the backbiting and bitchiness, a genuine, if torturous affection can exist between these women."[8] While this may overstate the relationship, the comedy rests not on romance, but on the women's continued relations.

"Backbiting and bitchiness" describes *The Women* even better than *Our Betters.* With its cast of well over one hundred women—including a bevy of central female stars of the day, its blending of melodrama and comedy, and its focus on multiple female friendships, *The Women* provides a particularly contentious proving ground for theories about the woman's film and the issue of female bonding. That the film was a sort of consolation prize after Cukor lost *Gone with the Wind* (1939) also speaks to the connection of these issues to the label of "woman's director."

Through its tagline—"It's All About Men!"—and setting in privileged-class domestic spaces and female-oriented public settings (e.g., beauty salon, perfume counter, fashion show), this adaptation by Anita Loos of a play by Clare Booth Luce simultaneously illustrates the vitality and decries the treachery of female friendships. Through a menagerie of opening credits, *The Women* classifies its female characters as predator or prey and as domestic or wild animals. Gender-inflected binary oppositions operate from start to finish in *The Women,* from virgin/whore and wife/old maid to comfortably privileged versus graspingly working class. Hence, it is not surprising that Clarens declares that *Our Betters* offers "interplay [that is] more concise and intricate" through characterization that is "much more subtle" than that of *The Women.*[9] Despite these just assertions, however, there are varied female bonds and same-sex alliances worthy of close reading for their social commentary in the early Code era.

The Women tells the story of Mrs. Stephen (Mary) Haines (Norma Shearer), a woman married to a wealthy "Adonis" of a businessman and raising, with ample domestic help, their precocious daughter, Little Mary (Virginia Weidler). The central conflict for our gentle, amiable protagonist comes when she discovers—through the meddling of her gossipy best friend/cousin Sylvia Fowler (Rosalind Russell)—that Stephen is cheating on her with hard-nosed, gold-digging salesgirl Crystal Allen (Joan Crawford). As Mary tries to chart the best path to peace and stability for herself and her daughter, female family and friends all offer their opinions. (Servants even comment with sisterly supportiveness—aware of their vastly different class status—below stairs.) Mary first decides to take an ocean voyage with her wise, old-fashioned owl of a mother in order to give her husband time to get over his infatuation and return to loving family life. When her absence fails to "cure" Stephen, Mary decides to keep her pride rather than her philandering spouse, much against her mother's advice that what matters most is where a couple ends up, not the bumps along the way. That her "wisdom" is of a former generation and inappropriate for our heroine seems evident if we note, along with Maureen Turim, that "Mary's mother represents the strength of self-contained solitude. . . . Yet her strength has cost her. She has no women friends, no feminist interaction with women."[10]

The setting shifts to a dude ranch with a boisterous, hard-drinking, working-class caretaker (Marjorie Main) in Reno, Nevada. She functions as a practical and fun-loving mother substitute for the film's second act. She tells of her own ill-fated love for a red-headed man and keeps busy with chores and a nip from the jug. Mary and other disenchanted wives attain residency in Reno to speed their divorce proceedings. Here, Mary makes new female friends and reunites with familiar faces as well, including lamb-like Peggy (Joan Fontaine), who decides to divorce her beloved husband, Johnny, when he refuses to let her spend her own money to aid their finances, and Sylvia, who is shocked to find her husband suddenly wants a divorce. Once Mary does attain her own divorce, however, she is disappointed to find that rather than begging her to come back, Stephen has married Crystal. Time passes, and in the final act only a slip of the lip by Little Mary lets Mary know Stephen is unhappily attached and still loves her just as much as she loves him. We also learn that Crystal is already cheating on him. Mary can now come to the rescue, having suffered lonely pridefulness long enough to welcome the opportunity to fight for her man. Active competition with Crystal is symbolized by Mary "growing claws" painted "jungle red." She will now enter the fray, becoming predator rather than prey, finding agency only against other women.

Sylvia, meanwhile, has become Crystal's best friend after learning Mary has unknowingly befriended Miriam Aarons (Paulette Goddard), the young divorcée for whom Sylvia's husband, Howard, left her. Miriam is arguably wiser than the rest, coming from a more middle-class background and having learned through the loss of the one man she loved how to play the romance game in this "gilded asphalt jungle."[11] Miriam offers a more sincere friendship to Mary than Sylvia can provide Crystal, for both of the latter are too self-absorbed. Nonetheless, the film does not end with a focus on friendship. Instead, after some effective scheming that puts an end to the Stephen/Crystal relationship, *The Women* concludes with Mary rushing up a flight of stairs to forgive her Adonis, who waits just out of shot. Her arms are outstretched as she faces the camera and calls his name, voice quivering with melodramatic effusiveness.

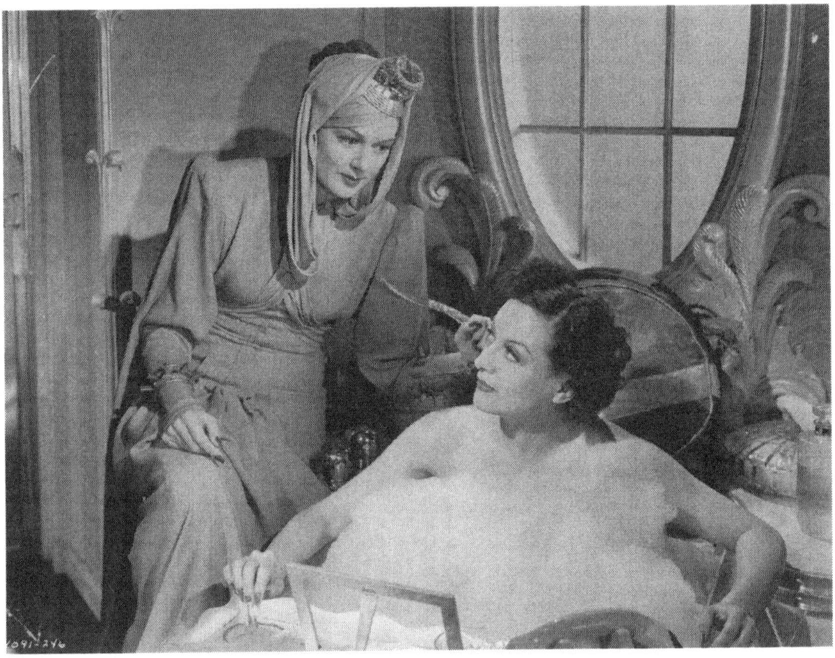

Sylvia (Rosalind Russell) befriends social-climbing homewrecker Crystal (Joan Crawford) as petty revenge against former friends in *The Women* (1939).

A superficial reading of *The Women* posits that female friendships are mostly temporary or strategic, and always of less importance than attaining and keeping a man. We may judge women for this or not, as befits our perspective. Certainly, both Luce and Loos intend a heavy dose of satire in their scripts. In the chess game of *The Women,* female friends serve primarily as pawns who enable or thwart a queen in her attempts to claim the king. Sylvia claims special closeness with Mary, but she is more often gossiping with brainless and fecund "cow" Edith (Phyllis Povah) than showing true fondness or sympathy for Mary. When Sylvia abandons Mary for social-climbing, hard-as-nails Crystal, it is both a form of petty revenge and a way to get better gossip. Then there are the Reno women, including Miriam and Flora, the Countess de Lave. While Miriam laments having let her first lover get away, the elderly Flora has turned love into an absurdity, marrying ill-advisedly and often, using wealth attained at the death of her first husband, the Count, to lure each new husband. Leaving *Girls About Town* far behind in its innocence, there are multiple similarities between *The Women* and *Our Betters,* including the duplicity of ambitious women (Pearl and Crystal), wealthy older women who "buy" their men (Minnie and Flora), and the faithlessness of these bought men (Buck and Pepi).

The significance of such similarities becomes even clearer when we bring *The Women* and *Our Betters* into conversation with *Rich and Famous,* a film produced nearly five decades after the earlier two but featuring portrayals of female friendship with many similarities in style. At first glance, the three films seem to share only a few surface features. The main characters in all three films are rich and involved in competitive relationships with other women related to broken marriages. We do see career women across the years; although, today, we would not use such a label for Pearl, a scandalous hostess living on men's money. Moreover, while the other two films do both feature professional writers, *The Women*'s Nancy Blake (Florence Nash) is a secondary character, as is gossip columnist Dolly Dupuyster (Hedda Hopper). By contrast, as a film made after the height of the second wave of the women's movement, *Rich and Famous* can offer more: a friendship dyad composed of two strong, mature women with vocations beyond wife and mother—though not beyond cattiness. Liz Hamilton (Jacqueline Bisset) is a well-respected author of literature and a single woman, and Merry Noel (Candice Bergen) is a wife and mother who becomes a famous author of popular fiction and loses her "neglected" spouse. The two, we learn, lost touch after a college friendship, but have never been far from one another's thoughts. Liz wondered about Merry's rewarding domestic life, and Merry wished she had a career like Liz. When at last they are reunited, it is as though they have never been apart; yet gushing affection soon turns to jealousy and competition related as much to men as to writing. The pair do come together at the end of the film, disillusioned but determined to live their lives well. In some ways, *Rich and Famous* seems every one of its decades beyond *The Women* and *Our Betters.* In others, however, this remake of a 1940s melodrama relies on many of the norms of classic Hollywood and shows, in what would prove to be Cukor's final directing project, his commitment to the traditional heart of the Hollywood romance.

The Liz/Merry relationship is surprisingly comparable to that of Mary/Sylvia in *The Women* and Pearl/Minnie in *Our Betters.* None of the three films, for example, explains the origin of the friendship or what makes it so close. As just discussed, Pearl sleeps with Minnie's lover and

Minnie uses the opportunity to try to destroy Pearl's livelihood. Sylvia talks behind Mary's back and seems jealous and petty even as she declares her devotion. As with Pearl and Minnie, Sylvia and Mary are generally referenced as long-term friends of a shared social set (although, at one point, Mary casually references Sylvia as a cousin, without clarification; Sylvia has no relationship with Little Mary that we can see, for instance). For Liz and Merry, there is a similar vagueness of connection in that they are college friends whose lasting affection has no clear rationale. In fact, Pearl, Minnie, Sylvia, Liz, and Merry all show a tendency to overreact and squabble that makes each friendship dyad nearly indefensible (even with Mary as a lone rational voice), notwithstanding references to solidarity and loyalty in *Rich and Famous.*[12]

Furthering the comparison, we see that each film features a climactic conflict that threatens or ends the friendship, including significant positioning of the characters as objects of the male gaze. In both *The Women* and *Rich and Famous,* bickering turns to catfight, a representational method particularly relevant to the 1980s, when it would become central to prime-time television dramas and their depictions of female friendship, reflective of antifeminist backlash.[13] A prescient example, the fight between Liz and Merry combines fetishism and sadism through humiliation, central forms of resolution to male anxiety according to gaze theory as Laura Mulvey originally posited it. Liz and Merry fling their bodies and sexualized curses (including "cunt") at one another with angry relish in an extended scene. Through the gaze, we can read this as a scene of mutual abuse. The scene is a male fantasy of female confrontation that Lucy Fischer likens to female mud wrestlers.[14]

Such a reference encourages comparison to a similar scene that takes place in the Reno dirt in *The Women.* The catfight in the 1939 film centers on Sylvia. As a character, Sylvia stands out in the grotesque physicality of her performance. When she auditioned for the part, Rosalind Russell tried several different styles, from quiet to outlandish. Cukor preferred the latter. He felt that excess in her performance would ensure the viewer retains some affection and sympathy for Sylvia (identified with a housecat in the film's opening credits bestiary), particularly in comparison to "villain" Crystal (linked in the credits with a wildcat). When Sylvia fights, therefore, there is a comic absurdity to her actions, which include licking her lips and rolling her eyes before biting into the calf of Miriam, whom she has just learned is both Mary's new friend and the woman for whom her husband is leaving her. She also pulls down Miriam's shorts and has her hat pulled down over her face in return. Mary, meanwhile, stands by, trying to separate the combatants to little effect. In such display, we see women posed for sexualized display, for we get a good look at Paulette Goddard's shapely legs and lingerie-clad behind even as we focus on the purpose of the fight between the wife and the lover who has replaced her. Nonetheless, there is also pleasure in watching the scene's slapstick excess. Hence, traditional objectification meets unfeminine representation, revealing the flexible boundaries of Hollywood style.

If Russell leaps into buffoonery, Shearer does not. Mary stays out of the dirt, literally and figuratively, and even her seething dislike for Crystal never becomes physical. Even when Mary must "grow claws" to win her husband back, she does not literally use them. Through such genteel behavior, *The Women* distinguishes between "'good' passive and 'bad' aggressive femininity," typical for Hollywood films of the era.[15] By contrast, however conventional its narrative, Liz and Merry in their 1981 setting are not held to as rigid a traditional binary. Neither refrains from aggression nor does one emerge as particularly less sympathetic than the other. As James Morrison opines, the two share "a simultaneous susceptibility to romantic idealism and an ironic detachment from it," which bonds and equalizes them.[16] Bergen plays Merry comically and portrays her as oblivious, while Bisset's Liz is neither judged nor punished for her active sexuality. On this subject, Hollinger points to film reviews that laud *Rich and Famous* for its presentation of "sex scenes from the female point of view," "associating the camera's perspective with the female sexual gaze."[17]

In contrast to both *The Women* and *Rich and Famous*, in *Our Betters*, the fight between Pearl and Minnie is tempered, vicious in word but never deed. The comedy resists physical broadness and slapstick in favor of verbal wit. Nonetheless, the film's visual style is noteworthy for showing active response to the politics of the male gaze. Rather than coming down to be shamed in the sight of her friends and, in response, to show remorse for her misdeeds, Pearl remains off-screen. Her friends objectify and punish her with their words, but when she does appear they are more baffled than rewarded. Such staging reveals the power of refusing the gaze, with Pearl choosing when and how she will be seen. Of course, the actress is styled for objectification, even as the character emerges as in control, neither shamed nor humbled. And when she does respond to accusations of impropriety, she turns the tables and actively evokes pity or bemusement.

As with their portrayal of catfights, the resolution of the three films, along with *Girls About Town,* depicts a generally negative outcome for female friendship. While we have no doubt that Marie and Wanda care for each other, the friendship (necessarily) ends as Wanda moves to Michigan with Jim and Marie stays in New York, continuing her escort work. Friendship is lauded but left behind. In *Our Betters*, Pearl will no doubt sleep with Pepi again as the mood takes her, displaying the limits of honesty in her friendship with Minnie, and she will likely not see Bessie again. Mary in *The Women* will return to the traditional comfort of husband and family, while Sylvia's smug neglect of her husband has locked her out of this option; she had assumed he was happy while apparently not watching carefully enough to ensure it.

For Liz and Merry of *Rich and Famous*, we might expect a more fruitful conclusion, a negotiation of career versus romance versus friendship. Instead, however, the film focuses on escapist sexual escapades that the pair will "share," without intimate connection as writers or friends. Fit for both the 1940s era of the original on which the 1981 film is based, as well as what Susan Faludi calls the "backlash" of the early 1980s against second-wave feminism, *Rich and Famous* is mired in its classic Hollywood heritage.[18] Careers are unfulfilling, as are friendships among women. Liz unconvincingly declares, "We're terrific. We've accomplished one hell of a lot in one lifetime. We deserve a rest." But that rest involves escape into mindless sex. Liz suggests a sail around the Greek isles to pick up young men.

Interestingly, picking up young men is also part of classic Hollywood. Both *Girls About Town* and *Our Betters* feature central and even sympathetic characters who enjoy illicit affairs, and *The Women*'s Miriam is more sympathetic than Sylvia even though she has no qualms about "stealing" Howard Fowler from his first wife. Surprisingly, then, we do not see happiness for Liz in casual sex in *Rich and Famous.*[19]

There are other pleasures to be found in alternative readings of *Rich and Famous.* We may ask, is there lesbian (sub)text to be found within the friendship of Liz and Merry? Because Cukor's film is neither a lesbian romance nor a coming-out story, we must focus on reception. For

Hollinger, most persuasive is considering *Rich and Famous* through what she terms the female "erotic friendship" film. She argues that such films "sometimes take a more ambiguous form that renders them almost indistinguishable from representations of sentimental female friendship. In this variation, the sexuality of the two friends is left indeterminate."[20] On this subject, however, *Rich and Famous* appears more homophobic than *The Women* or *Our Betters*, with *Girls About Town* far more conducive to lesbian and bisexual readings. If the 1981 film more openly brings in the subject of same-sex attraction, Liz and Merry arguably turn to each other because they fear they have no other options. In the New Year's Eve scene in which Liz asks Merry to kiss her at the stroke of midnight, Merry retreats into discourse more associated with the homophobic panic of previous decades, as seen in such films as *The Children's Hour* (1961), than those made a decade after Stonewall. "After all these years, are you going to tell me that there's something strange about you?" Merry asks, leaving Liz to practically beg for "the press of human flesh," even as she notes that she seeks Merry's touch because she's "the only flesh around."

Mention of same-sex affection comes far more obliquely in *The Women.* The institution of the Motion Picture Code meant that a direct, serious request for a same-sex kiss, however homophobically expressed, would never make it to the big screen in 1939—or for decades after.[21] Instead, the era required indirection, double entendre, or dismissible comic excess. For Alexander Doty, all of this is present in *The Women* and is suggestive of lesbianism in both content and reception. "Certainly," Doty opines, "any film in which, for once, straight men are the ones literally out of the picture is a promising text for lesbian pleasure." Lesbians might interpret the fighting and cattiness of the friends in the film as "more indicative of the ways in which women have been forced by patriarchy into the roles of rivals rather than of any fundamental hatred and jealousy between women," argues Doty. In terms of content, Sylvia is central to a lesbian reading of the film. As Doty puts it, "Heterocentrism encourages us to read Sylvia's machinations as part of a plot to destroy Mary's marriage to Stephen Haines, supposedly because Sylvia can't stand to see someone in a happy marriage when her own marriage isn't fulfilling. But everything Sylvia does in the film can be read as easily—and justifiably—as attempts to break up Mary's marriage (and later her bonds with other women) in order to have Mary all to herself."[22]

A perspective such as that of the classic Hollywood film–loving Doty reveals queer pleasure for the viewer even as it does not offer a feminist alternative to the gendered status quo to which the film ultimately surrenders.

Following this pattern of reading queerly, we can assess Pearl's decision to sleep with Pepi as a plot to separate Minnie from her man in *Our Betters*. Pearl makes clear to both Pepi and Minnie that she has no serious interest in the gigolo. Might her reasoning be to have Minnie "all to herself," as Sylvia potentially desires from Mary? In this case, we can even argue that a queer reading has greater impact on heterosexist romance norms than in *The Women*, for Pearl's greatest concern as the film ends is having Minnie in her home, enjoying herself with a flamboyantly gay-coded dancing instructor. And that dancing instructor, named Ernest with inescapable Wildean overtones, inclines us to such a queer reading. As Pearl and Minnie embrace, he gushes, "What an exquisite spectacle! Two ladies of title, kissing one another!"

Even more directly open to queer interpretation is *Girls About Town*. Wanda happily jumps into bed with Marie and the two share a close, sisterly relationship, never trying to deceive or compete with one another over men. Additionally, the production is full of LGBT presence and references. Bill Krohn finds "heavily coded presuppositions about both gold-diggers' sexual orientation that the film calls up and overturns in every scene, and at every change of scene."[23] For instance, when Wanda declares her intent to marry Jim, Marie demands, "Are you going straight on me?" The line directly suggests Wanda was lesbian or bisexual before Jim, even if it may also be interpreted as relating to becoming a wife rather than a paid escort. Yet the scene does not end here. Marie continues the queer banter with "Did I ever tell you about my operation?" This joke adds a trans reference to the scene with lesbian implications, for as Krohn reveals, "a Danish artist had been making history, and international headlines, by undertaking sex reassignment surgery in 1930, and it seems that Marie's quip was in the air in gay circles."[24] In this context, how can we not interpret Marie as suggesting she can fill the male romantic role in Wanda's life, even as she shows understanding and support of her friend's ultimate heteronormative decision? In terms of production context, *Girls About Town* is also remarkably queer. Playwright Zoe Akins, who penned the script, was lesbian, as was Lilyan Tashman (who plays

Marie); and Kay Francis (Wanda) was known to be bisexual. Furthermore, Akins is said to have modeled Marie and Wanda on Tashman herself, in Tashman's relationship with Tallulah Bankhead.[25]

Not only queer and lesbian but gay readings are also relevant to interpretations of these films and their references to friendship and sexuality. Reading *Our Betters* through the perspectives of the two gay men who collaborated to make the picture—author Maugham and director Cukor—Dan Callahan argues for a reading in which Pearl and Minnie "could easily be two older gay men sharing [Pepi as] a trick."[26] More fully developed and persuasive in this context is James Morrison's reading of *Rich and Famous*, predicated on attention to Cukor's "persistence in a pre-Stonewall sensibility defined by obliquity and camp aestheticism" that "gives his last films an edge of nostalgia."[27] Rather than reading Liz and Merry as standing in for gay men, as does Pauline Kael in her infamous review of *Rich and Famous*, Morrison points to the need to avoid collapsing "a species of gay male identification with women into mere identity, an empathetic mirroring into a narcissistic projection."[28] He argues the distinction by attending the film's sex scenes. "They may be the most homoerotic depictions of heterosexuality in American cinema, yet they highlight the difference between the women's pleasure in the male body and the camera's way of looking at the same body." With the camera posed as what Morrison describes as an "excluded third party in a figurative menage-à-trois," men are frequently shot from behind in *Rich and Famous*, arguably suggesting "an anal eroticism nowhere registered in the manifest content." For Morrison, one conclusion to be drawn is overtly feminist: Liz's sexual activity reveals an inner-focused desire, a "self-sufficiency" of pleasure, that shows women's "erotic 'problems' as matters of social definition more than of women's sexuality." Morrison's reading of the film from a gay studies perspective posits that even as Cukor continued to direct in the post-Stonewall era, his portrayals of sexuality remained "more congruent with Classical Hollywood and the Celluloid Closet than with the New Hollywood and its self-declared 'frankness.'"[29]

A final area of focus through which to compare female friendships in the films under consideration is the issue of remakes. *The Women* was remade in 2008 and *Rich and Famous*, as already noted, is a remake of the Hollywood classic *Old Acquaintance* (1943). In both cases, the original film far eclipsed the remake in both box office and popular admiration. The reasons for this say much about each Cukor picture and its commentary on female friendship. *Old Acquaintance* is a Bette Davis and Miriam Hopkins vehicle, directed by Vincent Sherman (born Abraham Orovitz), another American son of Jewish immigrant parents who worked with major and sometimes "difficult" stars. The core of the original film is, like its remake, the tense friendship between two high-strung writers, one single and an author of high literature, the other married and penning popular fiction. A significant difference in the two depictions of the pair is their relationship to their writing. In *Old Acquaintance,* the women's friendship is based on their shared vocation. In the original 1940 play by John van Druten on which the film is based, both are happy with their chosen marital status and enjoy engaging with each other's work despite their differences. In both the original film adaptation and in *Rich and Famous,* by contrast, the friendship is based on rivalry and loneliness. Both films also end with the two alone together, friends once more. However, where the remake has the two focused entirely on escapism through an imagined worldwide tour of casual sex with men, the original returns to the subject of writing, with the pair toasting the title of the new book by the Liz character (Kit in the original film). "Why not call it 'Old Acquaintance'?" Bette Davis's Milly (the Merry character) suggests, and the two drink. In the play, the ending is even tenderer, including Milly's apology for blaming her friend for the problems in her marriage and mother-child relationship. Still, the heart of the friendship in the 1943 film is not the shared unhappiness we see in *Rich and Famous* but a mutual investment in and support of one another's writing, however tense and catty they may get. As Barbara Koenig Quart argues, the remake thus "[derives] spiritually entirely from old Hollywood."[30]

Like *Rich and Famous,* the 2008 remake of *The Women* can also be effectively defined as reliant on the classical Hollywood woman's film. The picture was directed by Diane English, the creator of *Murphy Brown* (1998–1999), the television program that would establish Candice Bergen as a post-feminist comedy icon.[31] Bergen herself played the mother of Mary Haines in the remake of *The Women.* Moreover, particular inspiration for the film's production was the success of the equally post-feminist television series *Sex and the City* (1998–2004), noteworthy for portraying privileged-class female friendships as all about men. The Women Film Critics Circle dubbed the 2008 remake of *The Women* "Sex, Lies and Shopping" and gave it their annual Hall of Shame Award. That year, the Alliance of Women Film Journalists also bestowed upon *The Women* their dubious 2008 awards for "Remake That Shouldn't Have Been Made" and "Movie You Wanted to Love, But Just Couldn't." The latter prize is particularly interesting as it reveals the pleasures of classic Hollywood cinema even when made in the twenty-first century.

Finally, although *Girls About Town* was never remade, one can certainly point to similarities between it and *Gentlemen Prefer Blondes* (1953), from its brunette and blonde duo, in which the blonde remains a gold-digger while the brunette falls for true love, to its lesbian and bisexual implications.[32] Only *Our Betters* seems destined never to be remade or even compared to other films by critics, given its focus on a particular historical moment's cross-cultural trend. Even adapting it for film from the original play during the pre-Code era had limited success, as audiences did not respond well to its British-style humor and attack on American women. Instead, the legacy of *Our Betters*, like *Rich and Famous*, is, for James Morrison at least, limited to its engagement with closeted gay sensibility, exemplified in the extended life of dance instructor Ernest, with his prissiness, fussy demeanor, and lip rouge, revived in Vito Russo's *The Celluloid Closet* (1995) and now on YouTube to illustrate what many call the most offensive gay stereotype ever filmed.

As a coda to this chapter, I now briefly turn to discuss one additional Cukor film, *The Chapman Report* (1962). Based on a 1960 novel by Irving Wallace, *The Chapman Report* tells the story of four (trimmed from six in the book) suburban women, both married and divorced, who volunteer to be interviewed by a visiting sexologist seeking data, the titular Dr. Chapman (Andrew Duggan) and his assistant Paul Radford (Efrem Zimbalist Jr.). Opposing them is a local doctor, played by Henry Daniell, a frequent presence in earlier Cukor films, including *Holiday* (1938), *The Philadelphia Story* (1940), and *A Woman's Face* (1943). The doctor warns that asking for detailed information about women's sex lives—especially without attention to the subject of love—may have troubling psychological impact and effects that Chapman is unprepared and unwilling to deal with. Against this backdrop appear the women themselves, portrayed by three high-caliber stars (Shelley Winters, Glynis Johns, and Claire Bloom) and one newcomer, soon to become a major celebrity herself (Jane Fonda).

With its suburban setting and focus on a group of women, we might expect to see multiple scenes in which the characters mingle as friends or

The four main characters of *The Chapman Report* (1962), together for the only time in a film that forecloses the possibility of women's friendships.

at least neighbors, to chat, gossip, or share more complex interactions. This proves not to be the case. The isolation of the suburbs and the discontent of wives and divorcées—to varying degrees—dominate the picture. Nevertheless, there are notable similarities to other Cukor pictures of earlier eras that make the few scenes between women in the film stand out. Friendship is arguably central to Bill Krohn's reading of sex as a red herring in *The Chapman Report* and *Girls About Town*.[33] More substantial is Gavin Lambert's comparison of the picture to *The Women* in discussion with Cukor. Lambert interprets the two films as sharing emphasis on "the lives of fairly well-to-do but discontented ladies." Cukor openly agrees with this assessment, differing only in his opinion that the suburban women of *The Chapman Report* are "more bourgeois" than the New York set of *The Women*, whom he identifies as "a cut higher."[34] Gene D. Phillips concurs, claiming that *The Chapman Report* "has sometimes been called *The Women-II*, since it also boasts a host of top actresses, and like the earlier film is about the personal problems of a select group of ladies."[35] To this, we might add that the character who chooses the most conventional path relative to her era ends the film most happily. In *The Chapman Report*, this is Jane Fonda's Kathleen Barclay, who goes from "frigid" widow to fulfilled wife with Paul, who has changed from dispassionate interviewer to devoted, if paternalistic, partner.

Remarkably, Lambert, Phillips, and even Cukor himself do not attend to tone in the comparison of the films. The light drama and broad comedy that combine in *The Women* are perhaps best compared to the most superficial of the four women's tales, that of Glynis Johns's baby-voiced Teresa Harnish, whose feigned classical romanticism receives a significant if comically portrayed blow when she pursues an affair with a classically built hick of a beach bum. When he takes her up on her offer, she is repulsed by his attempt at crude lovemaking and literally runs home to her tame, pretentious husband, Geoffrey (TV actor John Dehner, doing a sort of John Barrymore riff).

Nothing in *The Women*, however, prepares a viewer for the startlingly sharp contrast between Teresa's adventures and those of Naomi (Claire Bloom), a compulsive sexual masochist (what the film calls a "nymphomaniac"). Bloom's portrayal of this complex character is disturbing throughout. We see in the camera's attention to her body language and subtle facial expressions a woman who is not in control of herself, literally swaying in the presence of the two male strangers she meets over the course of the film. The result is not only sex with alcoholic, married musician Wash Dillon (Corey Allen), but gang rape at the hands of his friends.

This violent, traumatic encounter—however cut by censors—brings one of only two scenes between women in the film. After the rape, Naomi is tossed out of a car curbside in the early morning hours by Wash, who has enjoyed a drunken tryst with her, followed by her rape by his friends. Neighbor Kathleen (Jane Fonda) hears car tires squeal as Wash takes off without a backward glance. She rushes into a robe and outside to see what has happened. Naomi is sobbing, her clothes torn and body bruised. Kathleen takes her to her home, in which she lives alone, and gently helps her to undress. In an effective portrayal of a rape victim, Naomi visibly panics and flinches at every touch. Kathleen's firm gestures and quiet patience show her to be entirely sympathetic, actively desiring to be helpful, but Naomi cannot accept it. She resists being put to bed or seeing a doctor and cannot or will not discuss what has happened. After asking Kathleen to draw her a hot bath, she roughly demands to be left alone, and Kathleen acquiesces. The two do not meet again, and the lonely, self-loathing Naomi ultimately commits suicide with pills and alcohol after first calling Wash and inviting her rapists over for another session.

Failed connection between women is also revealed in the only other extended scene between women. This scene involves affection-craving middle-aged housewife and amateur actress Sarah Garnell (Shelley Winters) and Ruth (Hope Cameron), the on-again, off-again wife of philandering theatrical director Fred Linden (Ray Danton), with whom Sarah is having an affair. Sarah has decided to leave her bland but kind couch potato of a husband, Frank (Harold J. Stone), for the exciting Fred, but Fred likes his freedom and has fled his houseboat rather than face the clinging Sarah. Ruth waits on board, having been tasked by Fred to explain everything to Sarah. She humiliates herself, explaining to Sarah that she takes her husband back between affairs, and even takes on his dirty work—including confronting Sarah with the truth that he is no longer interested in her. Sarah denies the truth and dismisses Ruth's advice and her perspective. Both women have chosen the limited affections of a faithless, cruel man over self-worth, over recognition of their similar situations, and over any potential sympathy with one another.

In both painful scenes, we see potential for connection between women that might turn to friendship, to healing, or at least support. Instead, we witness isolated and isolating moments, reflecting the white suburban malaise of the era that led to the publication of Betty Friedan's *The Feminine Mystique* in 1963 and the second wave of the women's movement. Of course, as we have seen, even this major cultural shift did not lead to idyllic feminist female friendships, as the backlash of the 1980s and a problematic film such as *Rich and Famous* illustrate.

2

Collaboration and Chastisement

Cukor Directs Hepburn

While the previous chapter in its attention to female friendships required sustained attention to film content, this chapter's focus on Cukor films starring Katharine Hepburn emphasizes historical and production context as they inflect content and style. Cukor's relationship with Hepburn was his closest with any star, spanning most of her adult life and ten films together. The two came to Hollywood around the same time, and Cukor cast Hepburn in her first film role, as an ingenue daughter opposite John Barrymore in *A Bill of Divorcement* (1932). Director and actress shared a perspective on Hollywood that bound them thereafter. As Hepburn put it, they "had the same set of standards. We both adored the business—we loved to work—we admired each other."[1] Together, they found a powerful collaborative energy, and Cukor helped to elicit some of Hepburn's most lauded and memorable performances, as well as one of her biggest box office flops, as he directed her career in significant ways. She is arguably the closest the director came to featuring an identifiable "Cukor woman."[2]

Cukor directed Hepburn in excellent work opposite strong male costars, including Cary Grant, Spencer Tracy, and eventually Laurence Olivier. She also earned critical and popular scorn for aloofness and affectedness. In the three films to be discussed in this chapter, director and actor worked together within the restrictive framework of the romantic comedy genre to revive Hepburn's image with the movie-going public, from alienation to applause. Their collaborative work helped Hepburn become an iconoclast who could nonetheless succeed in Hollywood. Opposite Grant in *The Philadelphia Story* (1940), director and actor collaborated to rid Hepburn of the "box office poison" label she had earned in the late 1930s. With Tracy in *Adam's Rib* (1949), they cemented her new, mature, career-woman image without depicting her as man-hating. Finally, opposite Olivier in the television feature *Love Among the Ruins* (1975), the two worked to extend her appeal as a loveably snappish and fiercely independent older woman. In this trio of pivotal collaborations, we can see how strength and independence of mind define the Hepburn lead as an echo of the star herself, a determined woman fighting throughout her career for power and respect within a male-dominated Hollywood, as supported by established director Cukor.

In compelling ways, the trajectory of Hepburn's characters in these pictures emphasizes neither steady growth nor comfortable repose. Instead, in all three films, stretching but not breaking classic Hollywood narrative strictures, the bold Hepburn protagonist finds herself chastised within an unforgiving patriarchal structure. Moreover, the character's authority is undercut by a man whose dominant tendencies—identified as love—require him to demonstrate to her, in no uncertain terms, the dangers of a woman's pursuit of equality and independence. As young Tracy Lord in *The Philadelphia Story*, forty-something Amanda Bonner in *Adam's Rib*, and aging Jessica Medlicott in *Love Among the Ruins*, we see Cukor direct Hepburn the star and the characters she plays through artificially demeaning lessons on proper privileged-class femininity. Through this filmic chastisement, however, Hepburn's Tracy, Amanda, and Jessica emerge personally triumphant, reforming romantic relationships that will be based upon relative equality rather than dominance and submission. If, as Hepburn claims of her relationship with Cukor, the two had "the same liberal point of view—the same sense of right and wrong," they also shared the knowledge of how best to negotiate such a perspective within a sexist and homophobic Hollywood.[3] The three films discussed in this chapter illustrate the pleasures of this negotiation.

From her earliest performances, Katharine Hepburn's acting career had its ups and downs. On stage and screen, she had both grand ambitions and marked failures, both artistically and financially. Hollywood, in turn, had a difficult time fitting Hepburn into a successful type as a performer. She had an atypical look for a female star as well as imposing mannerisms and a distinctive voice. RKO, with whom she originally signed, could not seem to find a stable niche for her, even as she became, along with Fred Astaire and Ginger Rogers, the studio's strongest product. Her success in *A Bill of Divorcement* was followed by two strong performances in Zoe Akins's scripts. First came *Christopher Strong* (1933), in which Hepburn played an Earhart-like aviatrix for lesbian director Dorothy Arzner, and then she played an ingenue actress in *Morning Glory* (1933), for which she won her first of four Academy Awards. Despite such popular successes, Hepburn already had her detractors, including film critics and gossip columnists who dubbed her "snooty typhoon Kate" and "Katharine of Arrogance."[4] They felt she broke Hollywood's rules for proper female star demeanor and appearance, from wearing pants to demanding control over scripts. She was generally adored or despised for the same reasons. In the words of biographer Sheridan Morley (1984), Hepburn "was both physically and emotionally . . . unlike any other actress working in Hollywood in the early thirties."[5]

In many ways, Hepburn's strong personality and appearance were the opposite of Cukor's, who sought to fit in rather than stand out. The two came together in their desire to work, and they did so superbly. For their second film together, Hepburn was well cast as Jo in *Little Women* (1933), an androgynous, energetic, lovable role that made the most of her talent. After this work, Hepburn faced her first significant downturn, both on Broadway in *The Lake* and in Hollywood in *Spitfire* (1934). For Hollywood, she was too stagey; on Broadway, she had been ruined by Hollywood. Her next performance, in the ill-received *The Little Minister* (1934), led previously stalwart Hepburn supporter Pandro Berman to reconsider her contract. He claimed she was a hit only if the picture was a hit and blamed her for often choosing the wrong vehicles.[6]

Such experiences led many to conclude that Hepburn was both an indisputable talent and one of the most poorly used in Hollywood. This sort of roller coaster ride was to mark Hepburn's studio career overall: feast and famine, costume drama and slapstick comedy, unique star appeal and box office poison. There was the sparkle of *Alice Adams* (1935) opposite the crash of Cukor's *Sylvia Scarlett* (1935) and then the dull thud of *Mary of Scotland* (1936). A perfect turn as someone quite like herself (almost a parody) in the ensemble drama *Stage Door* (1937) led to the relative letdown of both *Bringing Up Baby* (1938) and Cukor's *Holiday* (1938). While some critics and many fans have come to adore these last two films even more than her box office triumphs, in the era of their production this indeterminacy in her output resulted in a break from film for Hepburn as she reconsidered her goals and her options.

Cukor, meanwhile, seemed to have learned much from their early work together, particularly the failures. From *Sylvia Scarlett*, he learned not to take overt risks related to gender and sexuality. Tomboyish Jo of *Little Women* playing male characters in a show for her family fared quite differently from Sylvia becoming Sylvester for the duration of an odd romantic comedy with melodramatic notes, for example.[7] From *Holiday*, he learned the value of collaboration among talented artists, not only with Hepburn but the entire cast, as well as screenwriter David Ogden Stewart.[8] His next film with Hepburn would bring all such awareness to the fore.

Like *Holiday*, *The Philadelphia Story* is based on a play by Philip Barry; both feature the wealthy and are romantic comedies that have dramatic notes. The part of Tracy Lord was specially written for Hepburn by Barry, who loved her work in *Holiday*. The script takes advantage of her aristocratic demeanor and strong will in a tale of a divorcée who must learn a vital lesson about vulnerability and love to achieve happiness within a mature, companionate marriage. Hepburn performed the role on the Broadway stage over four hundred times, and then bought the film rights so she would be able to play Tracy on screen as well. Hollywood was absolutely interested in the play, but less so in Hepburn. Warner Brothers, MGM, and Twentieth Century-Fox all wanted to purchase the rights, but for their own stars.[9] With some intercession by Howard Hughes and an outline developed by Joseph L. Mankiewicz, MGM finally agreed to Hepburn's terms, which included bringing in David Ogden Stewart to develop the screenplay and Cukor to direct.

The production was successful in many ways and is generally thought to be Cukor's strongest comedy and the film for which he should have won an Oscar. It features a witty, fast-paced script and a strong ensemble cast—including a fiancé for Tracy as well as two love interests, played by James Stewart and Cary Grant. The collaboration, while less truly democratic than that of *Holiday*, was strong behind the screen as well as on it. Moreover, both Cukor and Hepburn had matured. Producer Joseph L. Mankiewicz posits, "Kate, in her early years, was on the verge of being very mannered. Cukor wasn't going to call her on that—because those were his early years, too. I think he had as much to do with her being 'box-office poison' as she did. So when they came together on *The*

Philadelphia Story, they were both older and wiser, and they worked together well."[10]

For the viewer most interested in gender norms within classic Hollywood vehicles and the career of Hepburn, even more can be said. While the acting, script, and congenial working relationships made *The Philadelphia Story* a success, earning the film five Academy Award nominations and two awards (for James Stewart and David Ogden Stewart), the film also proved a powerful and well-handled vehicle for addressing Hepburn's toxic celebrity reputation. The character arc for Tracy Lord features arrogance giving way to amiability, selfishness shifting to generosity, and isolated independence yielding to romantic companionship without the kind of domestic passivity so often seen in Hollywood. It is easy to see why Andrew Sarris declares, "*The Philadelphia Story* is quite simply the breaking, reining, and saddling of an unruly thoroughbred for the big races to come on Broadway and in Hollywood. It is Katharine Hepburn getting her comeuppance at long last, and accepting it like the good sport she was."[11] Like Sarris's horseracing metaphor, the lesson taught can be off-putting to a contemporary, politically sophisticated audience. However, a more historically grounded feminism can encourage us to consider that Hepburn's choice to remarry Grant's Dexter Haven at the film's conclusion is not simply yielding to a comeuppance but learning that reworking her first marriage may ultimately provide greater satisfaction for her than fleeing into infatuation with Mike or, worse yet, stifling her desires with nouveau-riche social climber George Kittredge. The play and film rethink marriage, asking what a modern woman wants or needs from a husband.

Such a perspective enables us to challenge many critics' disparagement of Hepburn and her need for chastisement as an actress. As Cukor describes her, Hepburn was never a "'love me, I'm a lovable little girl' kind of actress. She always challenged the audience, and that wasn't the fashion in those days. On the hoof, when people first saw her, they felt something arrogant in her playing. Later, by sheer feeling and skill, she bent them to her will. Of course, her quality of not asking for pity, not caring whether people liked her or not, was ideal for *The Philadelphia Story*."[12] For Molly Haskell, Hepburn "was neither a 'regular guy' (in fact, she never won any popularity prizes in Hollywood) nor a representative of the American woman." Haskell describes a "cutting edge" in her roles, "a kind of ruthless, upper-class eccentricity, that was more a revenge on, than an expression of, her personality."[13] Robert B. Ray describes Hepburn as having an "edgy self-awareness."[14] He argues that this smacked of class prejudice and therefore needed, as Richard Lippe puts it, "democratizing." Hepburn's active collaboration on the role of Tracy Lord with playwright Philip Barry and the fact that she purchased the film rights and brought the package to Cukor, however, lead me to disagree with Lippe when he calls the film "the ultimate and most perverse illustration of Cukor the sexist/misogynist."[15] The film certainly *involves* sexism, but there is more commentary *on* sexism than uncritical display. Furthermore, we must read the production through the collaborative context that proceeds from Hepburn's active awareness of how to best move her career forward within Hollywood under the sympathetic direction of Cukor.

The most problematic moment for the film's sexual politics begins in a flashback that offers a shorthand depiction of the violent break-up of the marriage of Tracy and Dexter. Bags packed and ready to go, Dexter exits the front door with his last two cases. Clad in her nightgown and an angry, smug grin that arguably personifies Hepburn's "no pity" attitude toward audience disfavor as well as Tracy's exasperation with marital disappointment, Tracy follows Dexter out and throws his pipe rack and all but one of his golf clubs on the ground before him, phallic symbols of masculine leisure. She then performs a symbolic emasculation, breaking the remaining club over her knee. Dexter, in response, stomps up to Tracy in the doorway, accompanied by the sound of a militaristic drum roll. This audio accompaniment presents him as shoring up his wounded masculinity. Next, he mimes the punch he would like to give her, a potential act of violence or even rape metaphor that he ultimately shies from. Finally, he puts his hand fully over Tracy's face and pushes her backwards, hard. There is an echo of James Cagney's famous grapefruit-in-the-face scene opposite Mae Clark in *The Public Enemy* (1931), but it's played as tit-for-tat rather than as gratuitous hypermasculine aggression in this romantic comedy. We next cut to Tracy, sprawled in the entryway, rubbing a sore neck.

This teaser is the only completely new scene in the transition from play to film. It is a heavy-handed and purposeful introduction to the central couple. We see the characters at their worst, and audiences frequently lambaste the scene as misogynistic. She may attack his male-coded prized possessions, but he—even if he pulls his punch—attacks her, physically. Nonetheless, the scene is lightened by the soundtrack, which encourages a reading of the moment as slapstick comedy. Certainly, Tracy is chastised here, and audiences are encouraged to feel she deserved the push. However, in terms of comportment, Tracy can be read as triumphant, having forced Dexter to resort to brutish physical violence while she refrained from such excess (e.g., slapping him, as seen in so many romantic comedies). Maintaining this balance—Tracy/Hepburn being punished for cold haughtiness even as she ensures Dexter and the audience know she can hit him where it hurts, metaphorically—is central to the effectiveness of the picture. And the Hollywood tradition of the romantic comedy is essential to ensuring there is more pleasure than pain in the viewer's experience.

This scene also brings up a central, more serious question the film will answer in no uncertain terms by its conclusion: Who is to blame for the destruction of Tracy and Dexter's marriage? The pair seemingly had everything—love, money, youth, looks—and they threw it away. We can be certain they were well matched because they end up back together at the end, satisfying a desire for heteronormative closure. But what tore them apart? As chapter 4 explores in greater detail, Dexter's alcoholism is named as part of the problem, even as the film generally blames Tracy. While endearing in a self-satisfied, self-mocking way, Dexter is manipulative and pushy, but this is never portrayed as the source of his marital crisis with Tracy. Instead, Tracy is deemed at fault, attacked by more than one male character (and many film critics) for being an unsympathetic, frigid perfectionist. Dexter even manages to blame her for his drinking:

> Dexter: [You] never had any understanding of my deep and courageous thirst.
>
> Tracy: That was *your* problem.
>
> Dexter: Granted, but you took on that problem when you took me. You were no helpmate there; you were a scold.

Within this blame is language that the film will return to own at its conclusion. A wife must be a partner, a "helpmate," rather than an object of desire or scorn. And although we are encouraged to judge Tracy, this is in part because she is the most dynamic character—perhaps the only dynamic character—in the film.

By comparison, consider Tracy's father, Seth (John Halliday), another sort of addict in the film: a serial adulterer. His escapades are protected by the family, including his wife. Only Tracy condemns him for his behavior, yet he turns the situation around, blaming his own daughter for his affairs. "The best mainstay a man can have is the right kind of daughter," Seth argues, adding fuel to the fire that burns Tracy for her lack of sympathy for men's weaknesses. From a feminist perspective, as Marty Roth states, the offensive "project" of the film is "to get Tracy to accept her responsibility for both the father's affairs and Dexter's drinking."[16] "Beneath the comedy," Roth clarifies, "the work of sexual adjustment to an ideological status quo also goes on."[17] Many viewers, however, may feel Tracy is not ultimately responsible for her father or his generation. Tracy's mother, Margaret (Mary Nash), ultimately upholds patriarchal tradition in the home, making Dan Callahan's reading of the film persuasive as it identifies Tracy's experiences of "a specifically feminist nightmare . . . where Cukor catches the hell of sexist entrapment."[18] By contrast, one may not fully share Molly Haskell's grandiose pro-woman stance on the film: "This is the furtive revenge of mediocrity on excellence; [Tracy] is being convicted merely for being a superior creature."[19] The point, however, is in the multiple possibilities of interpretation. Ultimately, the collaboration between Hepburn and Cukor allows criticism of Tracy (and Hepburn) even as we see her triumph as the film's most compelling character. Hepburn gets to play a variety of moods, featuring crisp, witty dialogue. We see her strong and vulnerable, sober and drunk, icy and sizzling, angry and delighted. And she is ultimately even successful romantically, choosing to reunite with the man with whom she has the most potential for a sexual, companionate marriage.

We may draw similar conclusions regarding Hepburn's collaboration with Cukor on *Adam's Rib* nearly a decade later. Rather than Barry, the play was penned for the screen by Garson Kanin and Ruth Gordon, the husband-and-wife team's second of six collaborations with Cukor. The aim of the film was to create a strong vehicle for Tracy and Hepburn as a pair to match the success of George Stevens's *Woman of the Year* (1942) and to make up for lukewarm reception to their pairing in Cukor's *Keeper of the Flame* (1942). *The Philadelphia Story* and *Adam's Rib* productively bookend the 1940s for Hepburn and Cukor. The former restored her worth as a Hollywood leading lady, while the latter ensured her continued value by a shift from starring in glamor roles to being half of a compelling duo, in which she was balanced by strong male partner Spencer Tracy. The two worked together well, given their developing personal relationship, in which Hepburn focused on keeping the alcoholic Tracy sober and her career on the upswing. Beyond the personal, they paired particularly well as the decade came to a close and a former film emphasis on women's independence and equality with men gave way to a focus on equality through difference. Oppositionality became the dominant style of Hollywood gender representation in the 1940s, even as the romantic comedy remained a salient tradition, with fulfillment for a heterosexual couple coming primarily through negotiation of what is popularly called "the battle of the sexes."

From a more theoretical perspective, the rhetoric and images of *Adam's Rib* can be seen to rely on what Mimi Martinucci identifies as the hegemonic binary: "the coalescence of gender, sex, and sexuality into exactly two fundamentally distinct natural kinds: women and men," where the paradigmatic man is anatomically male, masculine in gender, and woman-oriented in sexuality and the paradigmatic woman is anatomically female, feminine in gender, and man-oriented in sexuality. This essentialist position is based on the traditional doctrine of "natural kinds," which divides the human world into two privileged, distinct, nonoverlapping categories.[20] While this opposition requires nuancing by race, class, and other determinants of identity, it describes well the white, male-dominated Hollywood perspective that Cukor and Hepburn had to navigate as they collaborated throughout their careers.

We can begin to explore foregrounding of the hegemonic binary in *Adam's Rib* with its title. An obvious reference to the Judeo-Christian biblical story of the first humans, *Adam's Rib* makes its position on gender and power clear before it even begins. According to the book of Genesis, Eve, the first woman, was created by a masculine God from one of the ribs of Adam, the first man. He is original; she is a lesser copy who owes him her very existence. This reference is reinforced when we learn that Tracy's character's name is Adam. Hepburn is not named Eve but "Amanda," which we might note begins with "a man." Will Amanda, read through Hepburn's star image and the figure of Eve, cause of humankind's downfall, attempt to be "a man" and usurp Adam's biblically inflected, legitimized male power in the film? Of course she will, and a delight in her comeuppance, followed by companionate triumph, is the fascinating and at times uncomfortable appeal of the picture. *Adam's Rib* relies, like *The Philadelphia Story*, on representation of women's struggles for equality within public and private patriarchal realms, even as it settles by the conclusion into its classic Hollywood closure.

The plot finds husband and wife Adam and Amanda Bonner in conflict over a trial in which Adam will prosecute while Amanda defends a woman (Judy Holliday) who has shot her husband (Tom Ewell) and the woman (Jean Hagen) with whom he was having an affair. Amanda argues that the wife was abused and posits that men are often considered justified when they commit such acts of jealous revenge. Adam, meanwhile, uses patriarchal privilege to argue that gender should not be part of such matters, claiming that the law is objective and they must use reason (masculine, but presented as nongendered) not emotion (feminine) to handle the case. Through various stunts—such as showing a woman's strength by having Adam lifted into the air by a woman bodybuilder and encouraging the jury to imagine the accused and the defendant as "opposite" sexes—Amanda wins the case. She is triumphant because she understands and can work the patriarchal system effectively. But the battle is not exclusive to the courtroom. At home, Adam wins. Disallowing for his male privilege, he shows he can play the gender binary game, too. First, he feigns jealousy over Amanda's friendship with neighbor Kip (David Wayne) and pulls a gun on the two, forcing Amanda to acknowledge that killing in such a case would be wrong, regardless of gender. He ends this stunt by taking a big bite out of his gun, which turns out to be made of licorice. Next, to woo her back, he resorts to the quintessential "womanly" trick of tears on demand.

Many viewers and critics rely on a patriarchal reading of the film. Emanuel Levy, for example, condemns Amanda for stooping to "unscrupulous methods," without mention of gender inequities. He posits that Adam is rightly "restored to dominance" when he is asked to run for judge despite Amanda winning the case. And, even as he argues that the film "celebrates accommodation and compromise," he uses the film's own gendered terms to differentiate the actors, comparing Hepburn's "intense, high-strung performance" to Tracy's "usual solid acting."[21] Reading within the boundaries of superficial Hollywood film prescriptions, such interpretations are one way a conservative reviewer can find pleasure in the text. However, there are other interpretations and other facets of the film to read.

In addition to dialogue, plot, and casting, we can consider the visual impact of gender on the film. Tracy looks gruffly masculine, but also portly, fatherly, and thus relatively desexualized. Hepburn appears angular, professional, and also arguably desexualized. However, their styles are quite different. Anita La Cruz points out that "Adam wears extremely non-descript suits in contrast to the varied, memorable attire of Amanda." Hepburn "both played and was in real life the professional, intellectual upper-middle-class woman and champion of the New Woman cause," she notes.[22] Because this position was unpopular in the postwar era, it is not surprising that interpretation of *Adam's Rib* hinges on the rebuking of behavior by Amanda that shows her ability to see patriarchal ideology and succeed in her profession despite it.

In contrast with *The Philadelphia Story*, Hepburn and Cukor had more freedom from the constraints on a leading lady and a "woman's director" by the late 1940s, as well as a shared "de-personalizing approach to identity" related to a "longstanding history of gender ambiguity," as David Jarraway puts it, related to both of their lives as Hollywood insiders with outsider lifestyles. Such context enables a reading of Adam's patriarchal chastisement of Amanda in *Adam's Rib* as tongue-in-cheek. With emphasis on performativity, Jarraway attends to elements of the film that resist gender binaries and absolutes, including the Bonners' shared nickname (Pinky/Pinkie) and the ability of both Adam and Amanda to produce tears when needed. He particularly attends to Adam's stammering and spoonerisms, which "open up a gap" in language, which shares with gender a "socially and sexually bound" structure.[23] Additionally, the biblical allusion of the film's title can be interpreted ironically, illustrative of the "characteristic anxiety of patriarchy."[24]

Form and style in the film also encourage feminist and queer readings. *Adam's Rib* is more broadly comic and fantastical than *The Philadelphia Story*, for example. If we consider "rib" as not only a noun but a verb, we may find that Adam and the male power he represents get "ribbed" by Hepburn's Amanda and Cukor's stylistic choices as a director. And, if we add to this mix the fact that Amanda's best friend is her gay-coded next-door neighbor Kip, we even find possibilities for camp reading. Such a position begins by noting that Cukor was drawn to theatricality as a theme as well as a source throughout his career (see chapter 6). By interpreting *Adam's Rib* through the artifice of the theatrical, we see gender as performance. The courtroom and the Bonner bedroom become stages, each with its own audience: fellow counsel, judge, and jury in the former and spouse in the latter. As Carlos Clarens describes, "There is no one truth, only powers of persuasion. Hepburn's decision to dramatize an injustice implies exactly that: the courtroom as a stage, the trial as a drama." He therefore concludes, "That the film is about performance of one sort or another is the point the critics missed at the time."[25]

Additional evidence for the impact of theatricality on gendered interpretation of the film can be found in attention to the opening credits, which are placed over the curtain of a Punch and Judy type stage. The parallel between Adam and Amanda and these well-known (and oppositionally gendered) comic figures is echoed in a bedroom argument scene in which a stationary camera views the action of characters, like puppets entering and exiting from the wings of a stage. Similarly, in the final scene, Adam draws the curtain of the couple's four-poster bed as if it is a closing curtain on their marriage as a staged performance. The film also uses intertitles, which frame scenes and challenge realism, and these intertitles are echoed by the use of titles within the Bonner's home movie vignettes. Jarraway adds a further layer to consideration of the film in noting Kip's running commentary when watching the home movies with Adam and Amanda.[26] Artificiality (in home moviemaking) and the director's hand (in Hollywood filmmaking) are acknowledged as Kip questions perspective: "Who took all these pictures, your cow?"

By the time Cukor directed *Love Among the Ruins* for television in 1975, much had changed about making movies, including acknowledgment of both the dominance of television and the second wave of the women's movement. Both in keeping with its era and in response to it, the feature offers Hepburn opposite Laurence Olivier in an Edwardian vehicle shot in London, full of theatrical nostalgia and tinged with broad humor. The production brought both public acclaim and multiple Emmy Awards, including prizes for Hepburn, Olivier, and Cukor. Most importantly for this chapter, *Love Among the Ruins* offers a compelling coda on feminism and the chastising of strong female stars within a film that retains a classic Hollywood style.

The picture is a somewhat frothy commentary on the foolishness of youth as well as of old age, along with romantic notions of undying love. Olivier plays eminent barrister Sir Arthur Granville-Jones, whom Hepburn's wealthy former actress Jessica Medlicott approaches to handle a breach of promise suit. Alfred Pratt (Leigh Lawson), a young gold digger, must be exposed if Miss Medlicott's dignity and fortune are to be saved. The complication is that Granville-Jones had a youthful affair with

Curtains around the double bed enhance the theatricality of *Adam's Rib* (1949).

Medlicott himself, although the grand lady claims to have no memory of it. He realizes he can only win the case by showing Medlicott to be a doddering dupe who fell prey to the conniving skills of a scheming gigolo, but he is loath to portray her in this light. Yet, after an explosive court scene from which Medlicott must eventually be removed for uproarious behavior, this is precisely what he does. Then, after a clever reveal, the two end up together, a happily-ever-after glint in their aging eyes.

Themes central to Cukor/Hepburn collaborations dominate *Love Among the Ruins.* Like Tracy in *The Philadelphia Story*, Medlicott is a haughty upper-class woman on the receiving end of a comeuppance at the hands of a former lover with whom she will reunite. Phillips's description of Medlicott as an "inaccessible goddess" echoes the language used about Tracy by both Dexter and Mike.[27] Such similarity echoes Clarens's perspective in identifying the script as "spiced-up Barrie [*sic*]." Clarens also points to *Adam's Rib* as similar in "terrain" to *Love Among the Ruins.*[28] The courtroom setting, its portrayal more theatrical than judicial, and the

The happily-ever-after of *Love Among the Ruins* (1975) comes after Jessica Medlicott (Katharine Hepburn) deftly manipulates Sir Arthur Granville-Jones (Laurence Olivier) into painting her as a crazy, credulous old woman in court.

"battle of the sexes" rhetoric in both the case and Granville-Jones's handling of Medlicott place the viewer on familiar Cukor/Hepburn ground, indeed. And the film's grand reveal announces its feminism, related directly to options available to a Hollywood television production in an Edwardian setting helmed by a classic studio director.

Hepburn's daffy, manic behavior in the courtroom, we learn in the end, is entirely a performance. She remembers only too well Granville-Jones and their brief, long-ago liaison and actively encourages him to humiliate her publicly to win the case. Sentimentality on his part might well have lost the case, so Medlicott must inspire him to outrage. Medlicott (like Hepburn and Cukor) knows that an old man with a young wife is acceptable (even admired by some), but an old woman with a young man is far less so, particularly in the Edwardian era. Even today, the "Cougar" and "MILF" are subjects more often of curiosity or ridicule than respect. Late in their long careers, in this otherwise sentimental romance, Cukor and Hepburn can come together in their fame and maturity, using this vehicle to pull back the curtain and reveal that the chastisement of strong women is and always has been no more than a strategic and temporary ruse. And they can do it without yielding the pleasures of the classic Hollywood romantic comedy.

3

Tone, Genre, and the Actor's Director

Achieving the appropriate tone is key to successful work with classic Hollywood's preferred practices. Across diverse genres and whether actively pushing boundaries or adhering closely to cinematic norms, effective establishment of mood and atmosphere can govern the appeal and relative success of a film. Such a claim is particularly salient when considering tone alongside gender issues as they relate to the success Cukor found with *The Women* (1939) and the critical and box office failures of both *Susan and God* (1940) and *Edward, My Son* (1948).

Chapter 1 considered *The Women* in terms of its depiction of female friendship, concluding that, despite potential queer readings, heteronormative romance trumps bonds between women in the end. But what if we read the film through its ambivalent tone rather than its content? We can begin consideration with the relationship between screenwriter Anita Loos and Cukor. The two shared a long friendship that was grounded, at least in part, in love of glamor and sharp wit. Cukor loved to entertain Hollywood stars, but only if they "contributed to the conversation": a lack of wit meant an individual, however beautiful, would soon be off his list.[1] Loos passed this test immediately for Cukor, as well as for most of the American public. Her brilliance shone, from her early silent scenarios and best-selling novel *Gentlemen Prefer Blondes* (1925) to her later return to screenwriting for the talkies. Her relationship with Cukor was enhanced when Loos composed the film scripts for both *The Women* (based on the original play by Clare Booth Luce) and *Susan and God* (based on the original 1937 novel by Rachel Carothers). In both cases, Loos was cramped by the Code, through which all jokes even remotely about sex were banned.

Nonetheless, she worked to keep her scripts full of stinging humor, ad-libbing as she worked beside Cukor.[2]

That Loos understood satire and its appeal is obvious from her work, particularly *Gentlemen Prefer Blondes*, but also in earlier advice she gave to aspiring screenwriters in *How to Write Photoplays* (1920).[3] At the end of chapter 19, entitled "What to Write and Not to Write," Loos advises, "At the present time, the material most in demand is the story with the emotional woman as the star, good light comedies, [and] satires upon society."[4] Such demand continued throughout the 1930s and into the 1940s in romantic comedies as well as witty social dramas offering sharp critiques of the privileged classes. Certainly, the presence of an emotional woman star, the use of light comedy, and a satiric intent describe well both *The Women* (1939) and *Susan and God* (1940). Nonetheless, a close look at the films reveals that Cukor's appreciation of Loos's bright wit did not necessarily translate into an ability to adapt her work as effective screen satire.

Clare Booth Luce's original *The Women* is a sharp and brittle comedy, harshly but wittily judging its objects of scrutiny. Rich, catty women in their natural habitat parade and pounce, fickle and backstabbing and ripe for ridicule. Whether at home for luncheon or at play in the beauty salon, rich, idle women are ruthlessly satirized. As noted above, Loos knew quite well how to adapt the tone of the work, even as Hollywood demanded some rounding of the harsher edges and MGM forced a romantic ending. The major difference between play and film, then, is not the step from Luce to Loos, but from Loos to MGM via Cukor. And the difference is centered on gender norms and the handling of satire.

Cukor's film begins well with the animal menagerie that introduces the cast of primary female characters. As noted in chapter 1, each woman is linked to a particular animal, from Norma Shearer (Mary Haines) as a doe to Joan Crawford (Crystal Allen) as a wildcat. Such diverse elements as Rosalind Russell's screwball portrayal of Sylvia Fowler and a fashion show scene shot in Technicolor, featuring female models and caged monkeys in matching outfits, add to the satirically toned romp. Despite these elements and glowing reviews in the *New York Times* and the *Los Angeles Times*, the film can also be read as missing the satirical mark in several key ways. The weakening of the satire emerges particularly through the film's devotion to the perspective of Mary and her emotionally dramatic portrayal by sympathetic and popular actress Norma Shearer. Shearer was not selected by Cukor but used her star power to claim the role. This casting, combined with MGM's insistence on a romantic ending, reduces the original play's thrust, which comes from its emphasis on wealthy married women's catty competitiveness and their reach for social status over love.

Certainly, in both play and film, Mary is our protagonist. Her plight as she addresses her own needs and her pride in the face of her husband Stephen's adultery is the production's centerpiece. The lesson she learns begins with advice indirectly offered by the lone unmarried careerist, Nancy Blake (Florence Nash). "Nature abhors an old maid," Nancy pronounces, just before she disappears from the film entirely. She doesn't even merit an animal partner in the film's opening. Mary's mother (Lucile Watson), by contrast, plays a stronger role. She is the wise owl of the female menagerie, and her advice is to follow the lessons of generations past. Mary's father was a philanderer, too, and she kept him and her family happy by simply, if painfully, ignoring it. This is the "wisdom" she shares with her daughter. Mary suffers greatly, unable to overlook what she justly sees as mistreatment, neglect, and betrayal. In the end, her decision to return to her husband, even after he marries crass perfume salesgirl Crystal, is more modern in method but not in ultimate result. Mary travels and weeps away her days until she ultimately opts to compete, playing as dirty as Crystal has. She unsheathes claws she did not realize she had (painted "jungle red") and finally wins back her man. That Crystal has cheated on Stephen aids her efforts.

Mary's earnestness throughout the film, notwithstanding the entertaining schemes and broadly comic portrayals of her friends (especially Mary Boland's absurd Flora, the Countess De Lave, chanting and eventually bemoaning "L'amour"), has a strong impact on the film's tone. She is a loving wife, a doting mother (albeit with a governess on stand-by), a healthy horsewoman, and a sincere friend. She is selfless and devoted to the happiness of others, but this means she is more a figure of romance than realism, especially to modern viewers.

The key to *The Women* as an effective satire is our attention to the larger cast of characters. From Sylvia we learn that simply announcing that your marriage is successful does not make it so. She is entirely oblivious, and we are likely to conclude that she is less unhappy to have lost her marriage than to have been shamed by the skills of Miriam Aaron, the younger beauty who "steals" her husband. Similarly, Flora clearly has more money than sense, and scarcely earns even a touch of sympathy from friends when she loses the fidelity of her new young freeloader of a husband, Buck. Crystal, however, is of a different breed than the rest of the film's women, accented by the casting of Joan Crawford. As Ellen Carol DuBois argues of the original play, "As 'good' as wife Mary is, schemer Crystal has the author's attention."[5] Luce herself went from working-class to wealthy wife, ultimately then becoming both a congresswoman and ambassador, both for the far right. She knows the characters she writes, and Crystal gets the best lines.

If we place our attention on the wildcat and not the doe, the satirical power of *The Women* shines more brightly. Pampered Mary may display what we call strength of character, but Crystal has the most at risk when she makes her play for Stephen. Yes, she lies where Mary is truthful; she cheats where Mary is faithful. Yet, even if she loses Stephen, Mary has all the money she needs, custody of her daughter, and the likelihood of other men's attention for remarriage whenever she desires. Crystal, by contrast, lives by her wits and what she can earn—at a sales counter or from a wealthy married man.

We see the stakes when we contrast the marked disparity in the attitudes of those who work for Mary and Crystal. Mary has devoted servants, including a maid and a cook who bemoan their mistress's dilemma more greatly than their own as they face imminent loss of employment. Of course, unlike Crystal, when they lose their positions, they are given letters of reference, handled by the assistant to Stephen's lawyer, a somber, serious woman not unlike "old maid" Nancy, although the assistant is beholden to her male employer and is not independent like Nancy, a novelist. Again, we are reminded of the fate of the unmarried, this time through the satirizing of the priggish career girl. She is professional but plain, her voice as monotonous as her appearance.

By contrast, Crystal has only a coworker, Pat (Virginia Grey), who ridicules Crystal's lies as she lures Stephen by phone, and an African American underling, Lulu (Butterfly McQueen, uncredited), whom Crystal bullies into making dinner at the lowest imaginable price in order to pretend she cooked for her man. The contrast between exploiter and exploited here hinges on an economy of race and class. Mary seems to do little to earn the devotion of her staff except behaving as a wealthy wife and mother is expected to behave. The only time Mary even speaks to her maid is to patronizingly soothe her when she is crying, worried about her mistress's future because of the divorce. By contrast, Crystal threatens Pat and bullies Lulu, relying on toughness rather than feigned friendship to get what she desires. Here, friendship and deference are signs of class status. Only when Crystal temporarily becomes the new Mrs. Haines does she merit or seem to desire a friend—Sylvia, who abandons Mary's coterie because it now includes Miriam, the new Mrs. Fowler. Moreover, when Crystal has the wealth to hire servants, she chooses a stereotyped French maid whom she mistreats in word and deed. She also dislikes playing stepmother to Stephen and Mary's daughter (Virginia Weidler) and quickly involves herself with Buck. Thus, when she loses Stephen to his former spouse, it has much to do with her inability to play the role of privileged wife "properly."

That upper-class marriage is a game with strict rules and boundaries for women is one message the film offers in the Mary/Crystal contrast. This said, I find Crystal to be *The Women*'s most graceful loser, which brings us back to satire. While Flora sobs and Sylvia is locked in a closet, Crystal delivers two lines that announce the satirical nature of the film—or would if they were not underplayed and overshadowed by the final scene and the character of Mary. Standing at the exit to the voluminous ladies' room, Crystal admits defeat directly, saying, "Well, girls, looks like it's back to the perfume counter for me." Clearly, Crystal knows how to compete for a man, but not how to relish the dullness of a wealthy wife's existence. In fact, Stephen was hers to lose, and her behavior arguably shows she did not much want him once she had him. Then, she adds, "There is a name for you ladies, but it's not used in high society outside of a kennel." Neither doe nor housecat, Crystal identifies her opponents as the bitches they are, Mary and her barely dry "jungle red" claws included. Unfortunately, we are not allowed to leave the film with this awareness, nor with a championing of women's desire. After all, Crystal is the only character in the film whose wealth includes indulging in boxes of chocolates, bubble baths, a French maid, rejection of stepparental duties, and an extramarital affair with a man as sexually reckless as she.

If a woman's aim is to make her own money and to experience her own pleasures, then Crystal is more our heroine than Mary. Her assessment of these "ladies" and her matter-of-fact recognition that she is not one of them nor does she care to be is overshadowed by the final scene of the picture. Even if we interpret the last scene as ridicule through excess when Mary shines with devoted love as she trips lightly up the stairs with arms extended toward the camera that stands in for Stephen, we are still encouraged to declare Mary the film's winner, unsatirically.

As Cukor himself declared, the film has a weak and "preposterous" story line. But is this not exactly what a satire demands? He laments in an interview with Gavin Lambert for *On Cukor*, "We sentimentalized it more in the movie." Lambert himself admits he finds the character of Mary "a bore . . . there to send the audience home happy." "So worthy and self-righteous!" Cukor replies, to which Lambert adds, "There's a point of view on all the comic characters—they're satirized. But no point of view at all on [Mary]." Acknowledging Lambert's accuracy, but not acknowledging that there might have been stylistic ways to keep a viewer's attention more fully on the satire, Cukor concludes, "Alas, that happens very often with a straight character."[6]

Perhaps more than anything else, the problem of tone in *The Women* reveals Cukor's efforts to balance difficult and sometimes conflicting objectives, including his dedication to the script, his pleasure in directing comedy, and his need to please the studio executives who kept him working. In this case, satire gave way to romantic comedy, with pleasing if less than radical results. A similar shift occurred with *Susan and God* (1940).

Susan and God also stars Joan Crawford, although in this film she is the protagonist and the subject of the satire. The original play was written by Rachel Carothers, known for addressing feminist themes, often through parody. This arguably lessened as the plays of her heyday in the 1920s became less forceful in the 1930s. Gary Carey describes the play as "almost an about face from her earlier plays; its heroine is criticized for putting her ideals before her family. Susan's ideals however, are those of a religious quack, and she herself is a silly, vain, frivolous woman, and the issue of the play is no issue at all."[7]

Like Luce's work, Carothers's play was reworked by Anita Loos for Cukor to direct. Loos added to the roles of other characters, including the lead character's husband and daughter, enhancing the focus on gender and family relations. The social issue taken up by *Susan and God* is faddish religious trends and their impact on women's lives and relationships. The fad in the play and film was specifically based upon Christian evangelist Frank Buchman's Oxford Group, which encouraged the intimate confession of sins with others in social settings. The film's protagonist is Susan Trexel, a wife who seeks escape from the duties of marriage and motherhood. She is deemed by others to be flighty, but at a deeper level we see signs that she finds it difficult to relate to her awkward daughter Blossom (Rita Quigley) and does not sympathize with her emotionally vulnerable husband, Barrie (Fredric March).

Interestingly, the film was intended as a Norma Shearer vehicle, but the actress refused, on the grounds that it made her look old to play a mother with a teenage daughter. Instead, after Greer Garson also rejected it, Crawford took up the role of Susan, who manages the conflicts in her life by fleeing them, traveling at whim and leaving husband and daughter behind. Crawford's tough woman image makes the character ripe for satire; as the film begins, she has just returned from a trip and is hiding at a friend's home to avoid husband and child. She boasts a new perspective on life, an allegedly spiritual perspective on openness and honesty that is entirely and immediately contradicted by her actions. In addition to avoiding her family responsibilities, we soon see that her fervor is primarily directed toward meddling in friends' lives and judging everyone but herself.

Susan insists her friend Leonora (Rita Hayworth, in an early role) leave her elderly husband (Nigel Bruce) to return to her stage career. And she insults her closest confidante Irene (Rose Hobart) by declaring she is unsuited to her lover Mike (Bruce Cabot). She also alienates her husband further when she agrees to spend the summer with him and their daughter. He has become an alcoholic and begs her forgiveness for it, although the audience is encouraged to judge Susan herself as the cause of his drinking.[8] Susan agrees to the summer arrangement on the condition that Barrie not take even a single drink, adding pressure on him while giving little of herself. Barrie at first delights in her new "religious" passion, hoping it is a sign of maturation; soon, however, he realizes she has not changed from her self-absorbed, shallow self.

If the film remained broadly comedic, with focus on Susan as a static, narcissistic fool in a fast-paced screwball role, it might have been an effective satire. A shift to melodrama and Hollywood-style romantic reconciliation in the film's third act, however, muddles character and tone and dampens social critique. Neither a feminist critique of the confines of traditional marriage nor an effective attack on faddish spiritualities, *Susan and God* cannot hold its ground. The picture ends with Susan finally somehow realizing the pain she has caused others. She punishes herself with remorse, even showing willingness to let Barrie be happy with another woman—the kind, patient Charlotte (Ruth Hussey). Of course, Susan's sudden magnanimity leaves the self-effacing Charlotte no choice but to release Barrie, who returns to Susan with a new resolve to be more dominant in their marriage.

As I interpret the film, satiric impact rests on Susan's inability to care about others' happiness more than her own selfish needs and on a broad display of this character defect. When the film slows its pace and shifts in tone from comic to melodramatic, the character of Susan becomes inconsistent rather than dynamic. Any statement on gender relations and women's issues is lost as well. Susan's sudden desire for a traditional marriage belies any feminist potential in her former resistance, and Barrie's shift from sensitive to strong reinforces the conservative message. In short, like *The Women* but even more so because of character inconsistencies, *Susan and God* fails as satire and becomes an oddly paced comedy of remarriage. In his original review of the film, Bosley Crowther sums up the problems of character, tone, and gender issues in stingingly sexist terms: "If ever a woman needed a beating—but good—that woman is the Susan Trexel of Joan Crawford in '*Susan and God*,' which arrived yesterday at the Capitol amid much jubilation of the Crawford fans, and the fact that she doesn't get it after almost two hours of steady meddling in the lives of other folk—plus the fact that her pitiful husband, a wan and submissive Fredric March, permits her to go on and on giving him the needle while she flings her own ego around—comprises the most disappointing letdown of a generally disappointing film."[9] That Cukor agreed with this sentiment and blamed the film's failure on poor dialogue and plot rather than inconsistent tone returns me to one central question of this chapter: Could Cukor direct effective satire, especially given the demands of the studios and despite his ability to manage classic Hollywood standards alongside flexible perspectives on gender representation?[10]

Perhaps the best answer to this question—for *The Women* remains one of Cukor's best-loved films and even *Susan and God* has its fans—is an examination of a less typical Cukor production that truly failed, one based on a harshly satirical play centered on a British male protagonist in the years after World War II. The film is *Edward, My Son*, adapted from

Noel Langley's 1947 stage success. Even more than with *The Women* and *Susan and God*, attention to the historical and production contexts of this rarely studied 1949 film offers a powerful opportunity to consider in depth the demands of satire and how difficult they could be for Cukor.

In his *New York Times* review, Crowther laments the failure of the film to achieve its iconoclastic potential. Unlike his attack on *Susan and God*, he admits *Edward, My Son*'s strong points, finding the picture "gripping in its exposé of the intimate life of a man in his ruthless rise from poverty to fabulous position and wealth," all ostensibly in service of making life perfect for his "inevitably corrupted" son. Nonetheless, Crowther claims that the screen adaptation of the stage play "has been drained of its most trenchant poison"—the ruthless ambition and "devilishly cruel" single-mindedness of the main character—through the casting of Spencer Tracy. Crowther compares vividly the performances of the two actors to inhabit the role:

> As Mr. Morley played him, he was a behemoth of baldfaced insolence, casually knocking down people with his candid arrogance and brass. He was flippant, indeed, in his demeanor, and completely, almost genially, self-assured. And he hadn't a shred of conscience nor concern over anyone's regard. But as Mr. Tracy plays him, he is a really decent sort who sells his soul for the sake of his beloved son and whose defection seems to haunt him for the rest of his life. His moments of hard and ruthless dealing, in which his eyes narrow coldly and his jaw sets, are heavily interlarded with gay and smiling gobs of Tracy charm.[11]

In both the original Noel Langley play and the film, Lord Arnold Boult (Holt on the stage) goes to extraordinary measures to make his son's path far too smooth. He commits acts of arson, blackmail, and betrayal in professional spheres and abandonment of women in the personal realm. Yet, where the play makes his lordship so boldly callous that we may question whether his ambitions are truly motivated by overzealous love for a son or just sociopathic greed, Tracy's portrayal tempers the image significantly, making the figure detestable but pitiable, too.

If we cannot entirely loathe the man, for Crowther this ambivalence comes from Tracy's inability to play a villain. Assisting in the dulling and muddling of the character is Motion Picture Code censorship, which, in Crowther's estimation, "absurdly bowdlerized" the ending by insisting that audiences see Lord Boult punished (with jail time) for his wrongdoings—or at least for his initial crime of burning down his business for the insurance money.[12]

Crowther's critique is shared by later critics within biographies and filmographies of Cukor. Carey, for instance, asserts, "The role in *Edward, My Son* doesn't fit Tracy, and he doesn't seem at home in it. His own personality, reinforced by the audience's knowledge of past roles, stubbornly refuses to coincide with the character."[13] Gene D. Phillips also focuses on credibility, commenting that "Tracy's screen image as an essentially good-natured kind of person was simply too firmly fixed in the minds of the mass audience to allow them to accept him as a vicious neurotic."[14] Even a highly productive atmosphere on set—for Cukor enjoyed his stay in England, and "Tracy was in a rare happy state," neither anxious nor overdrinking—could not salvage the picture.[15]

Attention to Cukor's direction enhances explanation of the film's problems. Throughout his career, Cukor was derisively, but in practical ways accurately, described as a "woman's director." Although sexism and homophobia are evident in the label, Cukor helmed very few pictures that featured male protagonists, and even fewer that included "fleshed-out fathers of any sort."[16] To be fair, as Stella Bruzzi explains, "Various films released in the late 1940s feature father figures, although conspicuously few of them enter into a discussion of fatherhood as such."[17] This context makes *Edward, My Son* unique for both Cukor and Hollywood cinema of the immediate post–World War II era.

With somewhat less offensive implications, Cukor was also known as an "actor's director." He foregrounds performance in his pictures, working closely with his actors to draw out their best work. Some argue that this made Cukor a director more of the stage, where he began, than the screen. However, few critics deny that he elicited magnificent performances from some of Hollywood's best, and stars racked up quite a few Oscars for their work with Cukor as well. Of the many male stars he directed, Cukor had a particularly solid professional relationship with Spencer Tracy. They worked together on five films over the course of a decade.[18] Although in some ways they did not see eye-to-eye on acting method or lifestyle, they were productive together—especially when Katharine

Hepburn was involved. In the case of *Edward, My Son*, we might argue that his role as "actor's director" came into direct conflict with the script and the tone it demanded.

The source play on which Cukor and Tracy collaborated for *Edward, My Son* was witty and satirical, its success based on the evocation of audience outrage. Even in the capable hands of screenwriter David Ogden Stewart, who worked well and frequently with Cukor, the figure of Holt/Boult did not suit Tracy's style nor Cukor's emphasis on close work with actors to draw deep and convincingly realistic portrayals from them. Moreover, this was not a witty, female-written comedy, but a dark drama. If *The Women* had a weak central plot and Mary was a bore, she was at least a sympathetic type familiar to Cukor, her dullness surrounded by broad comedy. By contrast, the pompous greed of Lord Holt/Boult offered no respite in familiar feminine foibles or screwball portrayals.

The limits of *Edward, My Son* begin, from this perspective, in Cukor's reading of the main character not as an offensive type but as "superficially conceived."[19] There is a one-dimensional, overblown quality to the persona, but Cukor never reflects awareness, either during or after the film's production, that this was intentional and purposeful. That Cukor was either uninterested in or unwilling to direct a male protagonist played for scorn is well illustrated in his selection of Spencer Tracy for the role. Clarens calls the film "the worst miscasting in Spencer Tracy's career"; however, unlike Crowther, he does not attack the performance. Clarens declares that Tracy's acting is "forceful and cunning," particularly effective in the way he "allows his usual bonhomie to seep through while still removing all trace of warmth and tenderness." What Clarens decries is the impact of cultural exchange, specifically the casting of an American actor in a role that was so entirely British in original conception.[20] The film glosses over this significant alteration, making Tracy's Arnold Boult a Canadian transplanted to England, a fact that is announced directly to the audience within the opening scene. For Cukor, this was necessary, for Tracy could not do a convincing British accent/persona. For Clarens, this is a misguided transformation, for it "upsets the social conflict of the original." When Lord Holt in the play threatens to foreclose on the mortgage of the exclusive public school his son Edward will be expelled from, for instance, he enacts a stereotype of the upper-class British gentleman bully. When, by contrast, Tracy inhabits the rewritten role with his rough

American demeanor, "the final effect is that of democratic pluck cutting through stuffy British class-consciousness."[21] Or, in the words of Bill Krohn, "We have a cast that pits the hapless English against a sonofabitch from the New World."[22]

Crowther laments the miscasting of Tracy mostly because he finds the film not only "intriguing in its details" but also in its "consistently interesting" supporting characters. Deborah Kerr revived her career after two MGM flops by playing tragic wife Evelyn Boult from youth to alcoholic middle-age in *Edward, My Son*; she earned an Oscar nomination for her performance. Crowther also praises Ian Hunter as abused family friend Dr. Larry Woodhope, Leueen MacGrath as amorous secretary Eileen Perrin (a role she originated on stage, though Katharine Hepburn hoped to play it on-screen), and other actors in smaller roles.[23] With its mixture of potential in supporting cast and failure in its lead, critics have ultimately not been surprised that this particular Cukor film "remains filed away and forgotten."[24] All generally lay the blame in the casting and/or performance of Tracy, whether because of the actor's limitations, audience bias, Cukor's direction, Code censorship, or some combination of these factors.

Greater depth of consideration of the cultural and production contexts provides more complex and satisfying answers to both the unpopularity of *Edward, My Son* and its worthiness as a subject of film study, particularly as a failed satire. We can read the film through American postwar anxieties, particularly over changing notions of familial gender roles—specifically fatherhood—and how this cultural context emerges in the methods of the film's director and lead actor.

In *Bringing Up Daddy: Fatherhood and Masculinity in Postwar Hollywood*, Stella Bruzzi posits, "Despite the emergence of more enlightened attitudes toward fathering in the first half of the twentieth century, the most significant event of the 1940s—the war—heightened the desire for a return to a more traditional patriarchal image." Hollywood films of the era, she argues, often display a repression of "caring, sensitive masculinity in favour of hyper-masculine toughness," exemplified by the proliferation of Westerns and patriarchal comedies "in which domestic tribulations become the source of comedy and sentimentality." In particular, 1949 was a year in which both "kindly, ineffectual" and "good upright" fathers gave way to what Bruzzi refers to as "strong, even abhorrently authoritarian patriarchs," seen in such Hollywood offerings as *Fort Apache* (1949), *The Heiress* (1949), and *House of Strangers* (1949), as well as the following year's *The Furies* (1950).[25]

In terms of its textual setting, *Edward, My Son* begins just after World War I, on Edward's first birthday. Arnold Boult is a man struggling to rise in class; he is ambitious but without funds. We do not know whether he is a war veteran, for this is never mentioned. The actual soldier in the family is ultimately Edward, who trains as a pilot for World War II service, although the character never actually appears in the film (echoing the technique of the original play). After more than two dozen years of having "the world your oyster" (a phrase that Arnold uses as a toast at year one and wife/mother Evelyn dislikes immediately for its implications of parental immoderation), Edward dies at twenty-three when he crashes his plane in a stunt to impress friends, before he even gets to battle. As an unnamed commander declares to family friend Larry when the doctor returns home for a break in military service: "Can't afford accidents like that these days. Destroying an aircraft while showing off over some girl's house. As if the Germans weren't doing enough damage."

This military record makes *Edward, My Son* unique for its era. Unlike most Hollywood films of the late 1940s that feature soldiers, this picture has no war heroes, neither father nor son. Moreover, its relationship to World War II is primarily one of displacement, in which Arnold rather than Edward signifies a troubled postwar masculinity, echoing the film's era of production rather than its setting. In other words, we can best understand the film as director Cukor's and screenwriter Stewart's Hollywood tale of a Canadian in London (whom audiences recognize immediately as American) set in the era between the world wars while featuring the unmistakable tone and attitudes of post–World War II America. Such a description is hardly recognizable as Langley's original satire.

We can best interpret the absence of heroes and heroism in *Edward, My Son* as a reflection of changing American gender roles after World War II. Useful is Bruzzi's assertion that "films that deal with the role of the father in the troubled aftermath of the war reflect the image of America as a nation in transition." Women who had experienced greater freedoms, meaningful work, and financial independence contended with returning men and their need to return to traditional masculine roles within the family and the workplace. Individual men might vary in their desires, but the media—from ladies' magazines to B thrillers—"established various incompatibilities between the man's war experience and the contemporaneous experience on the home front, again intimating that somehow fatherhood—the domestic masculine ideal—was likewise incompatible with being a 'man.'" In consequence, "Women were viewed as largely detrimental to the returning man's well-being"; they were blamed for either keeping their sons weak and immature or neglecting them, "having usurped the breadwinning role." Popular advice at the time advocated a return to patriarchal order in which mothers submitted to their husbands at home and all men in the public sphere.[26]

Interpreted within this context, *Edward, My Son* offers a powerful case study in the danger of heeding such advice. In displaced fashion, the arrogant, swaggering Lord Boult represents the postwar (American) man given sway in business, the home, and parenting, leaving little for wife and mother to do apart from obeying and hoping for the best. As a cautionary tale with Victorian overtones, the film teaches that the oppression of wives and mothers has a direct impact on not only the women themselves but their children (a lesson straight from Mary Wollstonecraft). That men are also wounded, even destroyed, by adherence to patriarchal hypermasculine norms is also evident when the film is considered from a modern feminist perspective.

Evelyn is clearly not the parent that actively keeps Edward weak and immature. A passive willingness to let her husband lead in every facet of their lives is her primary fault. Moreover, when she finally does rebel, it is because Arnold has had an affair with his secretary Eileen and thus, in traditional terms, failed in his patriarchal duties. Evelyn's lawyer has Arnold followed until they can collect adequate evidence to get her the divorce she seeks, with the assumption that she, as the mother, will gain custody of their son. Arnold, however, is unwilling to allow Evelyn or cultural biases related to motherhood to best him. He casually ends his affair without concern for his lover (who will lose both the man she loves and her relatively prestigious job) and denies Evelyn a divorce. To ensure her continued obedience to his will, he tells her flatly that if she proceeds with her plans to leave him and take Edward, he will ruin the life of Larry. Arnold knows the doctor is in love with Evelyn and, very likely, she with him. The blackmail succeeds, and Evelyn is, over time, reduced to a passive-aggressive alcoholic, trapped within the home and under Arnold's thumb, a displaced Victorian madwoman in the attic.

In a logical but surprising turn for the era, Arnold's extremes of patriarchal dominance mean he and not Evelyn is to blame for Edward's spoiled immaturity and, ultimately, death. Arnold, not Evelyn, is guilty of what Philip Wylie, in his 1943 critique of American ills, *Generation of Vipers*, calls "Momism," a maternal excessive attachment to sons that leaves them incapable of reaching independent adulthood.[27] Arnold has claimed all parental roles as well as the public realm, fitting the mold of the Hollywood-style postwar male as Bruzzi analyzes him, battling "to repress caring, sensitive masculinity in favour of hyper-masculine toughness."[28] Because of this, he destroys all around him. He bullies and torments Evelyn while overindulging Edward and builds his fortune on the exploitation and suffering—even death—of others. Ultimately, he emerges as the opposite of the typical Hollywood father figure of the era: an older, secondary character, harmless and ineffectual, letting his heroic son shine.[29] Instead, *Edward, My Son*, with its British setting but American pedigree, turns satire into political melodrama and ends up revealing that strict patriarchal control would be a disastrous direction for individuals and families within a nation in transition.

The film's dark mood that denies originally intended satire emerges not only in its content but its style. American cultural anxieties of the World War II and postwar era coalesced into the film cycle we have come to call film noir. Although *Edward, My Son* is not best identified as such, it does share postwar noir's general mood of anxiety and fatalism. Noir mise-en-scène, from dark urban settings and chiaroscuro lighting to Dutch angles and deep focus, are largely absent from the film, although there is a gothic noir feel to the family mansion as Evelyn deteriorates and the film moves to a close. Most noirish is the film's narrative framing device and structure. The picture opens with a black screen, then a massive door opening to expose blank whiteness behind it. An aging, somewhat frail looking Lord Boult is sharply silhouetted as he enters an empty, stage-like set through the door, leaning on his cane. Light pours in from behind him as he steps from a bright, empty space beyond the door into a wide and dark but shapeless entryway. He introduces himself to the audience against sympathetic music, emphasizing his wealth ("I probably own this theater") and his desire to establish "some sort of contact" with viewers. "I want your opinion," he declares flatly; "I want your response to a question." But he does not ask the question (except in the trailer to the film). A mood of discomfort typical of noir develops in this combination of expressionistic setting, direct audience address (as a kind of substitute for noir voiceover), and framing device leading into flashback.

As Raymond Borde and Étienne Chaumeton concluded, based on a group of 1940s American films screened just after the war in France, film noir "exists in response to a certain mood at large in this particular time and place," that is, postwar America. Anxiety in *Edward, My Son* flows through a combination of what Borde and Chaumeton describe as key elements of noir: an "ambiguous protagonist," an "uncertainty of motivations," and a "weird theme which creates the atmosphere of the nightmare." *Edward, My Son* also echoes their description of noir as a "film of death" through its emphasis on a "mix of foul play and murder." Certainly, death permeates the film, from the encouraged suicide of Boult's original business partner to Edward's selfish, lethal accident, spurred on by an overindulgent, irresponsible upbringing. The film thus fits surprisingly well into Hollywood's classical noir series, further reflecting its postwar relevance and simultaneous distance from the tone of the play from which it is adapted.[30]

The flashback structure of the film is particularly evocative. Throughout the film, Arnold has shown no ability to reflect on his ruthlessness and immorality or on the resulting suffering of others for which he is, ultimately, largely responsible. The closing return to the dark hall framing device has our protagonist ask the audience, "If you had been me, what would you have done?" The question is vague and ambiguous. We cannot put ourselves in this man's shoes, nor do we wish to. Yet, we pair in our minds this final rhetorical query with the unasked question of the opening scene, revealing Lord Boult's desperate desire to free himself of guilt and responsibility for the wrongs he has knowingly committed. The original stage play left no such vagueness, hence little anxiety: we despise Lord Holt and are meant to. By contrast, Cukor's postwar adaptation produces conflict, for the viewer and the protagonist.

Beyond the script and mise-en-scène, anxieties may be connected to the cinematic technique of the long take. As Charlie Keil explains in his study of Cukor/Tracy films, it is through the long take that "the director's role seems to fuse with the actor's most consistently." Interestingly, Keil discusses every Tracy performance in a Cukor film except *Edward, My Son*. Nonetheless, the films he does study help to clarify the problems of the one he does not. For Keil, the best evidence of the successful long take appears in Cukor's Tracy/Hepburn films, *Keeper of the Flame* (1942), *Adam's Rib* (1949), and *Pat and Mike* (1952). In these films, "Cukor builds the relationship between the two actors primarily through interplay conducted in unbroken shots," even as such shots also reflect his closeness to and confidence in the actors. Moreover, the three Cukor/Tracy/Hepburn collaborations all feature a romantic relationship in which issues of gender and power are addressed—to differing degrees and for differing reasons. Despite great differences in genre, plot, and tone, the long take serves in the trio of films to "keep the actors spatially connected" in moments of accord and in conflict. Ultimately, Keil is persuasive in arguing that through the long take Cukor showed that he "understood that the role of the camera was to reveal screen acting's myriad functions: establishing character, commenting on the narrative, and embodying emotional states." Nonetheless, this is precisely the approach most likely to ruin the intended ironic detachment central to the satire of the original play.[31]

For a potent example of the emotional impact of the long take in *Edward, My Son*, we can consider the scene in which Arnold refuses to give Evelyn a divorce as they fight over Edward's future. The camera follows the couple as they pace the room, verbally attacking one another until Arnold resorts to physical violence, throwing Evelyn roughly to the sofa in two unbalanced shots that display their discord. Only after this violence does Evelyn give in to Arnold's blackmail. She then wanders from the foreground of the shot to the open bedroom at the back of the set. Focus lingers on angry, smug Arnold, now alone in the foreground. Through the long take and its changing positioning of the actors, imbalanced gender relations are clearly demarcated. As Cukor biographer Gene Phillips describes, relative distance from the camera "symbolically defines the relationship of tyrannical domination and abject submission that exists between them."[32] This stylistic preference shows purposeful direction, yet it detracts from the film's overall effectiveness, for it emphasizes dramatic intensity in a script that neither sustains nor intends it. The long take reveals a character to its audience well, especially as that character has compelling emotions to show. Once Arnold Boult becomes little more than the embodiment of icy, immoral determination, however, lingering shots can be unproductive or misleading.

The long take, then, is one more example of how Cukor's style and relationship with actors in general and Tracy in particular are problematic

In *Edward, My Son* (1949), an unbalanced two shot of Arnold (Spencer Tracy) and Evelyn (Deborah Kerr) illustrates dramatic intensity that detracts from ironic detachment. (Photofest)

for the film. With no screen experience as a villain, taking joy in his productive work and brief respite from personal anxiety and alcoholism, and being directed by a man who knew him well and sought to get a deeply impactful performance out of him, the Arnold Boult of Cukor's long take shifts from the play's insolent monster to the film's lonely and misguided postwar patriarch, whose inability to connect with others has cost him everything. Together, such elements deny the possibility of reading the film as the satire of an odious figure of overweening greed. Instead, we have a failed tragedy about a father's moral decline or a flawed cautionary tale about postwar anxiety over masculinity taken to extremes.

Therefore, when the heavy-handed framing device follows Lord Boult as he ends his tale and says good night in the concluding frame, we likely agree with Crowther that "he is lugging a heavy conscience down that weary last mile."[33] We sympathize with or pity him, even if just a little. From the postwar context and its commentary on gender roles to the film's style and tone, including noirish anxiety and reliance on the long take, we can see Arnold's stagey departure as a congenial actor's remorse at being unable to persuasively embody a cruel and excessive patriarchal role at such a transitional time in American history, and a director's dissatisfaction at having to center a film on such a figure.

When read together, *The Women*, *Susan and God*, and *Edward, My Son* illustrate the complexities of producing satire for Cukor over the course of a decade and within very different collaborative contexts. The "woman's director" of romantic comedies was forced to accede to the demands of sexist happy endings that drew attention away from social critique in *The Women* and *Susan and God*. The "actor's director" of the late 1940s achieved comfort with an offensive representation of asocial masculinity via casting, form, and style that undercut the intended satirical effect. Whether the pictures were forgiven and appreciated despite their problems (*The Women*), dismissed (*Susan and God*), or forgotten (*Edward, My Son*), we see the vital importance of tone to classic Hollywood. Although he did experiment with gender in engaging ways, satire was too harsh a lens for his preferred methods.

4

Masculinity and the Man Who Drinks

As previous discussions of *The Philadelphia Story* and *Susan and God* have hinted, the figure of the male alcoholic appeared frequently in classical Hollywood cinema. From the man troubled by marital insecurities to the fading celebrity icon, the subject of masculinity is placed under the filmic microscope across genres in the films of George Cukor.

The representation of alcoholism and perspective on the figure of the alcoholic has varied throughout Hollywood history. The good-spirited boozer and laughable lush gave way to the pitiable drunk and, later, as cultural attitudes and awareness shifted, to the problem drinker whose alcoholism was blamed first on social and interpersonal pressures and eventually on disease. A troublingly common figure is that of the slapstick romantic comedy drunk of the 1930s. The attitude of the genre and era is perhaps best illustrated by George and Marion Kerby (Cary Grant and Constance Bennett) in *Topper* (1937), in which death by drunk driving barely dampens the spirits and ultimately adds to the adventurous times of the fun-loving central couple.

During this same era, as screwball yielded to romantic comedies with a bit more drama, heavily influenced by the strictures of the Motion Picture Code, the giddy tippler and the lecherous boozehound were joined by more realistically portrayed addicts, particularly in the figures of central male characters. Hollywood was more interested in showing some of the real consequences of alcoholism, without yielding its sense of humor or happy ending. Thus, for example, Cukor's *The Philadelphia Story* (1940) features both the bawdy Uncle Willie (Roland Young) and the somber if not sober C. K. Dexter Haven (Cary Grant). The film has no difficulty balancing the lovable lecher and meddling ex in one picture. Moreover, drinking is central to the transformation of the film's protagonist, Tracy Lord (Katharine Hepburn). She pays for her drunken lesson opposite young Macaulay Connor (James Stewart) with a doozy of a hangover and the loss of a fiancé, but only Dexter is denoted as a problem drinker.

Cukor's other film released in 1940, *Susan and God*, another romantic comedy, is even heavier on the dramatic element, as discussed in the previous chapter. Here, alcoholism is treated less as a subject of entertainment and humorous comeuppance than as a sign of the distress and alienation felt by Susan's husband. While Dexter acknowledges that his drinking problem is not of his ex-wife's making, Barrie (Fredric March) turns to the bottle directly because of his marital woes in *Susan and God.* In both cases, the distant wives must come to accept responsibility for their marriages, and this includes the tendencies of their alcoholic husbands.

Generally, if the genre is romantic comedy, the male drunk must be cured or his ailment ignored to reach satisfying Hollywood-style closure. This makes serious consideration of alcoholism difficult. In "Something Wild: The Fruits of Filmic Intoxication," Marty Roth identifies Hollywood as a major source for mainstream America's "culture of denial" because its films posit that "life's problems are transitory or remediable." As concerns alcoholism, such pathology becomes portrayed as "temporary comic complication."[1] Such an approach suits Cukor's work in romantic comedy well. In a discussion of his work with the plays of Philip Barry—author of both *The Philadelphia Story* (1940) and *Holiday* (1938)—Cukor stated, "I find it wonderful to take a serious subject and treat it with a kind of impertinence and gaiety."[2] Specifically, we see such trivialization in both *Susan and God* and *The Philadelphia Story*, which results in lifting the alcoholics' burden to shift it onto women who reject them.

That Hepburn's Tracy has a night of drunken regret helps her to sympathize with Dexter's problem. In fact, when he sees her topple from her tower of teetotaling uptightness, his "deep and gorgeous thirst" swiftly subsides. Their remarriage can be read as a reuniting of minds and lives that are now more in accord. In *Susan and God*, however, Susan not only recognizes that she has "failed" her husband, but she even wishes him happiness with another woman. Like Tracy, she has had a revelation about her personal selfishness and harsh judgments of others, but the film handles her transformation with heavy-handed melodrama. First, she praises Barrie for his (miraculous, willpower-driven) ability to quit

Susan (Joan Crawford) goes from irresponsible and willful to tearful and guilt-ridden in *Susan and God* (1940), represented by her sitting at her estranged husband's feet in this publicity shot.

drinking. Then, seated while her husband looks down from above (at his feet in a publicity photo of the scene), she begs with tremulous voice, "Please let me try again. I want to be so much more to you than I've ever been before. I know now, dearest. If only I'd done myself what I was asking everyone else to do. God couldn't help me, not one little bit. Because I wouldn't dig and dig to get the rottenness out of me."

These post-screwball romantic comedies present female independence as destructive and companionate marriage as attainable only once patriarchal norms are at least acknowledged. However, dominance over others requires self-control, and an alcoholic man lacks this. When a film is not centrally about alcoholism, the illness must thus be trivialized, magically cured or shown not really to be alcoholism after all. Argues Roth, the "incongruity between a romantic and a clinical mode [of portraying alcoholism] is minimized because his [Dexter's] alcoholism is both marginalized and romanticized" in *The Philadelphia Story*.[3] This mystification turns an addiction to liquor into what Stanley Cavell describes as Dexter's "thirst for truth, or for self-knowledge, as well as for her [Tracy's] desire."[4] Alcohol is here a symbol; alcoholism is a condition whose cure is a woman's love in both films.[5]

To draw conclusions about these representations of the alcoholic male within romantic comedies, we can turn more generally to historical context. Cukor developed as a director within a "generally booze-soaked generation and moved in a liquor-heavy social set. He was a moderate drinker, but he was obviously fascinated by alcohol and why people needed it." Drink, after all, can lead to "edifying follies."[6] Such "follies" and the way they link drink to the challenges of living up to the norms of white, privileged-class masculinity within domestic settings definitely occupy Cukor's early romantic comedies. However, Cukor had even harsher opinions on the subject. He described alcoholism as "the kiss of death" that "destroys people."[7] And we see this most pointedly and poignantly in his depictions of the male alcoholic in Hollywood, the figure on whom the remainder of this chapter will focus.

If comedic approaches allow for almost magical solutions to drinking problems to bring about romantic solutions, what happens when the scenario is more darkly dramatic? Whether in an early drama with comedic elements, such as *Dinner at Eight* (1933), or a tragedy, such as *What Price Hollywood?* (1932) and Cukor's later film inspired by it, *A Star Is Born* (1954), the Hollywood alcoholic male marks the impact of drink upon the Hollywood set, particularly the figures of aging male actors and directors.

Traditional Hollywood imagery presents "proper" white, privileged-class manhood as best illustrated by a man's ability to demonstrate success (often dominance) in both heterosexual relationships and the workplace. Simultaneously, he must display confidence and talent professionally, socially, and interpersonally. Ineffectiveness in either private or public realms dooms most major male characters in both dramatic and comedy narratives from classic Hollywood to the present. Such a distinction is important to the films of George Cukor because much of his material lacks stereotypically heroic men, especially in relationship to his women, who tend to be relatively strong and sympathetic. Sympathy, however, often emerges in a woman's pity for a man who cannot fulfill high levels of heteronormative masculine gender expectations. The central metaphor for representing such figures in Cukor films is alcoholism.

When addressed dramatically, this investment comes through fictionalizations of those he knew best: men in Hollywood.

When films foreground incurable alcoholics, they are more likely to consider the psychological and social issues that lead to their self-destruction. In the figure of the male Hollywood alcoholic, Cukor reflects a trend to evoke emotional identification from viewers. Hollywood's particular pressures both inspire and encourage drinking, even if alcoholism is derided. Abuse of liquor, especially when displayed publicly, damns Hollywood stars. Within films such as the three on which the rest of this chapter will focus and many others throughout Hollywood history, these men are depicted as lacking self-control, weak-willed, and antisocial. Nonetheless, Cukor almost exclusively directed films that ensured viewer sympathy with characters, including those portrayed as failures.[8]

The means by which Cukor achieves compassion for his doomed male Hollywood alcoholics is in their pairing with and response to women. Working with classic Hollywood films, I share the perspective of sociologist Norman K. Denzin, who, in *Hollywood Shot by Shot: Alcoholism in American Cinema*, posits that "stories of the social, 'natural' relations between (alcoholic) men and women have typically been told, seen, and written about through the masculine gaze and voice."[9] Of course, the male gaze and voice dominate most classic Hollywood pictures, as has been explicated by many a feminist film critic. Important here is how the patriarchal perspectives control the figure of the woman in response to the dominant male alcoholic. Denzin finds women generally function as "the barometer of alcoholism's effects on family, love, intimacy, self-respect, and work."[10] They are sometimes the victim of the drunk, yet they are often held to blame for the drinking. Before the 1960s, when alcoholism began to be treated as a disease requiring treatment, Hollywood cinema generally adopted the "alcoholism alibi," blaming drinkers for their own problems, as we have seen through consideration of male alcoholics within romantic comedy above.[11] Within pre-1960s drama and melodrama, however, there was a tendency to blame the woman who loves the man who drinks. Only a certain type of woman would be drawn to an addict, runs the logic. Hence, these films suggest that such women are also "sick."[12]

To nuance study of gender norms and filmic representations of alcoholics in Cukor, I find it useful to adopt Denzin's general conclusions and qualify them by genre and setting. For films centered on alcoholism, the most common genre is the social problem film. Cukor, however, did not direct such films. Instead, he most often directed dramas and romantic comedies that feature alcoholic characters, often blending the genres in the films in which they can be found. Such disparate films as *What Price Hollywood?* (1932), *Dinner at Eight* (1933), and *Susan and God* (1940), for example, begin with comic excess but shift to (melo)drama. *A Star Is Born* (1954) adds discordant elements of the musical to its dramatic narrative, while earlier romantic comedies *Holiday* (1938) and *The Philadelphia Story* (1940) reveal darkness beneath the surface of their happy endings.

The setting of films that feature male alcoholics is equally critical to their methods and messages. *What Price Hollywood?*, *Dinner at Eight*, and *A Star Is Born* all link alcoholism directly to the demands of Hollywood. The three present a similar type in Max Carey (Lowell Sherman), Larry Renault (John Barrymore), and Norman Maine (James Mason), respectively.[13] At the level of narrative, all three films involve a story of a star-struck young woman enamored of an older male Hollywood star who inspires her, though this is most obvious in the transition from *What Price Hollywood?* to both the 1937 and 1954 versions of *A Star Is Born*, where the only significant shift from film to film is the blending of the Hollywood star and the love object into one man, who becomes a fellow actor rather than a director. (Cukor did not direct the 1937 film, arguing it was too similar to *What Price Hollywood?* Instead, the picture was directed by William Wellman.) *Dinner at Eight* features a less ambitious but entirely awed young woman who wants only the former matinee idol's attention and affection, and their story is a subplot rather than the film's centerpiece. Nonetheless, all three couplings fit the description of love destroyed by alcoholism against a backdrop of Hollywood pressures.

If love is killed in these films, so are men. All three of the alcoholic characters to be discussed die, and their narratives evoke sympathy. In part, this relates to the seriousness with which the films take their critique of Hollywood itself. Even with moments of slapstick and ridicule, for example, producer David Selznick (who produced *What Price Hollywood?* and *Dinner at Eight*) insisted upon credibility. As Cukor states, "Most of the other pictures make it [Hollywood] a kind of crazy, kooky place, but to David it was absolutely real, he believed in it. I think that's why *What Price Hollywood?* was one of the few successful pictures about the place, in the face of a tradition that they never succeed."[14]

Because filmic depictions of suicide can evoke audience sympathy—however contrived they may be—the deaths of the male alcoholics in Cukor's films about Hollywood are a central part of their impact and availability for interpretation as cautionary tales. Perhaps most important in this context is that the deaths function as important catalysts for the forward movement of others' lives, particularly the women who were closest to them. Mary Evans (Constance Bennett) reunites with her estranged husband after Carey's death in *What Price Hollywood?* Paula Jordan (Madge Evans) seems likely to marry her former fiancé in *Dinner at Eight*, and even more broadly, Renault's death indirectly leads to an ending in which the central dramatic characters face reality.[15] Finally, Esther Blodgett's (Judy Garland) star rises even higher after Norman is finally gone. Cukor reflects his intention to emphasize this effect in *A Star Is Born* in his description of one of many scenes cut from the original film: "Right after that agonizing scene in her dressing room, after Mason's death, she goes straight out and, in one shot, does a very cheerful number on the soundstage. It was wonderful the way she went straight into it."[16] In the final cut, we see Esther's awareness of the role of her husband's death in her decision to identify herself in the film's final scene not as Vicki Lester or even Esther Blodgett but as "Mrs. Norman Maine."[17] In many ways, he made her the sober, mature star that she is.

An additional factor in the success of these films is their reliance on details from the lives of actual Hollywood personalities. Actor/director Lowell Sherman was known to have bouts of drunkenness, for example, although critics generally point to John Barrymore, his then brother-in-law, for inspiring his character in *What Price Hollywood?*[18] Gary Carey notes, for instance, that "Sherman brings to the early section of the film that light self-mockery with which Barrymore frequently guyed the ineptitudes of his late comedy roles."[19] The film's primary screenwriter, Gene Fowler, may have intended this specific connection, for he was a friend of Barrymore's and also his biographer.[20] In addition, Emanuel Levy reveals that the original Adela Rogers St. Johns story originated in the relationship between silent film star Colleen Moore and her producer-husband, John McCormick. Moreover, Levy adds, "Sherman's character also echoes the lives of Marshall 'Mickey' Neilan, a silent movie director with a drinking problem, and John Barrymore (who would play a similar role in Cukor's 1933 *Dinner at Eight*)."[21]

Playwrights Edna Ferber and George Kaufman may well have written the role of Renault with Barrymore in mind, as they did with Tony Cavendish in *The Royal Family of Broadway*, the film version of which Cukor directed (1930), featuring Fredric March as Tony. Barrymore himself claimed to be playing the role of Renault as "a combination of his father-in-law (Broadway matinee idol Maurice Costello), his brother-in-law (Lowell Sherman, married to Helene Costello, sister of one of Barrymore's wives), and himself."[22] That Sherman portrayed Max Carey as Barrymore while Barrymore played Larry Renault as Sherman illustrates that there was enough alcoholism within Hollywood—indeed, within the extended Barrymore family alone—to variously inspire these early film representations. Moreover, twenty plus years later, even Cukor's *A Star Is Born* offers traces of Barrymore in its imagery. Cukor tells an anecdote about the source for the agent character's visit to Norman Maine in a sanitarium:

> Years ago, when I was going to direct *Camille* [1936], I went to see Jack Barrymore about playing De Varville. . . . Jack had put himself into some kind of home in Culver City to stop drinking. . . . It was an old frame house that called itself a rest home. I went into some dreary, depressing room. . . . Then Jack came in, with a sort of aide called Kelly. He took us into a gloomy sitting room and said, "Can we sit in here, Kelly? Nobody's going to come through and disturb us by pretending he's Napoleon." I reported this episode to David Selznick, who was preparing the first *A Star Is Born* with William Wellman. They liked the scene so much they included it in the picture. Then, years later, I found myself redoing it.[23]

According to Denzin's sociological viewpoint, of the three films, *What Price Hollywood?* is most noteworthy for offering "the first major analysis of its [Hollywood's] own star system and the occupational causes of alcoholism."[24] The film critiques the big studios for their heartlessness, with both humor and moments of biting irony. Clarens praises the film for its "detachment and precision" in this regard. He further notes pointed parody in that "Max appears to have wasted his one considerable talent as a director just as Mary will waste hers in a series of tear-jerkers of the kind Bennett made popular in this period."[25]

Critics also frequently identify *What Price Hollywood?* as the first in the *Star Is Born* cycle, limiting analysis of the Max Carey character to its origins and tragicomic presentation. Lambert emphasizes Sherman's "slightly odious quality" as an actor, which played well in the film; and Cukor adds, "Yes, you felt his drunkenness and disagreeable behavior came out of a bitterness and feeling he was a basically unattractive person."[26] While scarcely a developed explanation of cause, this description does address issues of inadequacy and links failure to fulfill masculine norms with alcoholism, particularly in the Hollywood milieu. This is accentuated in the professional differences between the characters of Max Carey and producer Julius Saxe (Gregory Ratoff). Saxe takes a cutthroat approach and blusters, "If you can't tell it in fifty words, it's not a story!" Max, by contrast, can be read, as does Denzin, as a product of the popular cultural myth, begun by the *Star Is Born* cycle, that creative men abuse drugs and alcohol.[27]

To reflect this myth, Max's death is romanticized. First, Mary fulfills the requirement of feminine nurturance of a motherly sort by insisting, "You are going to be dry from now on." When alone, however, Max drinks two shots, and then compares the image of himself in the mirror with a photo of himself in his prime. As he lights a cigarette, images of drinking scenes from his past flash by in the mirror. To enhance its emotional impact, the scene—praised highly by reviewers of the time—features visual and aural creativity of an expressionist sort, including an eerie whirring sound effect. Next, Max turns away, returns with a gun, and shoots himself in the chest. We are encouraged to sympathize with this man who had so much talent and wasted it, and the fact that Mary leaves Hollywood in response tells us that she understands the real danger in spending one's life chasing stardom.

A harsher, less sympathetic portrayal of the doomed male Hollywood star appears a year later in a Cukor film. If both Max Carey and Larry Renault live and die in denial, Max is shown to have had genuine talent, while Larry grossly overestimates his abilities and appeal. Barrymore received top male billing for his work in *Dinner at Eight*, and although his character appears in several brief moments and only one extended scene that does not include most of the rest of the cast of this ensemble drama, his death is the central tragedy of the film. However important to the picture, there is some difference of opinion on how best to interpret the tone of John Barrymore's embodiment of second-rate, has-been matinee idol Larry Renault. The cynicism of the role differed significantly from the comedic tribute to Barrymore in Cukor's *The Royal Family of Broadway* or even the self-mockery of his own work in Walter Lang's *The Great Profile* (1940). Cukor biographers have generally characterized Barrymore's portrayal in *Dinner at Eight* as both self-effacing and emotionally moving. Typical are perspectives such as Patrick McGilligan's: "The part of the cheap actor was eerily close to a self-portrait, odious like the character of the director in *What Price Hollywood?* yet poignant." Hence, "Barrymore's bleak study of a drink-doomed Lothario anchored the film somberly."[28] And Carey reminds us that "Barrymore was not, at this point, a has-been, as is Larry Renault, but his reputation was already suffering from a disappointing film career and increasing alcoholic misconduct." He thus concludes, "It's a little embarrassing seeing an actor playing a character based so unflatteringly on his own life."[29]

Cukor's stated perspective on Barrymore's portrayal differs significantly from these critical assessments. When young, Cukor had seen the Barrymores on Broadway and admired them greatly. Moreover, he and John Barrymore built the role of Renault together, with intentional distance from the actor's life. "He played a cheapish, second-rate actor, which, God knows, he wasn't," Cukor states in Richard Schickel's 1973 PBS documentary, *The Men Who Made the Movies* (to accompany his book of the same name). The director particularly praises the way Barrymore handled the role "with enormous wit and very subtly." Together, director and actor sought to accentuate the arrogant foolishness of the character. As Cukor declares, Barrymore "put things in to make himself hammier, more ignorant," while Cukor ramped up the ridicule, particularly in his suicide. Cukor blamed Renault for his own failures and said, "We thought that although he wanted to die in a picturesque way, he should fuck that up, too."[30] Cukor came up with the idea for Renault to trip over a footstool into "this very ugly, middle-aged, awkward sprawl" before he turns on the gas and dies in an armchair, with a lamp purposefully tilted to accentuate his famous profile.[31]

Arguably, this pompous, slapstick death scene illustrates that Cukor's approach to Larry Renault's character relies upon the traditional "alcoholism alibi." Most critics agree, arguing that Renault's self-deluding pride dooms him more than his age or his drinking. If so, then why, we may ask, do so many viewers find sympathy or at least pity for the character? Most persuasively, this comes through a biographical reading, where Renault reflects Barrymore's own downward spiral that would ultimately have a tragic end. The realities of Hollywood belie its filmic fictions. Additionally, we may posit that this "lie" is part of Cukor's own perspective as an admirer of actors and their abilities. As Phillips concludes, "If Cukor is unsympathetic to the unreal dreams of wealth, fame, or respectability that so many of the characters in his films cherish, he nevertheless treats the dreamers themselves with compassion, as he does with Renault."[32] We can even substitute "Barrymore" for "Renault" in the above quotation, given the overlap in actor and character.

To address this conflation fully, we can turn to gender roles and relations, particularly Renault's treatment of women in *Dinner at Eight.* Before we even meet him, we are told by Hattie Loomis (Louise Closser Hale), the middle-class cousin of central female character Millicent Jordan (Billie Burke), that Renault's career ended with the talkies. Still, Hattie enthuses, "I'll say this for him: in his photographs, he has the most heavenly profile." The scene fades to an image of this famous profile, and then to the rest of Larry Renault, sporting a distinguished moustache and smoking jacket. Barrymore and Renault, we soon learn, share a nickname from their celebrated youth, the "Great Profile."

Forty-something Larry Renault appears in his first scene entertaining nineteen-year-old Paula Jordan (Madge Evans), daughter of Millicent and Oliver (Lionel Barrymore), bragging about the play he is wrongly certain he is about to star in. "The play's not much," he brags, "but I think I can put it over." He identifies his role as the "only" male character, noting as an aside that he will "dominate" the one scene featuring a "bit actor" as a beachcomber. As Renault speaks, he drinks, and, when the bottle is empty, he receives the delivery of a full one from the bellboy, whom he pays to run "errands" for him. Paula shows concern as he imbibes, rendering Renault instantly defensive. "Any reason I shouldn't?" he demands. When she reminds him that he is to dine with her family that night (for the titular "dinner at eight"), she gently urges, "I want them to see you at your best" and then puts her hand on his full glass and says, "Larry, don't." Renault snaps, telling Paula to mind her own business. Paula stands up for herself, telling him not to speak to her that way, but Renault replies with a petulant "I'll do as I please" and downs his drink. Here, Renault's temper reveals how addicted to drink he is and how connected his addiction is to his ego, both as an actor and as relates to his sense of masculine pride.

Renault does apologize soon after this exchange, noting that he is on edge as regards the play, "and everything." We see his temporary ability to play the confident, secure man, particularly for the "kid of 19," who thinks of him as "one of those million-dollar movie stars." However, his cover quickly slips again. If why Renault drinks is not already clear, he clarifies directly for Paula and the audience: "You don't know what it means to be up against it. To keep fighting them every second." Pouring himself another stiff one, he continues: "To pull yourself up, hand over hand, while they're waiting with a knife to cut the rope." Paula stands, stunned. "I'm not through yet," Renault adds, as if in answer to her silence. "I'll show 'em, if they think I'm finished."

He and Paula had been speaking of their relationship, and she attempts to return him to the subject. That he has drifted from the topic of love reveals what is most important to his confidence and sense of self. A young woman's affection might have sustained him in the past, but it cannot now. As a silent film star, he tells Paula, he was swarmed by female fans "of every age, kind, and description," but romance no longer means anything to him. "What do you want with me?" he asks. Then, holding the bottle, he admits the truth: "You're young and fresh, and I'm burned out." He wants her to leave him and get on with her life. Suddenly, he feels at least momentarily in control: "Paula, this is the first decent thing I ever did in my life. You listen to what I'm telling you." While perhaps "decent" and even generous, Renault's motives are, of course, still self-centered. His discursive style is performative, his gestures theatrical; together they speak of self-pity far more than Paula's happiness. The scene concludes with a link drawn between Renault's pride and a patronizing attitude toward women.

After Paula leaves, Renault's agent arrives to make clear that Renault has no chance at the lead in the play but that he may be able to get the beachcomber role. In response, a desperate Renault wraps up a remaining cuff link and belt buckle and the silver picture frame that holds Paula's photo with hopes the bellboy will be able to hock them for more liquor. The scene then cuts to the office of Dr. Wayne Talbot (Edmund Lowe), philandering physician to the wealthy, and then to aging ex-starlet Carlotta Vance (Marie Dressler). While the two interrupting scenes seem at first unrelated to issues of Hollywood-style gender norms and the accompanying dangers of male alcoholism, they are not. Both, in fact, serve as direct commentary on these matters.

Midway through the Talbot scene, the doctor's wife, Lucy (Karen Morley), overhears him romancing Kitty Packard (Jean Harlow) on the phone. Apparently, Kitty is far from the first extramarital liaison her husband has enjoyed, and Lucy confronts him about his "pathetic" tendencies. She calls him a "masher" with a split personality: one part of him is "magnificent, and the other's so shoddy." She also declares her intention to stay married to him, not only for their children but also because she loves him. Displaying her long-suffering nature, she lightens her judgment, asserting that her husband is "still a little boy." At this, the doctor breaks down and confesses his weakness, likening adultery to other "social" ills: "These other women. It's like gambling or drinking or drugs. You just keep on." His wife turns the matter to more clinical analysis, suggesting, "I hear it can be cured, if the patient wants to." Again, the "alcoholism alibi" appears, this time under the analogous guise of the "adultery alibi." Wayne declares his love and desire to be "cured," and we are encouraged by the sincerity of both to believe they may have a chance of living happily ever after.

Reconsidering Larry Renault's previous scene in this context, we may affirm that his love of booze and relationship with young Paula are linked addictions and are curable; both drinking and the pursuit of women are something he does out of habit. Wayne, however, is not a Hollywood type. He is a successful doctor and a father, a man who has proven his worth by fulfilling masculine roles both public and private. Renault, by contrast, is an actor, a profession at which one must continually prove oneself, particularly when leading-male roles rest more on looks than talent. Ageism will eventually affect Dr. Talbot, but not with the speed and devastation with which it hits the Hollywood star. We may enjoy the happy ending as the two reunite, but we are not encouraged to feel the depth of pathos Cukor brings to the resolution of Renault's crisis.

Before returning to the "Great Profile" in his final scene, there is a brief moment featuring Carlotta Vance, who stops in to visit the Jordans to let Oliver know she has been forced by economic need to sell her stock in his company. Unlike Renault, actress Carlotta fully acknowledges her age. In part, she is constantly reminded of it by young people telling her how much their fathers and grandfathers enjoyed her performances. In

Larry Renault (John Barrymore) drunkenly demands respect from émigré producer Jo Stengel (Jean Hersholt) as his fed-up agent (Lee Tracy) tries to hold him back in *Dinner at Eight* (1933).

addition, she is older than Larry and is fat; she can no longer boast even a great profile in Hollywood terms. Her goal in life now is singular: to retain enough wealth to live in the independent, privileged style to which she has become accustomed. This self-awareness, however, does not keep her from drinking to excess. When Millicent informs her that Oliver is not at home, she makes herself comfortable, breaking social niceties by removing her shoes and boldly asking for a whiskey and soda. A servant pours her a stiff glass, but she forcefully pushes away the soda before it can "ruin" her drink. Carlotta no longer cares who sees her drink or how much, for she recognizes her has-been status. She, like Larry Renault, is bitter, and we see this in her acerbic sense of humor. However, she seems always to have been less of a dreamer, having used her youthful charms to attain the stocks and bonds she now sells to survive. Renault made no such provisions, deluding himself that he would always retain his star value. As he tells émigré-producer Jo Stengel (Jean Hersholt), "I'm a name!"

Taken together, these two intervening scenes link disparate characters and situations into an interwoven commentary, with Renault and his situation at its center. Economic pressures have an impact on Oliver as a businessman (who seems about to lose his family shipping company), Carlotta as a weary-but-wise ex-celebrity, and Renault as a prideful actor whose star has fallen. Intimate relationship pressures affect Renault and Dr. Talbot—as well as the women who love them (Paula and Lucy). And Hollywood's sexism and ageism have an impact on both Carlotta and Renault—literally driving them to drink. Through these links and constellations, we see two alternatives to Renault's perspective, both of which hinge on gender. First, we see how the romantic comedy alternative is unavailable to Renault. The actor eschews the gifts of a long-suffering wife who can save him from himself and provide, through her presence, the promise of a magical cure to his ills. In part, this is because having a partner will dim his goals to remain a matinee idol, however unrealistic and bygone such ambition is. Second, we see the burden of the hypermasculine ego of the matinee idol contrasted with the opportunities and awareness linked with the figure of the leading lady. Like the wise Mary in *What Price Hollywood?* and Esther in *A Star Is Born*, recognition of the destructive pressures of Hollywood can suggest the importance of emotional and sometimes physical distance from stardom. Carlotta is older and wiser than the heroines of the other two films under discussion, and her experiences are played for humor rather than pathos, for the most part. Even more significantly, Carlotta was less serious in her artistic goals, using youthful feminine wiles to provide sustenance for her later years. Practicality in Cukor's films about Hollywood stardom seems a woman's purview.

When *Dinner at Eight* returns to Renault's hotel room, the scene begins by adding arguable nuance to the portrayal and the alcoholism alibi through attention to issues of ethnicity. While he is clearly drunk and demands respect he does not earn, his rudeness to Stengel illustrates more than just loutish behavior. "I'm drunk and I know I'm drunk," Renault states, "but I know what I'm talking about." Unimpressed and embarrassed, Stengel exits, with Renault shouting after him: "I'm an important artist, and you're nothing but a cheap pushcart producer. Pushcart!" However drunk and desperate he is, there may be some "truth" in Renault's sentiment. Actor Jean Hersholt was a Danish-born actor who would become most famous for playing Shirley Temple's grandfather in *Heidi* (1937). Though not Jewish, Stengel is obviously playing an immigrant and through his producer's role can be read as Broadway stand-in for the greedy Hollywood moguls. As discussed by Neal Gabler, these powerful men had indeed been peddlers and pushcart vendors in their youths.[33] In light of this awareness, American-born Larry Renault, no longer a salable product, vents his resentment at the powerful immigrant success story that created Hollywood and has driven him to drink when he failed to make the transition to the talkies. We see, by contrast, that Stengel is old and fat, and still has his old-world accent; yet, because he remains behind the scenes, the masculine appearance and age norms of Hollywood (here transposed onto the Broadway stage) do not affect his career as they do Renault's.

Such a perspective also reflects Cukor's own experiences. Renault is a ham, but he is played by New York theatrical nobility. Cukor was not an immigrant, but he (the child of Western European parents) fought often with Eastern European Hollywood producers over their interference in his work. Moreover, as briefly mentioned in the introduction, Cukor lamented his "ethnic" looks and body size when he was young and surrounded by Hollywood beauty and glamor. Pitting a former matinee idol who longs for continued work against a polite but distant "pushcart salesman" of a producer indicts not only Larry Renault but also Hollywood's origins—even if, as Renault's agent says, the actor is "a low-down ham" and a walking "corpse." After Renault's suicide, we see his agent's opinion echoed by the film-going audience, personified in Hattie's dull husband, Ed (Grant Mitchell). He is forced to attend Millicent's dinner party to round out the numbers after a sought-after high-class couple declines at the last minute, although he wanted to see a Garbo picture.[34] Hattie tries to cheer him up, reminding him that he will get to meet Larry Renault and Carlotta Vance in person. In response, Ed calls Renault a "has-been" and alludes to Vance's age when he asks whether Jenny Lind (a nineteenth-century opera star) is also going to make an appearance.

The association of Renault and Carlotta in this exchange, soon before the relatively happy ending of the film for most of the characters, returns us to their similarities and differences. If both celebrities are old, unattractive hams, why is Renault hurt so much more by his circumstances than Carlotta? Why is he driven to suicide when Carlotta is not? Gender norms explain much. Having been told he was leading man material in his silent-film years, Renault's identity becomes rooted in his physical appearance and rigid celebrity independence. He once dominated both women and mass audiences, and this defines him. He has no self beyond his stardom. Carlotta is more cynical, apparently aware from a young age that she would one day be passé. We thus see a contrast of stereotypical expectations of women versus men within the Hollywood celebrity context. Women can marry a successful man and rest their identity in being wives and mothers (as Lucy does and as Paula wishes to do). Men (from Wayne Talbot and Oliver Jordan to Larry Renault himself), by contrast, must be providers—at least for themselves. In comparison to wily and resilient Carlotta, Renault's more stubborn and fragile masculinity could not admit to the dependence and isolation aging would bring, and so he continued to treat women as objects and men as pawns as he acted the part of the "Great Profile" until it killed him.

The third and most powerful of Cukor's films about Hollywood and its ills, which he considered his singular (ruined) masterpiece, was 1954's *A Star Is Born*. He had opted out of directing the original 1937 film version, but once Judy Garland was established as the remake's star, he happily returned to the cycle he had started twenty-two years earlier. Musical numbers affect the tone and appeal of the film, but Cukor's *A Star Is Born* is clearly a tragedy with an emotional depth not shared by *What Price Hollywood?* or *Dinner at Eight*. The film directly highlights the causes of alcoholism in the pressures faced by the lonely male Hollywood artist and emphasizes its impact on the long-suffering wife. Certainly, women's suffering is shown in the earlier films. It is pointedly reflected by Mary's retreat from stardom in *What Price Hollywood?* and Paula's return to the arms of a less volatile man in *Dinner at Eight*. By comparison, however, the relationship between Esther and Norman is the melodramatic heart of *A Star Is Born*, and the film reveals in excruciating detail the guilt and blame placed on the wife for her husband's failings. In fact, the stronger Norman's self-loathing grows and the more self-destructive his behavior, the harder Esther labors to endure and ease his pain and anger.

Both ironically and tragically, as Denzin posits regarding gender and drinking in Hollywood cinema, "This alcoholic male gave Hollywood and America the new, modern working woman. She upheld the traditional values of family, while she pursued a work career. Her work career, however, was one that was played out in the Hollywood dream factory, itself a totalitarian, racist, sexist social structure."[35] As in *What Price Hollywood?*, we find again in *A Star Is Born* that the female experience of Hollywood is similar to, yet is coped with differently than, the male experience, and the rise to fame of the film's female star and male alcoholic are independent of one another.[36] Neither Mary nor Esther *should* feel responsible for the way shame and a loss of self-respect are linked with lack of control over addiction for the Hollywood star in her life, yet both do. Both are deeply beholden to their talented mentors, and Esther is in love with Norman. She cannot escape the pressures of Hollywood by retreating into marriage as Mary can, for Esther's marriage is intertwined, even synonymous, with Hollywood.

As in the previous examples, the specifics of the alcoholic's death scene are illustrative of the workings of gender in Cukor films that feature male Hollywood alcoholics. Norman has been trying to get help, but he cannot stop drinking. He does not share the denial of Max Carey or Larry Renault, and he is even more obviously full of self-loathing. Norman tells Esther, "Happiness is one thing I never had. . . . It has come, but too late. You can't throw away everything in your life the way I have and have anything left that is good enough." Like Max, Norman sees that he has wasted his life by neither valuing what he has nor devoting himself adequately to what he wants. And, like Renault, he recognizes that love is no longer enough to sustain him. Thus, his words implicate Esther even more than Renault's do Paula. Esther is the "anything left" that is not "good enough," after all. If Esther goes on to perform directly after the news of her husband's death (in the original, undistributed version of the film) and chooses to identify herself to an international radio audience as "Mrs. Norman Maine," how much of this comes from a feeling of responsibility for his unhappiness and death? She must go on as our "modern working woman," vaulting ever higher into stardom, even as she protests misjudgment by using her married name. She can thus avoid or at least challenge her devaluation as a widow, a woman without a man and home to care for.

Extending its relevance from content to production context, we see the ill effects of Hollywood pressures, not only on Esther as the wife of an alcoholic star but also on the actress who portrays her, Judy Garland. In the persuasive words of critic Tim Armstrong, if "self-commodification is the aim of the modern performer, then *A Star Is Born* surely suggests a return of the repressed: the star who rises is portrayed by an actor who is herself a victim and addict, whose story of decline and occasional revival it becomes part of." In this configuration, "'Judy Garland' stands, in movie mythology, for Hollywood's tendency to 'waste' its products by isolation and the denial of 'real' human needs."[37]

Considered together, *What Price Hollywood?*, *Dinner at Eight*, and *A Star Is Born* illustrate Cukor's attachment to both the appeal and the dangers of stardom. Illusion becomes a world of its own in Hollywood, and those who cannot escape its grasp until they are flung violently from it suffer tremendously when they finally see their folly. Men, in Cukor's films, suffer the most from this delusion, for they are Hollywood's primary creators, and with some powerful exceptions, stars. Alcoholism figures as a central means of portraying the harmful and sometimes lethal impact upon such men.

5

Edelkayt

A Jewish Angle on the Cukor Male

Picking up from chapter 4, this chapter begins with what is, arguably, Cukor's most sympathetic male alcoholic figure, a character who also exemplifies an alternate display of masculinity in the studio era of Hollywood film. The tragic secondary character Ned Seton (Lew Ayres) appears in the romantic drama *Holiday* (1938), the second and more successful motion picture production of Philip Barry's 1928 play about a stifling aristocratic East Coast family and those who seek to escape from its strictures. The central figures include the "black sheep" of the family, Linda Seaton (Katharine Hepburn), her materialistic younger sister Julia (Doris Nolan), and Julia's fiancé, working-class boy made good, Johnny Case (Cary Grant), for whom older sister Linda also falls. After a sincere but failed effort to convince head of the family Edward Seaton (Henry Kolker) that Johnny needs the freedom to do more with his life than make money in the family banking business, Johnny and Linda both revolt against the dynasty. Julia releases Johnny from his promise of marriage, which allows Linda to confess her love and belief in him. Immediately afterward, she rushes off to join her beloved and his friends—a middle-class academic couple—for a ship voyage away from marble pillars and corporate greed.

Left behind by Johnny and Linda, however, is younger brother Ned. Linda does invite him on the cruise, but Ned cannot comply, for he is trapped by his status as male heir to the family business. Ned is shown to lack the strength of will that Johnny has; we witness his weakness throughout the film in his copious drinking, self-effacing humor, and emotional isolation. Ned, we learn, has long ago given up his creative ambitions, illustrated by a neglected room full of musical instruments he can play—including banjo, drums, and piano. There is even an original piano concerto he never finished. Alcohol functions for Ned as solace for his loneliness and unhappiness and allows him to release anger through pointed jokes.[1]

Of any character in the film, Ned is closest to Linda, who loves and pities him, a moving feature that Cukor recognized in the script and enhanced in his film.[2] Ned is as worthy of affection as Linda, we might conclude, but he is male and therefore cannot, as Linda can, be rescued by the male hero. In conjunction with this pitying tone, the picture offers no easy cure for or denial of alcoholism. Weakness is the primary characteristic that critics point to in their discussions of Ned. Carlos Clarens argues, "Ned is too weak and timorous to break away from the family cocoon."[3] Gene Phillips goes further, blaming Ned for his own suffering: "Ned (Lew Ayres) has ruined his life by constantly knuckling under to the family's imperious demands on him, and he has thus retreated into alcoholism as his particular form of escape."[4]

Escapism is certainly central to the coping strategies of both Linda and Ned (not unlike Dexter in *The Philadelphia Story* and Barrie in *Susan and God*). Then, Johnny arrives to shake up the family with his working-class origins; he has just enough wealth to be antimaterialistic in Hollywood terms. Linda tells Johnny she has tried painting, nursing, and volunteer work, though Phillips describes as more purely escapist her tendency to spend time in the playroom that her dead mother created as her own necessary escape from the cold opulence of the family brownstone.[5] But Linda is escaping because she is trapped by the limited options available to a woman of her class, just as class expectations arguably turn Julia into a woman determined to live through her husband's success.

More can be made of Ned's alcoholism than labeling it a sad, temporary escape or even a means of summoning the gumption to display frustration through biting humor. Ned's pernicious drinking may best be explained when we read him as a coded homosexual. Late in the film, father Edward, frustrated and annoyed by Linda's sarcasm and directly expressed unhappiness, recommends she go on a trip somewhere. By contrast, he wishes Ned would not drink but never demands abstinence. He forces Ned to stay at the office even when there is no work to do, but he

In *Holiday* (1938), Ned (Lew Ayres) drinks copiously at the engagement party of Johnny (Cary Grant) and sister Julia (Doris Nolan), but why?

can have his drinks after. Why is drinking not prohibited or even curtailed? Does Edward know something we do not, something of which he cannot speak more directly? General clues can be found in the darker elements of Barry/Cukor romantic comedies, including depictions of divorce, infidelity, and self-destructiveness, including alcoholism. The sometimes tense dialogue is also suggestive. As Gary Carey describes, the characters speak "a kind of elegant banter, but under it is an abruptness and tension that suggests that the characters are withholding more than they are telling."[6] And one form of specific "withholding" in *Holiday* seems to be the fact that Ned is as drawn to Johnny as is Linda.

On the night of Julia's New Year's Eve engagement party, Linda is depressed. Ned takes the opportunity to get drunk. Alone with him in the playroom, Linda is moved to ask Ned about drinking:

> Linda: What's it like to get drunk, Ned?
>
> Ned: Well, I . . . how drunk?

Linda: Good and drunk.

Ned: Oh, it's wonderful. You think clear as crystal. But every move, every situation is a problem. It gets pretty interesting . . .

Linda: You get beaten in the end, though, don't you?

Ned: Sure, but that's okay.

Linda: Where do you wind up?

Ned: Where does anybody wind up? You die, and that's okay, too.

Linda: Oh, Ned. That's awful.

Ned: Think so? Other things are worse.

The query leads Ned to wonder why Linda wants to drink. She confesses, "I love the boy, Neddy." His very quiet reply is "Great, isn't he?" It is difficult not to read this as barely masked homoerotic desire. Certainly, Ned may admire Johnny, even wish to be more like him. He has seen how much his father has come to admire the man. However, when we read Ned's admiration alongside showing no interest whatsoever in the opposite sex (or even being encouraged to), alcoholism related to closeted homosexuality is a logical interpretation.

Classical psychoanalytic approaches current at the filming of *Holiday* tended to blame alcoholism on an "inability to resolve Oedipal conflicts and develop healthy, normal sexual, emotional relationships with a suitable, morally strong mother or father substitute figure."[7] This relates drink to failed masculinity; but, as opposed to failed gender performance, with Ned the situation relates more obviously to sexual orientation. In *Holiday*, drinking may be "an attempt to reduce anxiety over one's masculinity, as a means of coping with over-identification with one's father (an indication of latent homosexuality), or as a way of dealing with an irrational fear of heterosexual relationships."[8] Although Ned does not identify with his father—quite the opposite, in fact—he has internalized his father's judgment. Ned knows he is unlikely to fulfill his father's expectations as his heir, both in business and in reproduction of a next generation. Of greater relevance, in the 1930s, "classic psychological bromides" were likely to explain substance use "as a defense against homosexuality" and "as slow suicide."[9] This seems to represent Ned's quandary with tragic precision.

The production context of the film adds further nuance to the role of Ned. Cukor chose to cast Lew Ayres in the part, nine years after they first worked together when Cukor served as dialogue coach for *All Quiet on the Western Front* (1930), in which Ayres played the role that shot him to stardom—the sensitive, disillusioned German soldier Paul Bäumer. Moreover, Cukor decided to expand the supporting role of Ned beyond the boundaries of the Barry play. This was part of a largely collaborative production in which Cukor, screenwriter David Ogden Stewart, and the central cast (particularly Hepburn) challenged traditional studio norms related to power and film creation. As Candace Mirza describes in her detailed film history, *Holiday* emerged as an "act of resistance to and intervention into the construction of popular ideology."[10]

If he is a tragic alcoholic and closeted gay man trapped by gender and class dictates, Ned can also be interpreted beyond these boundaries. A more positive, alternative masculinity (however decried by family) emerges if we read Ned through the concept of *Edelkayt* as nuanced by Daniel Boyarin in *Unheroic Conduct: The Rise of Heterosexuality and the Invention of the Jewish Man*. *Edelkayt* literally means "nobility," but a nobility that emphasizes delicacy and gentleness over courage and gallantry. Specifically, Boyarin sees such traits in "the Eastern European Jewish ideal of a gentle, timid, and studious male."[11] Enhanced through Cukor's direction, we can read Ned through this alternative stereotype, useful for both feminist and queer studies of masculinity. Ned is not literally Jewish but is arguably Judaized in such a reading; he is quiet and gentle, with his musical talent and ambition to be a composer linkable to the figure of the scholar. Sadly, Ned lives within a (gentile) culture and family that champions the norm of active, dominant, aggressive masculinity. Johnny, too, resists typical masculinity in his lack of financial ambition, but he fulfills it in his vigorous heteronormativity (attracting both Seton sisters) and aggressiveness when he finally leaves Julia. Linda admires his determination and can escape her family's dictates by following him. Moreover, Johnny and Linda's perspective dominate the film and original play. We are intended to judge harshly the greed of the Setons and the pressure they put on those in their sphere to fit their rigid class and gender absolutes. Nonetheless, both the Seton greed and Johnny's active masculine confidence doom the more passive, quiet Ned to isolation.

Applying Boyarin's concept of *Edelkayt* to *Holiday* requires that we read Ned through the figure of the Jew within the dominant western paradigm. Historically, Jews have been viewed and judged from outside their own traditions. The Jewish male has generally been conceptualized as lesser, different, and Other. Being so marginalized, one of very few options is to deny his own identity, a struggle in which we see Ned comparably trapped. As Linda declares her freedom from the family, she does toss a lifeline to her beloved brother, offering to take him along. When he says he cannot go, she pats his shoulder and declares, "Oh, never you fear, I'll be back for you, my fine bucko." She offers her perspective, that Ned is a "fine bucko," an ally who shares her worldview (and Johnny's)—a perspective that we in the audience share. If only he could see himself as she does. But heteronormativity means that he would not truly fit. Johnny and Linda sail off with his married friends, Nick and Susan Potter, while widower Edward Seton has his ambitious daughter Julia to reflect his views. Ned, by contrast, stands truly alone in the film, his desires disallowed and his identity drowned in alcohol.

Were the film to enable Ned to attain a worldview centered in his own desires, a gaze from which he could find an identity to counter the norms that isolate him, it might well look like Boyarin's take on the premodern Jewish male ideal, a countertype that renders specular relationships more complex. His object of study is the ancient rabbi, a figure that is linked with gentleness, studiousness, and sexual attractiveness but that rejects aggression and dominance. Boyarin does not deny the patriarchal, sexist, and even misogynistic elements of Judaism and Jewish history, but the concept of *Edelkayt* in the figure of the rabbi offers a feminized antidote to the hypermasculine (gentile) male that has dominated western culture since the classical Roman era.[12]

George Cukor faced his share of Othering as a gay Jewish American Hollywood director. He saw firsthand, from his earliest years, an America steeped in adoration of traditional gentile masculine norms, echoed in many a Broadway play and the majority of Hollywood films. "He was an outsider as a gay person, as a not-attractive person, and as a Jewish person," claims Gavin Lambert.[13] He was also resourceful and determined, however. Cukor's performance of Jewish masculinity rejected any flourishes that would have linked him with stereotypes of effeminate homosexuality, for example. The language with which actor Bill Bakewell defends Cukor's public persona is worth noting: "He couldn't have been straighter. He was not effeminate or swishy."[14] Clarifying such a declaration, Patrick McGilligan asserts that Cukor was "patently homosexual," not for how he acted, but for how he did not. He was identifiably gay primarily because he was not one of the "swaggering, cigar-chomping polo-playing, deep-sea and safari-adventuring manly men who notched their leading ladies on their belt."[15] That he was also confident, charming, determined, and quickly successful in the cutthroat business of Hollywood did not mitigate the gender-stereotyped expectations and homophobia Cukor faced.

Lew Ayres, for example, praised Cukor for his "tremendous presence—and presence of mind."[16] However, the actor also expressed fear of Cukor's sexuality in clearly homophobic terms. When Cukor, Bakewell, and Ayres were working together on *All Quiet on the Western Front*, Cukor invited Ayres to his apartment for extra dialogue work. Ayres was anxious, fearing Cukor might make a pass at him, validating a common homophobic notion that gay men pursue straight men. Nothing sexual did happen, and Bakewell attributed this to the fact that Cukor was "too intelligent, too nice, too professional" to pursue Ayres.[17] Here we can see how establishing *Edelkayt* mitigates homophobia.

If Cukor had concerns about being seen and labeled as gay within a homophobic culture and played down his Jewishness to avoid gentile (and even Jewish) judgment, he was one of many who yielded to the dictates of the day. Outsider or not, Cukor had great success and earned great praise from many with whom he worked. Gavin Lambert affirms that "George was basically optimistic about life."[18] Such optimism may have led him to create characters through which the impact of Othering might be mitigated. Specifically, several of his most memorable characters can be interpreted as exemplifying traits linked with *Edelkayt* in ways that echo Boyarin's description of a traditionally Jewish male counter-ideal that destabilizes the performances of hypermasculinity around it.

I have earlier explored *The Philadelphia Story* for its role in retrieving Katharine Hepburn from the box office poison list and for its comedic (and gender problematic) resolution to the problem of the alcoholic male as played by Cary Grant. The film was important to a third actor as well, James Stewart, who won the Best Actor Oscar for his role as Macaulay "Mike" Connor. Mike is a creative writer whose ambition to achieve literary notice is crushed when his volume of fiction achieves critical praise but little financial success. He turns to tabloid journalism for *Spy* magazine to pay the bills and ends up at the home of Tracy Lord (Hepburn) to cover her second marriage. He and photographer Liz Imbrie (Ruth

Hussey) are invited under the guise of friendship with Tracy's ex, Dexter (Grant), who is being blackmailed by the tabloid's editor.

Cynicism dominates Mike's perspective for much of the film. He dislikes the excesses of materialism practiced by the wealthy, even as he detests the job he must do to survive. He considers himself morally superior to Tracy, Dexter, and their wealthy ilk, and remains aloof even from the similarly cynical Liz, who clearly cares for Mike and has an eye on marrying him, if she can only get him to propose. When he does become enamored of a woman, however, he desires a drunken Tracy. She is unique in his experience, especially as she welcomes him into an alluring fantasy of emotional and physical escape. As she tells Mike how she feels when released from class pretension and defensiveness and invites him for a wee-hours dip in the pool, he is entranced. Importantly, he is not the aggressor here, but neither is he desexualized. Within the subgenre of the comedy of remarriage that explores the impermanence of matrimony, drunken moments of infidelity, multiple love interests, and fluid gender presentation, these traits link Mike with *Edelkayt* and the kind of queer feminist reconsideration of male subjectivity it enables.

Such a reading is particularly apt if we read Mike's sarcasm as armor for a man who feels prohibited from living the gentle, creative life of a serious writer and especially if we explore his relationship not with Tracy or Liz but with Dexter.[19] The latter relationship develops in a late-night drunken confrontation scene. Having reassessed his feelings for Tracy, Mike accuses Dexter of having sold her out to *Spy* to hurt her for moving on emotionally and marrying someone else. Mike arrives at Dexter's door before dawn. As he steps out of the car that has driven him, he declares, "Well, this is where Cinderella gets off." Here, he metaphorically configures himself as the humble girl with Dexter as the prince. He then proceeds to defend Tracy as if he is the injured party. Dexter, in expensive bathrobe rather than royal robes, welcomes him in and remains patient and indulgent beyond what we might expect from someone awakened from his sleep and accused of betrayal. Confrontation between the men leads Mike to an unconvincing aggression, in which he claims, "Either I'm gonna sock you or you're gonna sock me." But there is little conviction in his voice, leading Dexter to casually reply, "Shall we toss a coin?" The queerness of the interaction emerges when we read this scene as metaphor for forbidden intimacy, but it becomes even richer when Dexter

Mike (James Stewart), a drunken Cinderella, tells all to a princely Dexter (Cary Grant) in *The Philadelphia Story* (1940).

goes on to confess he has read and enjoyed Mike's published volume of short fiction. If a powerful, dominant type like Dexter can see and appreciate Mike's more quiet, creative masculinity without rejecting or judging it, then Mike can drop his imitation of normative masculinity and be a more genuine countertype rather than a demeaned stereotype.

Furthermore, Mike in *The Philadelphia Story* is recuperated into heteronormativity by the trajectory of the film as demanded by its genre. Tracy rejects Mike's offer of marriage, and he declares that he has not only never proposed to a woman but has actively avoided it. Tracy is the one who must direct him onto the expected romantic comedy path, declaring she has rejected him "because I don't think Liz would like it . . . and I'm not sure you would . . . and I'm even a little doubtful about myself." Mike blusters further about a room full of waiting wedding guests, and Liz acts, silencing him by declaring, "Don't get too conventional all at once; there'll be a reaction." She clearly sees he is attempting traditional masculinity (again) but failing with Tracy. From her seat on the edge of a sofa, she takes Mike's arm and pulls him to her. Mike acquiesces, puts his hand over hers, and, head downturned, smiles bashfully. Clearly, the film's conclusion shows, the man to possess strong-willed Tracy is not this exemplar of *Edelkayt* but rather the gentile ideal, the man of confident, dominant masculinity, Dexter.

If Stewart's Mike Connor exemplifies what Boyarin calls an "'unmanned' but not desexualized" type, *Born Yesterday*'s Paul Verrall (William Holden) is even less queer but more potentially complex in gender terms, rejecting hypermasculinity both conceptually and behaviorally.[20] Of Cukor's male leads, Paul may be the most effectively constructed through the feminist (but not queer) potential of the Jewish male countertype. I devote space to Jewishness in *Born Yesterday* in chapter 9, addressing central characters Billie Dawn (Judy Holliday) and Harry Brock (Broderick Crawford) through stereotypes of New York Ashkenazi Jews. Within this context, however, Paul Verrall—a patriotic journalist and Billie's tutor—is the least Jewish character in the film. He has a flat midwestern accent and is quiet, yet assertive, and smart, yet more a critic than a scholar.

Nonetheless, through Boyarin's Jewish masculine countertype, we can instead consider Paul within a continuum of Jewish types: he is in many ways the opposite of Harry Brock. Where Harry is aggressive, loud, and domineering, for example, Paul is quietly assertive and invested in equality. He may represent to audiences of the film's era (it was released in 1950) the handsome professional, his surname, Verrall, a potential tweak of "virile"; but he is also awkward and timid with Billie, dazzled by her looks and openly sexual demeanor and eventually dazed in response to her determination to understand the wide gap between Washington politics and American constitutional ideals. She encourages Paul's timidness even as she seeks to breach it. For example, she summons him to her bedside rather than her living room to discuss what she does not understand in the newspaper. At the earliest opportunity, she offers her lips rather than the pages of the paper.

As they develop a relationship based on trust and increasing respect, we experience Paul as honorable, humble, and desirable rather than dominant or arrogant. We can see this vividly in a full-page magazine ad for the film, which identifies each character with specific traits and thumbnail headshots. Judy Holliday as Billie Dawn is "beautiful, blonde, brazen, and oh-h-brother!" Her images show expressions from smiling to angry

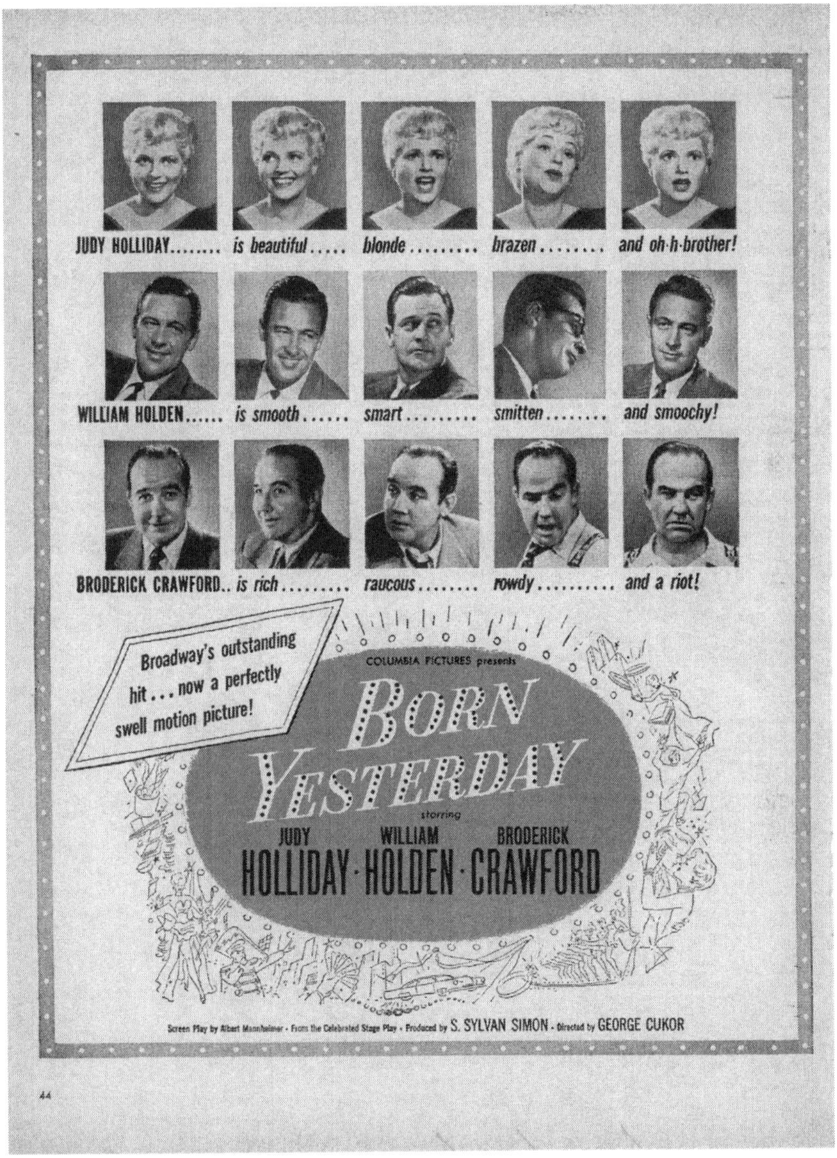

A magazine ad for *Born Yesterday* (1950) marks the main actors/characters by image and descriptors.

to sarcastic to shocked. Broderick Crawford's Harry Brock, by contrast is "rich, raucous, rowdy, and a riot!" He is shown smiling slyly, shouting, and grimacing. Between the two rows is William Holden. His Paul Verrall is "smooth, smart, smitten, and smoochy!" This description affirms his sex appeal and intelligence. However, he is also described as "smitten," a role that makes the woman dominant in the pairing. Furthermore, in his five headshots Holden is never shown looking directly into the camera, in distinction to aggressive Crawford. Paul can live happily ever after with Billie as the film concludes, without the arrogant swagger of the gentile (Hollywood) male (or the aggressive Jewish street bully), linking him with the category of Boyarin's alternative, the countertype possessed of *Edelkayt*.

Reading characters such as Ned, Mike, and Paul in Cukor films from the late 1930s to 1950 offers the opportunity to rethink the stereotyped rigidity we may at first see in such studio-era portrayals of men and masculinity. They may be queer and isolated, complexly positioned within heteronormative genre demands, or successful as gendered countertypes. Having alternative conceptions through which to explore male characters, such as those that Boyarin provides, widens possibilities for understanding what and how we see as film viewers.

6

The Theatricality of Gender and Drag Performance

The first chapters of this volume have centered primarily on issues of gender representation within Cukor's films, with attention to images of women and men, male/female relations, and conceptions of normative femininity and masculinity. Attention to genre, tone, and production context has inflected this approach and my conclusions. This chapter, however, offers a pivot point, reading gender performatively, where the feminine and the masculine are artificial, unconnected to biology. Drag is a heightened form of performance, useful for illustrating the concept of gender-as-performance, especially as explored by Judith Butler in *Gender Trouble*.[1] Here, drag parodies the perspective of gender as inherent or natural to human beings. Drag acts emphasize mimicry of "true" identity. By doing so, they reflect the absence of an authentic source for gender. A surprising number of female-to-male drag acts appear in the films of George Cukor, from musical numbers and fantasy sequences to moments of lived experience. Such performances bring to spectators an awareness of the artificiality of gender and the attendant pleasures of such recognition.

Across distinctive historical periods and film industry circumstances, through diverse styles, and at divergent points in Cukor's career, multiple films invite critical readings of gender roles and relations through drag. Films discussed in chapter 2, including Katharine Hepburn's Jo playing a mustachioed villain in *Little Women* (1933) and her work in *Adam's Rib* (1952), with its courtroom fantasy of gender reversal, are familiar to Cukor fans for their playful pleasure. However, additional films even more fully illustrate the radical potential of gender performance via female-to-male drag, including *Sylvia Scarlett* (1935), the previously discussed *A Star Is Born* (1954), and *Heller in Pink Tights* (1960). A 1930s picaresque romantic comedy, a 1950s melodrama with music, and a 1960 Western centered on a traveling troupe of stage performers all share gender bending and gender reconceptualization to significant feminist and queer effect. And all do so while retaining the traditional Hollywood narrative structure and style.

For its time and perhaps to this day, *Sylvia Scarlett* is unapologetically risk-taking, portraying with wit and good humor bisexual and other queer attractions.[2] I would not, as does Lesley Chow, go so far as to call it "amazingly avant garde," for it ultimately fulfills the expectations of the romantic comedy genre as it pairs off all of its central characters, but I understand her motives.[3] *Sylvia Scarlett* is not an easy film project to describe. From Cukor's perspective and despite compromises from the source material, the film was a "goddamned daring" enterprise, whose negative public reception caused the director to turn away from ostentatious display of sexual difference in his films in future.[4] In Molly Haskell's words, "This is Cukor's first film (and last for a while) in which he dared to challenge, in a lyrical stage whisper, our traditional assumptions about male-female roles."[5] More gleefully, Alexander Doty identifies it as simply "one of the queerest films ever made in Hollywood."[6]

In brief, Katharine Hepburn portrays a cross-dressing young woman (Sylvia/Sylvester) traveling with her hard-luck father Henry (Edmund Gwenn). Along their way, they meet con artist Jimmy Monkley (Cary Grant in his first lead role), philandering maid Maudie (Dennie Moore), playboy artist Michael Fane (Brian Aherne), and arrogant expatriate Lily Levetsky (Natalie Paley). The setting for this adventure is dreamlike, with cinematography full of wipes and dissolves that help to establish identity as more akin to "rehearsals or explorations of behavior" than fixed or absolute.[7]

Even in this "daring" film, however, drag requires explanation. Sylvia takes on the Sylvester persona to travel openly and safely with her father as he flees his creditors. By contrast, in the 1918 Compton Mackenzie novel upon which it is based, Sylvia's cross-dressing is for personal pleasure and lasts for only a short segment of a long novel.[8] For Cukor, the heart of the story clearly involves this section of the novel, and the picture emphasizes Sylvia becoming and retaining key elements of the Sylvester persona throughout the character's adventures, including romance. Cukor decried the fact that the studio refused to allow the film "to give the impression that she liked it [cross-dressing], or that she's done it before, or that it came naturally."[9]

Despite studio demands, however, *Sylvia Scarlett* does feature drag as a centerpiece. Cross-dressing and its pleasures are featured throughout, with its most significant impact offstage, particularly in the relationship that develops between Sylvia/Sylvester and Michael Fane. When we meet Michael, he is confident in his attraction to women, particularly foreign women of the upper class who play hard to get, exemplified in his infatuation with exiled Russian princess Lily. Michael is introduced as a carefree womanizer, inflected by his privileged class status; he is an artist living in the country who needs no other means of support. Our perspective on Michael quickly changes, however, when he meets Sylvester. Michael meets the "lad" when at his most queer: onstage, cross-dressed as a young man and also in the gender-bending costume of a "Pink Pierrot." I use the term "queer" here because, in such doubled garb, we cannot easily say this is gender "reversal," that is, a woman (actor) dressed as a man (character). Instead, the pink flouncy Pierrot costume is layered on top of the reversal, complicating gender presentation.

The callous artist ridicules the performances of Sylvester and his companions, principally Maudie, who badly croons "Who wants a kiss from me?" in her tight-bodiced pink dress. Given the spectacle of the men in their effeminate, frilly costumes and their ineffective chanteuse, Michael's scorn may be persuasively read as his attempt to distance himself from the gender confusion onstage. Adopting the masculine privilege that is his by performance, Sylvester shouts a demand for an apology from Michael and his fellow bohemians. Playing the gentleman, Michael formally acquiesces, and even invites the troupe to a party at his home. We can interpret the action as literally and symbolically welcoming gender disruption into his life.

The next shock for Michael occurs at his party, when Lily taunts a drunken Henry Scarlett about his jealousy over Maudie, with whom Henry has fallen in love. The rest of the guests enjoy the game she plays with the delirious man, but Sylvester does not. Sylvester scolds then slaps Lily, decrying a cruel femininity "he" eschews in women by once again performing male indignation—this time beyond gentlemanly bounds. Clearly, Hepburn's character has not internalized the rules of her assumed masculine gender. Lily's response is mixed, however. She holds her cheek,

In a Pink Pierrot costume, Sylvester (Katharine Hepburn) looks on with frustration as Michael (Brian Aherne) is dazzled by the cruel but beautiful expatriate Lily (Natalie Paley) in *Sylvia Scarlett* (1935).

horrified to be struck by a male; yet, she smiles, seemingly drawn to hypermasculine aggression. Michael responds entirely according to the traditional gentleman's code, by contrast, and throws the chaotic troupe out.

In the wee hours, when Sylvester returns to apologize after the party has ended, Michael reminds him that a man simply does not strike a woman. However, the two also bond at a deeper level based on sexist homosocial terms, acknowledging that perhaps Lily "deserved" the slap. Michael then invites Sylvester inside through a large second-story window. Together in his bedroom in the predawn light, Michael finds himself drawn to young Sylvester. He uses the excuse of wanting to paint Sylvester's portrait to utter the film's most infamous line: "I know what it is that gives me a queer feeling when I look at you." Sylvia blushes despite the drag, uncomfortable with Michael's friendly cajoling in his pajamas. Here the gender disruption of performativity wanes, for Hepburn's character seems to be displaying a "true" femininity beneath a masculine guise. Instead, the most destabilizing impact of drag is upon Michael, a man whose unaware queered desire for a drag performance leads to a transformed identity where Mr. Fane must feign his heteronormative masculinity.

It is not surprising in this context that Michael's relief when he finally learns that the young boy to whom he is attracted is actually a girl comes out in overwrought, "hysterical" laughter. Michael can, at least temporarily, think of Sylvia/Sylvester as a joke when she sits, legs widely spread, in a flowing summer dress. Sylvia herself (again with a seeming authentic feminine core) is deeply troubled. She desires Michael in gender normative terms. She is here a young, inexperienced girl with a crush on a sophisticated playboy. A touch of heteronormativity reminds us we are still in classic Hollywood. But drag soon takes both characters, and spectators who are willing, for a ride.

Late in the film, under the pretext of going to rescue Lily, who has been kidnapped by Jimmy Monkley, Michael and Sylvia/Sylvester (who is once again dressed in men's clothing, without explanation or justifiable need) hop a train and confess their love. In a comfortable, casual drag that is neither formal suit nor Pierrot costume, Sylvia finds the confidence to confess her feelings and win her man. This overt and transgressive presentation of gender suits her better than performative trickster or blushing girl, and it also attracts Michael. We can read the romance now as between a trans character rather than a woman in drag within a queered attraction that bends heteronormativity even while superficially fulfilling Hollywood romantic comedy expectations.

Additionally, these two are not the only characters to experience queerness related to drag. As Maudie seduces Henry, she also seeks to seduce his "son." She seeks him out to help wash dishes, draws a faux moustache on him, and then grabs hold of and kisses Sylvester passionately. The scene is unsubtly cut, suggesting it was even longer originally. The image, however, is clear: we have just witnessed two women kissing on the screen.

Even more than Maudie, Monkley knows how to use his working-class charm to get the object of his desire. Early in the film, he cons jewelry from Maudie's rich employers by embracing and flattering her. And the film ends with his aggressive, ultimately successful seduction of Lily. Nonetheless, this brutish persona is but one facet of Monkley's skills—and attractions. During their travels, he casually proposes a shared sleeping arrangement with Sylvester, whom he takes for a boy, calling him a

Soon after handsome young Sylvester (Kate Hepburn) finishes "his" thoughts, Maudie (Dennie Moore) will plant a passionate kiss on "him" in *Sylvia Scarlett* (1935).

"proper little hot water bottle." The calm confidence with which he expresses his sentiments cannot easily be read solely as part and parcel of his role as ne'er-do-well adventurer. On the contrary, Monkley's easy expression of male–male attraction (not present in Mackenzie's novel) serves to challenge compulsory heterosexuality as a central core of normative gender identity. Furthermore, Monkley seems attracted to the queerness of drag itself at one point in the film, when he secretly watches Sylvester transform into Sylvia. He offers to marry her when she flees Michael Fane's ridicule, citing their compatibility. We can read Monkley's attraction through a shared cultural outsider status, but it is equally compelling as a comment on gender and sexuality. Where Michael yields to Sylvia's multiply gendered desirability, Monkley seems aroused by gender performance itself.

Beyond queer textual interpretation, attention to the production context and the casting of Hepburn is also suggestive. As suggested in chapter 2, Hepburn was known for adopting "masculine" behaviors and appearance norms early in her Hollywood career, from her strident attitude to wearing pants around the studio. Alexander Doty links this persona back to Cukor and also to lesbian director Dorothy Arzner, pondering whether Hepburn's screen image would not have been established as "quite so appealingly butch, or androgynous if you like, if Cukor and Arzner hadn't been assigned to guide her through most of her early RKO star-making films."[10]

Poor studio and box office response alike determined that Cukor would never make as wild a film romp as *Sylvia Scarlett* again. Nonetheless, the director did return to drag and its destabilizing effects in two later films that also highlight gender performance and queerness through their use of theatrical settings. Perhaps the most complex of these examples in genre and intersection of text and star is 1954's *A Star Is Born.* Ostensibly, the film emphasizes the price of stardom via a format that fuses elements of the Hollywood musical with melodrama. However, the film is best known historically for its extratextual elements, especially the obvious parallels between the story line and the life of its star, Judy Garland, and Cukor's loss of control over the editing of the final product. Within this context and the era of its production, the film's importance and its pleasures for spectators benefit from study of its complex presentation of female-to-male drag.

In this Garland comeback vehicle, we see the agony of life lived through the presumption of naturalized gender roles and gendered bodies, including patriarchal marital norms and restrictive notions of "proper" masculine and feminine behavior. From the invocation of the figures of the self-sacrificing wife and the alcoholic husband (discussed in chapter 4) to the representation of gender and sexuality as uncomfortable and arbitrary masks, *A Star Is Born* powerfully marks and remarks upon the gender rigidity of 1950s America.[11] Far from the freedom of the gender-bending romp that is *Sylvia Scarlett*, the cautionary tale *A Star Is Born* reveals, through drag, the oppressive impact of traditional gender roles and heteronormativity.

Analysis of Judy Garland's performance of the character of Esther Blodgett (later Vicki Lester) begins, for most critics and biographers, with reference to the confluences of the film narrative and the life of Garland. If some critics assumed Katharine Hepburn was Sylvia Scarlett, many more read Blodgett as a thinly veiled Garland. This perspective produces the effect Richard Dyer calls a "total star text," a cultural constellation that encourages reading a star across multiple "media manifestations."[12] Made after MGM broke her contract in 1950, in the midst of Garland's ongoing battle with drugs and alcohol, *A Star Is Born* was produced by her then-husband Sidney Luft as a comeback picture. Pairing Garland with Cukor, however, made it something even richer from feminist and queer studies perspectives. Cukor, like his leading lady, knew and struggled with pressures to conform to social norms, including self-esteem issues related to body size and desirability. We can in this context productively read the film as actively foregrounding the gender norms of its era through drag in order to condemn them. Cukor pointedly directs a troubled star who had been disempowered and psychically and physiologically damaged by those norms to perform—through song, dance, and melodramatic acting—their lethal impact. That Cukor suffered greatly over losing creative control of the project, which he considered a singular masterpiece, we can read at least in part as an indication of how poignant the director found the film's themes and their presentation to a mid-1950s audience.

Beyond directorial authorship and star discourse, there is pleasure in watching the performance of gender—in and as drag—throughout the film. Garland's embodiment of Blodgett/Lester is fraught with anguished display of the burdens of traditional femininity. The film's most obvious moment of gender constraint comes when, largely through the intervention of her mentor, and later husband, Norman Maine (James Mason), Blodgett is given a screen test. Before she may be filmed (within the film), she is given over to the make-up department to be framed as a Hollywood starlet. Nothing of Blodgett (like Garland) is Hollywood-friendly, she quickly learns, and she suffers the emotional and physical trauma of scathing comments and a drastic makeover, from blonde wig and flowing bright pink dress to heavy cosmetics and even nose prosthetics.

The scene that follows invites us to understand this shift from female to feminine as a form of drag, imposed by Hollywood rather than decided upon by Blodgett. Women engage in feminine drag not for personally chosen purpose or pleasure, we see, but because they must. Upon presenting herself to Maine, Blodgett finds, first, that he does not even recognize her and, second, that he rejects her. Ostensibly, his rejection is of the transformation, not Blodgett herself. Yet Maine fails to consider the emotional state of his protégé as he reacts cruelly, with ample investment in controlling the already abused Blodgett, even if the film audience is more in sympathy with his purpose. He grabs Blodgett and forces her into a chair, unceremoniously pulls off her wig and nose prosthetic, then grabs handfuls of cold cream and roughly slathers them over her face, unconcerned whether she can see or even breathe. The act is difficult not to read as a symbolic rape, regaining control of her body from the studio. Maine demands she remove all the make-up and return to her usual look (not without cosmetics, just less thickly applied). Blodgett at first protests, a victim who has obviously come to identify with the criticisms of her sexist makeover oppressors, and then flounders and gives way to Maine's perspective, rushing to return to the self of which he approves before going to film her test. Here, drag is forced hyperfeminine excess, made necessary by stringent Hollywood norms in which being female is no guarantee of being properly feminine, and women yield to one form of patriarchal judgment or another. Blodgett has no control over self-presentation in this and other scenes.

In ways more akin to the performances in *Sylvia Scarlett*, however, *A Star Is Born* does actively offer challenges to gender norms and their devastating impact, specifically through staged drag images in musical numbers, including "Swanee" and "Lose That Long Face." Drag in some scenes signifies a freedom from the restrictions of traditional femininity—socially, psychologically, and physically. From high heels to flats and from tight skirts to loose pants, the act of female-to-male drag can be read in the film as a performance of gender liberation. And this is particularly significant when film text is read alongside star context. For most of her life on film, MGM demanded intense scrutiny of every aspect of Garland's physical being, from her height (too short), weight (too fat), and face (too flat) to her posture (too rounded) and movement (not balletic enough). Argues Adrienne L. McLean, "Garland's body was from the beginning manipulated out of its natural form."[13] This resulted in what many critics have interpreted as an uncomfortable, awkward, even anguished stage presence, exacerbated by her use of alcohol and drugs (including diet pills) and suicide attempts.[14] In this context, drag acts signify even more deeply as moments of freedom for Garland fans, where the actress escapes the constant studio manipulation she is reported to have undergone, a manipulation highlighted in the fictionalized context of *A Star Is Born*.

From this perspective, the most compelling drag type Garland performs is arguably the gender-ambiguous "tramp" figure. This figure is exemplified well in "A Couple of Swells" from 1948's *Easter Parade*, where Garland dances with Fred Astaire in a tattered tuxedo. From a feminist kinesthetic perspective, McLean emphasizes the impact of this costume: "The clothing is loose and unconstricting, and the body's shape is neither emphasized nor bound literally by a corset. Garland is thus free to exploit the full range of her body's motion and can take pleasure in her skill, the feeling of the movement itself, or the interaction with her partner, rather than worrying about whether she is minimizing her physical 'faults' sufficiently to avoid criticism. With the glamour stakes lowered as it were, Garland can dance more confidently, in greater tune with her body and its capabilities."[15] Garland is similarly freed from constriction in her drag numbers in *A Star Is Born*, with the addition of escape from pairing with a partner known for his slender grace playing a character within a traditional romance genre context.

As McLean makes clear, the gender ambiguity in Garland's drag performances is empowering in part through its bodily enactment. A more thorough exploration of queerness and gender subversion in the musical genre appears in chapter 7; for this chapter, we may simply note, as does critic Brett Farmer, that musicals frequently offer audiences moments of "gender or sexual subversion," particularly through cross-dressing in musical numbers.[16] Within this context, I want to explore the pleasures of the "Born in a Trunk" section of *A Star Is Born*. This portion of the film has received ample critical attention as Garland autobiography or, more precisely, as a "knowing précis of the image MGM had fostered" for her.[17]

Within the film, the multi-song sequence is presented as a biography of starlet Vicki Lester, who tells the story of her humble origins ("Pocatello, Idaho") in a tuxedoed stage performance with flashbacks. We watch Garland as Blodgett/Lester watching the opening night of Lester's first star-vehicle film, in which she plays an actress on a stage recounting her rise to stardom. The memory sequences are film numbers within the film that Blodgett/Lester watches within the film we are watching. Within this *mise en abyme* display, Garland/Blodgett/Lester deconstructs gender through drag, particularly when she performs the classic "Swanee," attired in top hat, jacket, tie, and white gloves. Richard Dyer links this number to Garland's "trampish" mode of androgynous drag performance, which appears in contrast to an alternate "stylish [and] vampish" mode, seen in *A Star Is Born* in the early "You Gotta Have Me Go with You" number. Here, Garland wears a tuxedo jacket with sheer tights instead of pants, where she is "both glamorous, sexy and one of the boys"—similar in style, Dyer argues, to the drag of Dietrich and Garbo.[18] This "vamp" drag requires attention to sexual allure and its accompanying restrictive clothing (e.g., tight tuxedo jacket—corseted beneath—and high heels). "You Gotta Have Me Go with You" begins with an objectifying shot of Garland from behind, preparing to perform by checking her stockings. By contrast, "Swanee," like Garland's other "tramp" performances, opens with Garland facing her audience, confidently and comfortably belting out her song.

The complexity of this drag number reaches beyond Dyer's compelling gender analysis. The costumes Garland wears are certainly available for "tramp" interpretation; however, the performance is also a seeming homage to Al Jolson, complete with what critic Brian Currid calls an "odd vocal drag" of Jolson, himself doing a racist vocal "drag" of stereotyped African American song style, making the number another *mise en abyme* display and a nostalgic gesture to American vaudeville minstrelsy. If, Currid argues, "the crossing of gender that Judy's drag performs stands in for the black face she is prohibited from putting on," then "Swanee" offers representation of freedom from gender norms at the expense of entrapment in racist nostalgia. It operates in what Currid calls an "economy of racist exchange," a formulation in which the feminism of gender performativity is enabled through racism.[19]

While we may find such a reading persuasive and the "Born in a Trunk" sequence important to the film's commentary on gender as a whole, it is noteworthy in the context of this book that Cukor did not direct this sequence. Instead, Cukor clarifies, this "great big divertissement" was likely directed by the film's choreographer, production designer, color advisor, and (uncredited) musical supervisor. In a 1964 interview, Cukor acknowledged that it "fits in quite well," even though it interferes with the "main flow of the narrative."[20] By 1969, however, he claimed the sequence was too long and "threw everything out of kilter."[21]

By contrast with the "Born in a Trunk" sequence, there is little critical discourse on the "Lose That Long Face" number, though I find it a powerful facet of the film. Dyer, for example, devotes only a sentence to it, linking its "ragamuffin look" with the tramp persona.[22] Currid ignores the number

Judy Garland (as Esther Blodgett) performs "Lose That Long Face" in prepubescent, boyish, ragamuffin garb in *A Star Is Born* (1954).

completely, despite its racist nostalgia in the use of pickaninny-styled African American children as momentary sidekicks to Garland's character in the scene. In terms of both gender and race, "Lose That Long Face" deserves investigation for its uniquely prepubescent drag character and its placement at a moment in the film that actively confronts the failure of gender roles that drive the film's ill-fated Hollywood romance. When she performs the number, Blodgett is a successful celebrity, struggling with a failing marriage to the aging, alcoholic Maine. Maine is increasingly despondent at the loss of his fame and resentful of his wife's success. Why Blodgett, now a glamorous cinema star, is doing a number dressed as a preadolescent boyish type with freckles and a straw hat is not a question the film asks. However, its presence and placement in the film is quite significant.

What makes "Lose That Long Face" particularly noteworthy is its reference to childhood, its portrayal of the freedom to be found in escape not only from feminine norms of movement and appearance but also from adulthood and its responsibilities more generally. In addition to costume and make-up, Ira Gershwin's lyrics are central to the importance of drag and the escape from adult femininity. The song opens with a suggestion to rearrange a long face because it's the "wrong face." Certainly, this can be interpreted as further commentary on the way Garland and Blodgett face forced molding to fit Hollywood feminine appearance norms. Yet, drag is another way to change and "rearrange" one's appearance to avoid censure. And when drag distances one further from the adult sphere of (gendered) criticism, all the better. Linking the Tom Sawyer–like character she plays with another famous androgynous boy, Garland sings, "Like Peter Pan, the sweeter pan / Wins the day." Loosed from the strictures of gender and adulthood, Garland/Blodgett/Lester here is momentarily as free as Peter Pan, the eternal boy so often portrayed on stage and screen by a woman. Sung and danced with abandon, this number exemplifies McLean's thesis that "to alter the way we dress, occupy space, and comport our bodies might be to alter the power structures that invest our bodies and their movements with the effects of that power."[23]

Equally important to reading this drag act is a consideration of its placement within the film's narrative trajectory. As Blodgett/Lester sits at her dressing room mirror, putting on her boyish make-up and wig, she is approached by studio head Oliver Niles (Charles Bickford), the man who advanced Norman Maine's career and is now threatening not to renew his contract. Niles goes to Blodgett/Lester not as a star commodity but as Maine's wife, to brace her and shift responsibility onto her for how the devastating news will affect her husband. The inappropriateness of approaching a performer about to film a scene with devastating news about her husband reflects the film's investment in 1950s American gender expectations. Niles clearly considers Blodgett/Lester as a wife first and star second, despite his financial investment in her. He interrupts her preparations and concentration without hesitation. And Blodgett offers the emotional breakdown expected in such a (filmic) context: she cries and openly confesses her anxieties and depression regarding marriage to a man who has become jealous, competitive, and increasingly emotionally abusive. Blodgett is unwilling to leave Maine but also unwilling to give up her work—at least at this point in the narrative. We can find feminist pleasure here: Blodgett rejects the pressure to conform to patriarchal norms that argue the husband's career must lead a Hollywood marriage in terms of wealth, prestige, and fame. To this is added a queer pleasure, as Blodgett dries her eyes and walks onto the film set as a boyish character, determined and confident.

That Garland performs this emotionally troubled scene while made up to look like a farm boy deserves further comment. If a stage setting (or film set) with a drag act foregrounds gender as a performance, there can be a tendency to read representations of gender outside of these overt theatrical settings as natural, even within the obviously constructed space of film narrative. Jane Feuer posits that "whenever a number commences in any musical, the world does become a stage."[24] If so, then how does a film maintain adequate staginess to avoid the appearance of gender authenticity in offstage moments—moments that comprise the bulk of *A Star Is Born?* I posit that if we wish to read the emotional breakdown of Blodgett as more "real" than the musical number that follows it, we must overcome the ridiculousness of the garb and make-up in which she acts the scene. Such juxtaposition may puzzle viewers, forcing them out of the narrative and into a critical dialogue with the film's imagery. Hence, as with so many examples discussed thus far, classic Hollywood prescriptions are filled even as subversive interpretations are possible.

The active tension offers opportunities to consider gender as a performance. That the film is more lament than celebration, however, is made plain by the film's emphasis on melodrama, particularly in its conclusion. Though she continues with her cinematic career, Blodgett feels increasingly guilty that her husband's star has fallen. Niles does cancel his contract and Maine struggles with alcoholism and rehabilitation, repeatedly humiliating himself and his wife. He is unable to reconcile himself to being supported by her or to find other ways to attain happiness. After a drinking binge that leaves his wife distraught and unsure whether he is alive or dead (or which would be better for him), he is found and returns home. Blodgett finally decides to put her career on hold to care for her husband, at last acquiescing to heteronormative gender roles. The film offers no subsequent drag moments to challenge this shift.

Standing on a veranda to their home overlooking the sea, Blodgett tells her plans to a sympathetic Niles. In this scene, she appears in the guise of traditional if privileged 1950s woman, wearing a form-fitting dress, her hair awkwardly styled to fit the era's beauty standards. She sports a short scarf knotted around her neck, a kind of noose that billows in the breeze, its appearance arguably echoing the way her life is being strangled by her marriage, by conformity to social norms that are killing both her and her husband.

Only one of the two must die, however, and in a highly performative manner, Maine outdoes his wife's self-sacrifice. After an agonized overhearing of Blodgett and Niles's discussion, Maine tells her that he is going off for a swim and drowns himself. Blodgett is paralyzed at first by his suicide, the guilt overwhelming and the desire to return to stardom gone. Her former band partner, Danny McGuire (Tommy Noonan), ultimately convinces her that she is not just her own person but Maine's legacy. While she accepts this patriarchal argument, the film does not allow her to perform onstage at the film's conclusion (in contrast to her two successors, Barbra Streisand and Lady Gaga, in the 1976 and 2018 remakes, respectively). Instead, Garland appears at an awards ceremony in the most obviously formal and constricting costume she has worn throughout the film, and in the most clearly gender-normative guise she has performed. She achieves a standing ovation not for a singing or acting performance but for a heteronormative gender performance. With grim confidence, Blodgett approaches the microphone and proudly announces, "This is Mrs. Norman Maine."

Indeed, it is obvious at this moment that she is "Mrs. Norman Maine," and what it means to be her. In the fur-sleeved, corseted gown before us, she is neither the optimistic yet awkward Esther Blodgett nor even the studio-created but talented Vicki Lester. Still, it is difficult not to see this as another hyperfeminine drag act. Applauded as the film ends is the spectacle of the long-suffering wife, the being whose career can never be as important as her domestic role, performed inside a wholly domesticated body. As Currid writes, "The force of the name is less a claim about her husband than an assertion of her domesticity in the public sphere."[25]

If *Sylvia Scarlett* celebrates theatricality and the transgression of gender norms in the 1930s and *A Star Is Born* uses drag to decry their claim on 1950s America, then 1960's *Heller in Pink Tights* can be read as championing drag excess to reveal the ultimate absurdity and artificiality of gender in all forms. If we use the criterion of "authenticity" for a comparison of the latter two films, we can argue, after Dyer, that in *A Star Is Born*, "The whole film shifts between acknowledging manufacture as the rule and asserting the authenticity of this particular case," while *Heller in Pink*

Tights champions artificiality, performance, and "manufacture."[26] *A Star Is Born* offers a deconstruction of Hollywood's production of stardom while it simultaneously champions its own star, Judy Garland, as the "real" thing. *Heller in Pink Tights*, by contrast, has no similar struggle. It is arguably all pleasure. There is no anguished history of star Sophia Loren lurking within this text, no melodramatic need to discover authenticity beneath the actress's wig and corsets. Interestingly, Richard Lippe argues that *Heller in Pink Tights* is a "companion piece" to *A Star Is Born*, ostensibly because both films highlight the way in which the stage can be both a professional and personal space—where Blodgett can declare that she is "Mrs. Norman Maine" and Loren's Angela Rossini can propose to Anthony Quinn's Tom Healy.[27] That said, my greatest pleasure in watching the film is in how it mobilizes Loren's star image as camp excess.

Playfulness drives *Heller in Pink Tights*, from its throwaway use of the Hollywood Western genre to Loren's intentionally unconvincing drag performance of *Mazeppa*. Based upon a pulp novel by Western genre writer Louis L'Amour, Loren plays a bewigged blonde bombshell, a heart-throb of the Old West. With a touring troupe of performers, her Angela Rossini is a seducer of men and vamp extraordinaire. She reigns triumphant in the film within its heteronormative paradigm: her over-the-top performance of femininity—in evidence equally onstage and off—wins her admiration, money, and the lust and love of every man she meets.

An analysis of *Heller in Pink Tights*, far less critically acclaimed than *A Star Is Born* and of lower cult status than *Sylvia Scarlett*, perhaps best begins with a synopsis. A down-on-its-luck vaudeville troupe travels through the Hollywood-styled Old West of the 1880s, with its star bringing in audiences and trouble with her sexual appeal and appetite for riches. Manager Tom Healy attempts to rein Rossini in (both sexually and behaviorally) and keep the troupe together—including the ingenue (Margaret O'Brien) and her bawdy stage mother (Eileen Heckart). Into the fray comes gunslinger Mabry (Steve Forrest), who wins Rossini herself when she overbets in a poker game; Healy strives to shield her from her fate despite this betrayal of their romantic commitment. All ends well when Mabry must be sneaked out of town and Rossini carries the day, buying a permanent theater for her troupe and marrying the pliant Healy.

Reviews of the film vary widely, from those who enjoy its humor and link it to other Cukor films to others who boggle at the mix of genres and choice of director and actors for the film, ultimately panning it.[28] Those who interpret the film as a comedy seem to praise it most, especially critics who understand Cukor's investment in theatricality and its relationship to gender.[29] Richard Lippe specifically reads the film as a rescripting of the Western. He argues that the picture "shifts the dramatic interest from the traditional emphasis on the hero defining himself by action to an investigation of Angie's [Rossini's] attempt to explore her identity." The film thus investigates "role reversal," where "regressive 'masculinity' is . . . signalled as a destructive force" and the woman is the "initiator of action" rather than the passive sexual object.[30]

Through a queer lens, the film may best be analyzed as broad comedy. The primary features of the Western genre are parodied or ignored: the woman, who usually represents a threat to male freedom, is rewritten as Western star, and a wonderland of theatrical sets and glamorous costumes is substituted for the wilderness of the Old West.[31] Thus, although the gunslinger character seems at first out of place in his threatening display of hypermasculinity, he is rendered ineffectual and ultimately irrelevant because the beautiful artifice of the theater conquers the danger he represents. Similarly, though we may wonder whether Rossini will at last destroy the doglike devotion of Healy, we suspect not and ultimately do not really care, for the film assures us, in tongue-in-cheek fashion, that the conventions of Hollywood romance will carry us where we need to go. Cukor himself identified the film as a "romantic comedy," rather than as Western or drama, and was drawn not to the story line but to the "subject" of a traveling theatrical troupe in "the pioneer days." In particular, the director remarked on the idea of the troupe "traveling in culture," bringing their way of being and seeing the world with them.[32] At least part of this perspective includes an unmasking of the Hollywood Western for the racist, sexist fantasy it always was, and drag conveys this message powerfully and playfully.

From the moment Loren's Angela Rossini is introduced to us, we are confronted by an outrageous show of glamorous feminine excess. She is female-to-feminine drag writ far larger than Esther Blodgett–as–Vicki Lester. The character steps down from a stagecoach, the camera panning from her elegantly shoed foot up her long legs and round hips to her tiny, corseted waist and ample bust. When we get to her face, we find it veiled by scarves, which she removes one by one, tantalizing viewers with brief

Donning red wig and toga with flesh-toned leotard beneath, Sophia Loren in *Heller in Pink Tights* (1960) plays fictional character Angela Rossini portraying Tartar Prince Mazeppa in homage to Adah Isaacs Menken, which distances the viewer from any notion of gender as "natural."

glimpses but no long glances at her heavily made-up features. At this introductory moment and throughout the film, Loren's appearance is entirely and clearly artificial and hypergendered, from her costume, make-up, and wig to her breathy voice, stylized walk, and desire for male attention. That gender is performative cannot be missed in the face of this excess, and, unlike the figure of the objectified pinup, the film invites the viewer into its playground.

If Rossini is playing Salome when we meet her, the film adds another layer of artifice through drag when she performs a show-stopping act as the Tartar Prince Mazeppa. This is an homage to nineteenth-century Jewish American star of theater and poetry Adah Isaacs Menken, identified as "America's Original Superstar" by biographers Michael Foster and Barbara Foster in their 2011 biography. Within *Heller in Pink Tights*, the performance involves a layering of gendered impersonations that entirely distances viewers from the concept of an essential gender. Loren performs as Rossini, a Cukor-directed version of L'Amour's literary version of Menken, and Loren/Rossini performs as Cukor's version, via L'Amour, of Menken's Mazeppa. Like the "Born in a Trunk" sequence in *A Star Is Born*, there is a *mise en abyme* quality to the performative strata here.

Moreover, the specifics of this drag performance require comment. Loren/Rossini's Mazeppa is firmly situated in Dyer's "vampish" mode. In a short but femininely coiffed red wig and a scanty toga that would expose one breast if she were not wearing a flesh-colored leotard beneath, Loren is anything but masculine. Unlike Garland in her tramp mode or Hepburn in her genderqueer baggy suit at the end of *Sylvia Scarlett*, Loren's Rossini-as-Mazeppa is more about wearing little than trying on masculinity. And the audience of men that watches the act finds her entirely seductive in this guise. Ultimately, I share Lippe's perspective that this spectacle "call[s] our attention both to [Loren's] identity on and off the screen as an actor, and to the artifice involved in both the theater and film."[33] Furthermore, the placement of this gender display within a genre film in which the conventions are confounded through emphasis on theatricality renders a "straight," patriarchal reading far less convincing.

Such terms are, similarly, the most persuasive way to read the film's heteronormative romantic conclusion, which sees the "heller" Rossini tamed and married off to Healy. The narrative of *Heller in Pink Tights* makes plain that it is the leading lady who controls the when, where, and why of marriage while also controlling the finances and future of her husband and the entire troupe of actors. Though she gives the new theater to her man and meekly offers to leave him just before she proposes marriage to him, Rossini does all of this as an act, to ensure the safety of her own existence. We have no evidence—apart from her out-of-character apology and staged humility—to suggest she will not continue to be the heller she has always been, in word, deed, and appearance. Experienced this way, the film is arguably one of the strongest feminist challenges to Hollywood norms within Cukor's oeuvre.

Reading this "romance" through gender performance and drag also relies on how we analyze the character of Healy, particularly as played by Anthony Quinn. Fawning after his star and acting more as mother hen type than traditional leading man, Healy is far from a representative of normative Hollywood masculinity. Throughout the film, Healy acquiesces to Rossini's demands, gets her out of difficult situations in which she shows open disrespect for the troupe's well-being as well as for Healy's devotion, and fails to get her to commit to marriage through his own efforts. This lack of masculine power is something Quinn himself found disturbing, perhaps explaining his poorly received performance. According to Emanuel Levy, the actor claimed he got little of the director's attention and did not know why he was cast. Furthermore, Levy reports Quinn stating, "I was basically playing a homosexual."[34] Queering the text in this fashion certainly fits within the playful mode of the film. However, Quinn's frustration with the role suggests he was playing against the kind of gender mischievousness in which the film engages. Most broadly, there is potential for reading all of the film's main characters as performers who see through gender-normative roles and take pleasure in confounding them on- and offstage. And the staged drag scene points this out most directly.

Ultimately, whether we emphasize similarities among *Sylvia Scarlett*, *A Star Is Born*, and *Heller in Pink Tights* or their differences, there is pleasure in the methods they employ to explore and challenge Hollywood gender norms. We see in the trio Cukor's engagement with female-to-male drag as it questions and at times refutes gender essentialism and heteronormativity. Within the contexts of playful adventure, dramatic social critique, and comedy, we have opportunity to see in Cukor's work how the politics of gender performativity emerge in ways that have rarely been carefully considered.

7

Queer Musical Excess

With the single, Academy Award–winning exception of *My Fair Lady* (1964), George Cukor is not well-known as a director of musicals. He was not a fan of the genre, and he did not feel he had the particular skills it demanded. "I am not a musical comedy director," he firmly declared in an interview given the year *My Fair Lady* was released.[1] Nonetheless, more than ten of the films Cukor directed to completion in his lifetime can be identified along the musical genre continuum, from comedies and dramas containing song and dance numbers to fully integrated musicals, both Broadway adaptations and Hollywood originals.

One of the central features of the American musical genre is its emphasis on theatricality and excess. Both, as the previous chapter explored, are central to Cukor's films. Nonetheless, when presented with a musical to direct, rather than enjoy the artificiality, Cukor struggled to include songs in a "natural" and "clever" way, claiming he aimed to be "very logical about music" and keep in mind that the audience "will not take any bull shit."[2] Such a perspective shows awareness of and adherence to Hollywood demands and the criterion of naturalization, even within a genre that Martin Rubin justly calls "impossible" for its frequent spontaneous and flawless performances of song and dance by unlikely characters or in incredible situations.[3] Cukor referenced such elements of the musical as the inevitable production of "a realism that has been egged up some way towards the realm of marvel," but he did not claim to enjoy working within this realm.[4]

Musicals are no more artificial than other Hollywood genres, but they can seem so. All genres have arbitrary requirements, from the forced happy ending of the romantic comedy to the emotional excess of the melodrama. Yet, the musical highlights theatricality in a broader, more self-conscious fashion, due to the "fractious elements of the genre—narrative and spectacle, dialogue and song."[5] Thus, while Cukor's experience led him to embrace the theatrical, the overt excess of the musical did not mesh well with his approach to filmmaking. Thus, argues Carlos Clarens, "Cukor seems less at home, never quite accepting a transposed theatrical convention which on film blurs the line between the real and the illusory, world and theatre, however imperceptible the transition between the spoken word and the sung lyric."[6]

Despite his declared discomfort, Cukor nonetheless directed multiple musical films, with varying degrees of critical and box office success. Hence, among his filmographies, for example, three include a chapter or subchapter devoted directly to the "Cukor musical." Gary Carey's *Cukor & Co.: The Films of George Cukor and His Collaborators* offers a chapter that brings together *A Star Is Born* (1954), *Les Girls* (1957), *Let's Make Love* (1960), and *My Fair Lady* (1964), for example. In his discussion of "New Directions" in Cukor's oeuvre, Clarens (1976) begins with focus on the musical, identifying the same four films as Carey. Gene Phillips's Twayne Filmmakers volume expands this focus; he begins his musicals chapter with *What Price Hollywood?* (1932), the nonmusical inspiration for Cukor's *A Star Is Born*, and follows his discussion of *Let's Make Love* with brief reference to *Something's Gotta Give* (1962), the uncompleted second Cukor–Monroe musical collaboration. He also includes *Les Girls* and concludes with discussion of the rarely discussed musical fairy tale *The Blue Bird* (1976), a star-studded but ill-fated Russian–American coproduction that had not been filmed when Carey and Clarens completed their books. Such unifying discussion demonstrates Cukor's involvement with the musical, however reluctant, even as his oeuvre makes plain that his work in the genre began after the peak of the classic, integrated Hollywood musical of the 1930s and 1940s.

A central facet of the classic musical is its drive toward heterosexual union, toward happiness earned after resolution of conflicts leading to heteronormatively satisfying closure. It shares this common focus with romantic dramas and comedies. Song and dance numbers aim for the kind of "heaven, of grand and glorious feeling" achieved when Fred Astaire and Ginger Rogers perform Irving Berlin's "Cheek to Cheek" in *Top Hat* (1935). Achieving their happy ending depends upon a particular understanding of heterosexual relations. Heterosexual complementarity is one of two dominant modes of textual representation and "generally implies that masculinity and femininity are themselves tantalisingly incomplete opposites that can be rapturously fused in an equal, loving relationship." The second mode emphasizes difference and inequality, correlating gender and power. Here, romantic intoxication comes from "men relishing having power" and "women luxuriating in surrender."[7] The latter came increasingly into prominence after the 1930s, and well describes the direction of both *Les Girls* and *My Fair Lady*.

Robert Altman emphasizes oppositionality as central to American culture beyond gender relations, seen in such binaries as "order/liberty, progress/stability, [and] work/entertainment." Musicals are a kind of text that serves to obscure the potential paradox in mutual exclusivity, fashioning "a myth out of the American courtship ritual."[8] The danger of such ritualization, of course, is its reliance on power imbalance, as one term must dominate over the other, however obscured. Richard Dyer explains that musical numbers often reveal that "someone is paying a price, and being asked to believe they love it." There are occasional alternatives, as in the example of couples' song and dance numbers that emphasize "sporty sparring" and demonstrate equal ability.[9]

By the late 1940s, there had been a cultural shift away from the equality of the 1930s (exemplified by the Fred and Ginger musicals). Films of the late 1940s and 1950s, despite or perhaps in reaction to the growth of (white, middle-class) female independence, show a "renewed insistence on the differences between women and men, sometimes pushed to the point of a virtual incompatibility."[10] We see this in all three films discussed in this chapter. In *Les Girls*, featuring Gene Kelly in his final MGM musical, womanizing performer Barry Nichols takes his pick of the three women who work under his direction (portrayed by Mitzi Gaynor, Kay Kendall, and Taina Elg), and goes even further, giving the final and definitive "truth" of his relationships in the context of a court trial within the film's *Rashomon*-style narrative. In *My Fair Lady*, the closest Henry Higgins and Eliza get to mutual understanding is Eliza's knowing return and Henry's demand for his slippers. And in *Let's Make Love*, so much deception occurs that a happy ending must be forced in an elevator.

Because these films are *musical* comedies, however, they feature moments of spectacular excess that point to their own artificiality, including the absurdity of (oppositional) gender roles, not unlike the extremes of *Heller in Pink Tights* as discussed in the previous chapter. Related to this is their availability for camp readings. The three films all feature exaggerated images suggesting nostalgia for past eras, whether it is the homage to pair dancing that obliquely links *Les Girls* with musicals of the 1930s, the Victorian setting and attitudes toward women of *My Fair Lady*, or Marilyn Monroe's reprise of Cole Porter's 1938 hit "My Heart Belongs to Daddy" for a 1960 audience.

Theories of camp discourse, as they explain the relationship among theatricality, gender, and sexuality, offer an important starting point for study of the role of the musical in Cukor's oeuvre. Popular perspectives may (following Susan Sontag's 1964 "Notes on Camp") have "downplayed, sanitized, and made safe for public consumption" camp's "homosexual connotations," argues Moe Meyer, but only temporarily. Avoiding the conflation of camp with "rhetorical and performative strategies such as irony, satire, burlesque, and travesty," requires attention to the "binding referent" of camp: the homosexual.[11] I find this attention paid in Cukor's musicals, and the following paragraphs will illustrate its presence through a queer/camp lens. Specifically, Meyer's vital "referent" is deployed in Gene Kelly's camp take on Marlon Brando in *The Wild One* (1953) in *Les Girls*, in Henry Higgins's solo numbers that cast light on his preferences for the company of men over women in *My Fair Lady*, and in Milton Berle's appearance in *Let's Make Love*.

A form of both production and reception, camp is, in the words of Richard Dyer, a "characteristically gay way of handling the values, images and products of the dominant culture through irony, exaggeration, trivialisation, theatricalisation and an ambivalent making fun of and out of the serious and respectable."[12] Camp reflects awareness of surfaces and the social construction of identity. "Its viewpoint suggests detachment from conventional standards," especially those of gender and sexuality.[13] This is especially so as its target is "the cultural basis of sexual and social identities in the masculine-feminine binary naturalizing heterosexuality as the single position of normality."[14] We may find that the musical, therefore, with "its open indulgence in sentiment, and its emphasis on atmosphere, mood, nostalgia, and the fantastic, is . . . a film genre that is saturated with camp."[15]

A more concise definition of camp is difficult to find. Most theorists and critics agree that it is a method of both constructing and interpreting texts, and its predominant discursive mode is excess. Its impact is also central. According to Alexander Doty, camp's politics "can be reactionary, liberal, or radical, depending on the example you are considering and your ideological agenda as a reader." Its most salient feature, Doty declares, is its queerness: "One thing about camp is certain—at least for me: Camp is queer. There is nothing straight about camp."[16] In *Flaming Classics* (2000), Doty enacts queer readings of various Hollywood classics, from *The Wizard of Oz* (1939) to *Psycho* (1960), including an exhaustively detailed camp reading of Cukor's romantic comedy *The Women*. Doty argues that "the coding of classic or otherwise 'mainstream' texts and personalities can often yield a wider range of non-straight readings [such as camp] because certain sexual things could not be stated baldly . . . thus often making it more difficult to categorize the erotics of a film or a star." Such a perspective, he is quick to point out, should not lead us to "valorize the closet" or to understand queerness as always suggested—that is, "never really there 'denotatively.'" Queerness, Doty posits, is "inside texts and production," for "any text is always already potentially queer."[17] Similarly, I read queerness, particularly via camp excess, as central to Cukor's musicals not because he was gay but because musicals are (at least in certain moments) queer. And in such subversive reading, I enjoy partaking in the pleasures of classic Hollywood.

Before engaging in this queer reading process, understanding the queer appeal of the musical genre is instructive. Brett Farmer's *Spectacular Passions: Cinema, Fantasy, Gay Male Spectatorships* offers a productive angle of approach, particularly if we read the queer studies critic in a position of affinity—though not of equivalence—to the gay spectator. Farmer's project vis-à-vis the musical is to explore its particular appeal to gay audiences without falling prey to the (potentially pathologizing) tendency to argue that musicals champion escapism and so do homosexuals. Although lavish song and dance numbers and the nonrealist structure of musicals may lead us to find queerness in them, we must remember that, "like most forms of mainstream cinema, the Hollywood musical is produced in, by, and for a culture that insists on the definitional primacy of heterosexuality and that, as a result, the utopian idylls it presents are most universally heterosexual." Instead, argues Farmer, it is within specific moments of textual rupture that we find the greatest potential for queerness in the text (or, for his project, explanation of gay attachment to the genre). If the musicals' "scenarios assume and promote a heterocentrist economy of meaning/desire," they also feature moments of cinematic excess that can be read as "marks of a signifying surplus that exceed the needs or demands of the dominant film narrative." We see such moments most often in musical numbers that disrupt narrative flow, when "the smooth functioning of the dominant representational convention breaks down and permits a momentary outburst of diegetically unaccommodated signification." For Farmer and other film/cultural critics (such as Stephen Heath, a primary theorist of the concept of "excess"), these moments offer a "symptomatic point of failure" that disrupts "not only the dominant structures of classical narrative film form but the structures of textual and spectatorial desire as well." For the (gay) spectator, concludes Famer, "prioritizing *other* moments—or moments of otherness" opens the film text "to the possibilities of alternative readings and desires."[18]

At first glance, Cukor's *Les Girls* offers typical Hollywood musical fare; it is positively giddy with traditional gender roles and heteronormativity. However, beneath the surface, much more is going on. With songs by Hollywood's favorite queer composer Cole Porter and incessant emphasis on theatricality, artifice, and duplicity, *Les Girls* is rich with "otherness" and ripe for camp readings. The title song begins the excess, with Kelly paying tribute to the charms and delights of femaleness in language as unoriginal as it is excessive, wording shamefully unworthy of the man that penned such witty, wicked delights as "Let's Misbehave" and "I Hate Men"—unless read as camp. From uninspired rhymes and hackneyed imagery ("Ah, what charms they disclose / From their hats to their hose") to the repetition of the phrase "Les Girls" nine times in the verse alone (while the chorus is made up almost entirely of a call and response centered on these two words), the song "Les Girls" opens a film that will posit so many sexual clichés that something queer simply must be going on.

The most compelling moment of narrative disruption in the film is the number "Why Am I So Gone (About That Gal)?" Here, Kelly's playboy performer engages in a staged couple's dance number with Mitzi Gaynor's small-town girl Joy Henderson that uses reversal of traditional gender roles to create a number with ample camp appeal. While it does not replace the film's heteronormative romantic ending, it does disrupt it momentarily, pointing through song and dance spectacle to the artificiality of the gender roles emphasized within the narrative and its forced closure.

To fully understand the disruption, however, let us begin with the tradition. Musicals of the 1950s and 1960s included fewer couple's dances than in previous decades and shifted from early burlesque (e.g., Busby Berkeley) and ballroom (e.g., Fred and Ginger) to ballet and folk (via tap), making way for greater athleticism (i.e., masculine display) in male solo dances alongside ongoing strong roles for women. The shift had political implications as well as textual, particularly in terms of gender. As Dyer describes, "A dance style developed that gave more prominence to men, permitted them to dance things other than love, free of the slur of effeminacy and worse; within couple-dances it also meant a renewed sense of gender polarity (to make the men look more like men) and female dependency." He thus concludes about the 1950s musical, "It was as if it was no longer possible to imagine in bodily terms a heterosexual happiness for which the star woman did not have to pay too high a price in terms of subordination."[19]

Les Girls does follow the trend of this era; Kelly sings and dances solo, for example, displaying his virtuosity and athletic style. However, the film also includes staged numbers, offering nostalgic pleasure even as homage becomes comedic parody, particularly in "Why Am I So Gone (About That Gal)?" A box set opens on a stylized diner scenario, featuring sketched-in doors, a soda fountain/counter, several small round tables and chairs, and a jukebox. Gaynor's Joy plays a waitress and Kelly's Barry is fashioned as a biker who bursts onto the set, looking for trouble. We are presented with a Hollywood-style working-class setup where the hypermasculinized bad boy can chase the hyperfeminized good girl in a setting safe for family audiences. Yet, this stereotyped heterosexual coupling quickly becomes more than that when read through notions of camp excess because the scene is clearly an allusion to the film *The Wild One* (1953), with Kelly evoking Marlon Brando's tough (for the era) biker, Johnny, and Gaynor as Mary Murphy's waitress, Kathie. However, detailed comparison of Brando's and Kelly's gendered portrayals makes parody a far more apt descriptor than homage here.[20]

Kelly enters the set with a self-conscious swagger, sporting an outfit that helped Orry-Kelly win the Academy Award for Best Costume Design for *Les Girls*. His leather jacket is cinched at the waist and accentuated with a white cravat. His slacks are cuffed like Brando's were, but they are neat, creased, and made to dance in, not the heavy, worn denim sported by the bikers of *The Wild One*. Stagy realism gives way to glamorized Hollywood in this performance within a performance. The conflation of a dancer's grace and femininity with the trope of effeminate homosexuality surfaces as Kelly saunters into the diner and removes a glove. His voice lacks convincing roughness as he tells Gaynor's character that he is a member of the "Clarport Rat Pack" and sets about seducing her. In 1957, "Rat Pack" would refer to a group of New York actor friends led by Humphrey Bogart, which later led to the 1960s group and its films. The name makes plain that Kelly is knowingly playing a role connected to Hollywood. That his seduction takes place in song and dance, however, is what most fully separates it from *The Wild One* and encourages a queer reading through excess.

Cole Porter's lyrics begin with appropriate reference to the mismatch between the biker from the wrong side of the tracks and the sweet diner waitress: "Lately I've been foolish enough to fall / For a doll . . . 'cause she isn't my type at all." After listing all her traits that oppose his usual preferences (blonde not brunette, straight hair not curly, etc.), he moves to a dissection of her flaws, including her rejection of his advances. This leads to a final stanza that includes reversal of expected gender roles, even a queering of the relationship. Kelly opines, "Her clo'es [*sic*] at any supper club are much too plain, / I'm for fancy satin and silk." We have lost entirely the working-class premise of *The Wild One*, certainly. There is also ambiguity in whether the satin and silk are his preferences for her clothes or his own, and this is echoed in Orry-Kelly's costume for Kelly in the scene. The final lines of the song have Kelly noting that he aches whenever he is near this woman, but that the ache occurs in particular "if she socks me when I'm on the make." While the theme of male sexual pursuit and female retreat continues, here it becomes an opportunity for female aggression. This "gal" that Kelly's biker character is so "gone about" is especially alluring for her ability not just to reject but to physically assault him.

Challenging gender norms as part of the camp elements of this musical number continues in the dance that follows the song. Gaynor repulses Kelly by pushing him over a table, and then Kelly lies on the floor while Gaynor sits above him, posing and waving to his prone form, for example. Then, invoking a stereotypical lion tamer image, Kelly holds out a chair to keep Gaynor from attacking him. Here we have a reversal of the male as wild animal and the woman as man tamer. However, we also see

Gene Kelly enacts the role of lion tamer against an atypically aggressive female (Mitzi Gaynor) in a dance sequence from *Les Girls* (1957).

moments of traditional heteronormative romance, as when Kelly leads Gaynor in traditional ballroom steps and shares a bit of 1930s style equality with her in paired jazz movements.

Traditional, too, is Gaynor's sadness when Kelly's character is called to return to his biker friends. We see the typical heterosexual paradigm of the bereft woman longing for the man she teased too long as the number ends, coupled with what can be read in Kelly's departure as an escape from heteronormativity into the homosocial realm of the biker gang. Overall, a queer perspective allows us to read the highly theatrical "Why Am I So Gone (About That Gal)?" number through its parodic allusion to *The Wild One* and emerge with a denaturalizing complication of traditionally gendered and sexualized romance codes that are central to the musical genre.

Although *My Fair Lady* is more invested in the kind of staged realism Cukor felt best suited the musical (though not, as previous chapters have shown, other genres), the film offers numerous moments of camp excess in its elaborate musical numbers and arguably clumsy rewriting of the ending of Shaw's *Pygmalion*. Of course, a more direct challenge to the oppositional gender roles and rigid heteronormativity of the film can be found in a feminist interpretation of Eliza, particularly the impact of her voice, spoken and sung. As critic Susan Smith asks, "To what extent, for example, does the charismatic strength of the woman's singing voice manage to effect some form of genuine recognition, or even transformation, in her influential male mentor figure or does the potency and autonomy of her voice ultimately result in the adoption of even more extreme or elaborate strategies of control?" Through close work with the film (including study of its narrative trajectory, specific songs, character relations, and Hepburn's star impact), Smith concludes that *My Fair Lady* features a "knowing" ending in which Henry and Eliza are "signalling to each other an ironic awareness of the class and gender structures underpinning their earlier relationship and their sense of distance from their former roles."[21]

A queer reading of the relationship between Henry Higgins and his sidekick Colonel Hugh Pickering offers a very different kind of pleasure in its evidence of "ironic awareness," based more on affinity than difference. In Shaw's original play *Pygmalion* as well as both Broadway and filmed versions of *My Fair Lady*, Higgins and Pickering share the pretensions of their social class and gender, feelings of self-importance, and a love of phonetics—not to mention a home, as Higgins invites Pickering to stay with him when they meet at the opening of the play and film. In Cukor's version of the musical, while talking to, at, and about Eliza Doolittle (Audrey Hepburn) in the opening scene, the men quickly find each other far more interesting: "I came from India to meet you," gushes Wilfrid Hyde-White's Pickering; "I was going to India to meet you," enthuses Rex Harrison's infamously stagy Henry Higgins. And they walk off, practically arm in arm, leaving Eliza with Higgins's tossed-off pocket change. This introduction blossoms into a close and easy friendship that boasts a delightful compatibility of mind and spirit. Pickering's calm and kind disposition balances Higgins's volatile, controlling demeanor in an idealized relationship easily compared to conventional wife and husband, respectively, while the two share a colonizing worldview that keeps either from seeing the full moral implications of manipulating a working-class woman's life and placing a bet on her fate.

The film, like its Broadway predecessor but unlike Shaw's original play, closes with Eliza deciding to return to life with Higgins (and, presumably, Pickering), exemplifying well the artificiality of the heteronormative romance imperative to the heart of the musical genre. We have no reason to believe marriage will take place—or sexual intimacy for that matter. This forced artificiality can encourage a feminist reading, with Eliza choosing life as scholar's assistant to that of trophy wife or flower shop salesgirl. Or perhaps it suggests a retreat into prepubescence as a daughter or younger sister type within a very nontraditional household indeed. However interpreted, the artificiality of the ending is plain.

We can begin to "go camping," as Doty puts it, by seeking queer excess through consideration of the song "An Ordinary Man."[22] Higgins's disposition encourages him to reject women who attempt to be anything more than servants or vehicles to prove his pedagogical talents. He concludes that he is, in such preferences, "an ordinary man," and then proceeds to clarify in a sung soliloquy that letting a woman into his life is to "invite eternal strife," and compares marriage to willingly letting a dentist's drill into his mouth. We have here a clear Hollywood example of the lifelong bachelor. He may be asexual, he may be misogynistic, or, just perhaps, he may be gay. If we choose to read this character's excessive anti-woman bias through camp, we find queerness in the song he then sings to Pickering: "A Hymn to Him," otherwise known as "Why Can't a Woman Be More Like a Man?"

After Eliza has passed herself off as royalty, winning Higgins's bet for him, she earns neither praise nor affection from Higgins or Pickering. She flees, trying to decide what she should—or can—now do with her life. Higgins is at a loss to understand Eliza; he finds her ungrateful and irrational, and identifies her incomprehensibility as entirely about her gender. Pickering, though more outwardly saddened at her departure, does not quite understand either. He phones the police to find her, admitting boldly that she is neither his wife nor a relation. Then, not liking the implications the officer on the phone draws, he barks, "What the girl does here is *our* affair!" This retort, within the context of Higgins's and Pickering's close relationship, situates Eliza as being in an intimate relationship of some sort with both men, or suggests that the "affair" is between the two men and Eliza is their charge as a couple. However interpreted, the song that follows this moment, talk-sung by Higgins as he walks in and out of his bedroom while Pickering attempts to phone an old friend for help, fuels queer implications based on traditional gender roles.

After railing against Eliza and women in general as "exasperating, irritating, vacillating, calculating, agitating, maddening, and infuriating hags," Higgins pauses to consider an alternative, and then shares his thoughts with Pickering. Men, he declares, are exactly the opposite of women: honest, straightforward, noble, and fair-minded. Pickering himself is Higgins's example of the excellence of men and delight in male–male relationships. Higgins then invites Pickering into the exchange by asking a series of questions, to which Pickering responds in supportive fashion. He wonders whether Pickering would feel slighted by long periods of silence or be angry if he had a few drinks or never gave him flowers. Pickering's responses are quick and firm: "Of course not," "Nonsense," and "Never!" Higgins then concludes, "Why can't a woman be like you?" As the song goes on, Higgins continues to praise men until he finally returns to Pickering: "Would you complain if I took out another fellow?" Pickering replies without hesitation, "Never!" Higgins concludes, in frustration, "Why can't a woman be like us?"

One interpretation of the song and the scene is a portrayal of the men's awareness of heteronormativity. They know a man *should* desire a woman, and they—especially Higgins—are infuriated that women are so unappealing to them. This said, having one man sing these lyrics to another directly brings an intimate connotation, especially as Higgins maneuvers during the song, dropping down beside Pickering on a small settee and putting his arm around the back of the sofa at Pickering's shoulder when noting how "Men are so friendly."

Cukor's cinematographical restraint in this number adds another level of camp interest. Apart from the moments mentioned above, the camera refrains from showing Pickering and Higgins intimately. For the first verses, Higgins either pops in and out of the shot or is the only one shown in frame. When Higgins and Pickering are filmed together, Pickering is shown in an almost protective stance, shying away, with the phone receiver between himself and Higgins and at a three-quarter angle, his eyes not visible throughout most of the song. It is engaging to read Pickering's posture as defensive, actively blocking the implications of the song and Higgins's aggressive stance and words. Yet, the choice of camera angles lets us read Higgins as the desiring subject, wielder of the gaze, aiming it not at Eliza but at Pickering now and, by implication, other sympathetic/queer men.

The song also asks another sort of queer question: Is there any reason a woman cannot be manlike? As discussed in the previous chapter, other Cukor films offer drag sequences that show women performing masculinity for various purposes, and Cukor's films often address questions of the role and meaning of gender, including what and how it signifies when a woman does act "more like a man"—or, as will next be explored in the context of Milton Berle in *Let's Make Love*, when a man acts like a woman. Within the story line of *My Fair Lady*, Eliza does arguably learn to challenge gender norms, in behavior if not appearance, as well as the class boundaries on which Higgins and Pickering are so focused. She refuses the idea of marriage to a wealthy man, understanding it as selling herself in a way she never had to do as a flower girl. Moreover, when she considers running off with the malleable Freddy Eynsford-Hill, she aggressively demands that he demonstrate his affection in "Show Me." Transgression of class and gender norms permeate the number, with Eliza telling and showing Freddy how she is "sick of words." Rather than offering romantic poetry or "undying vows," she demands, "Don't waste my time, / Show me!"

With its unsatisfying ending for those desiring more typical romantic bliss coupled with such gender transgressive moments in song, *My Fair Lady* offers a compelling example of how even a film cherished as a nostalgic heteronormative musical romance can display resistance to gender and sexual imperatives and be cherished for its queerness.

Far less cherished as a film but also rich with camp is *Let's Make Love* (1960). Its theatrical setting invites readings of gender-as-performance even as its narrative follows the typical Hollywood romance trajectory. However, like the moments of excess in *Les Girls* and *My Fair Lady*, this Marilyn Monroe and Yves Montand vehicle has its own explosive scenes of queerness. We can certainly "go camping" in Marilyn Monroe's pole-dancing, *Lolita*-referencing rendition of Cole Porter's "My Heart Belongs to Daddy," for example. Here, her dancing in a childishly oversized cable-knit sweater coupled with sexy black tights is composed mostly of coy posing and running around a stage with a group of male dancers. In many ways, this updates her "Diamonds Are a Girl's Best Friend" number in *Gentlemen Prefer Blondes* (1953), even as it feels more like the very queer Jane Russell number "Ain't There Anyone Here for Love?" (1953). Like

Milton Berle brings high camp to *Let's Make Love* (1960) as he attempts to teach Jean-Marie Clément (Yves Montand) what to do with a woman.

Russell, who ogles and flirts but is ultimately rejected by the entire male Olympic athletic team, Monroe simultaneously advertises heterosexual availability while questioning the inevitability of heterosexual unions as she tempts and teases yet discards the group of men for "Daddy."

Beyond this suggestive number, the richest source of camp in *Let's Make Love* is arguably in the film's mobilization of Milton Berle's television persona. Impersonation is central to the film generally, where the "Theater in the Round" show in which Amanda (Monroe) performs includes professional imitators of the famous, including enactments of real celebrities, such as Elvis and Maria Callas, as well as of fictional billionaire Jean-Marie Clément, played by Yves Montand both as a character and then as an impersonator when he is mistaken for an out-of-work actor and joins the show to get close to Amanda, taking the stage name Alexandre Dumas. Into this fantasy space come other Hollywood stars in cameos, including Bing Crosby and Gene Kelly. As Bill Krohn declares, "The layers of illusion and reality that the theater metaphor enables are dizzying," and this combination of artifice and excess leads directly to a superb camp performance by Berle as Uncle Miltie, "doing a version of his 'swish' act that is not for prime time." Clément opens the act by pretending he is waiting for his girlfriend, and Berle enters, impersonating Amanda/Monroe and making a play for Clément. The pretext for the scene is Clément asking Berle to show him "what to do with a woman," which can be read as a double entendre, for Clément means he wants to know how to tell that joke.[23] Clément displays homophobic horror as Berle first "mistakes" him for gay and then tries to teach him a lesson about Amanda, fumbling purposefully over who is (playing) the girl, multiplying the queer complications through high camp performance.

To deepen understanding of the importance of this scene's potential queer pleasures, the era and production context is worthy of note. The greater popularity of television at home over films in the movie theater was a well-known obstacle to studios in 1960. Thus, we can see the camp excess of *Let's Make Love* as an active attempt at intervention. As Krohn argues, "The Code is still in place, but the threat of television has the studios fighting back by showing anything they can get away with (Monroe's body, Uncle Miltie's swish offensive) that can't be seen on television."[24]

When considered together, the queer moments and mobilization of camp in readings of Cukor's musicals should be interpreted as saying more about the film business and genre than about Cukor's own identity. It may be tempting to read biographically and psychologically, but a broader interpretation of genre and era offers more. Queerness, as this chapter has endeavored to illustrate, is part of the musical genre itself and, thereby, of Cukor's engagement with the genre in *Les Girls*, *My Fair Lady*, and *Let's Make Love*. As Doty persuasively observes, "In order to appeal to the largest audience possible, it behooves the film and television industries to allow queerness some sort of expression much of the time. I'm not saying this is a deliberate or conscious capitalist marketing ploy (although sometimes it is), but there seems to be room for queerness in many 'mainstream' films and television programs—and I find it difficult to believe that all this queerness comes from reading practices alone."[25]

8

Race, Nation, and Gendered Noir Anxiety

The previous chapters have, in ways both direct and indirect, illustrated Cukor's facility with Hollywood genres, including romantic comedy and melodrama, through emphasis on theatricality, Hollywood life, and gender roles and relations. As we have seen, much of his output centers on films that feature happy, heteronormative endings. Such closure extends into Cukor's forays into directing musicals and even a theatrically enhanced version of the Western. If there is a single classic genre Cukor is least known for, it is the crime film and its progeny in style, film noir. One reason for this limitation is that Cukor eschewed film violence. He called it a "cop-out" and argued, "You have to get violence and tension from the situation, rather than imposing or indulging it."[1] Another reason for his distance from tough, action-centered pictures like the crime thriller is that he was pigeonholed by the studios, limited to pictures best suited to a "woman's director." Despite this branding, Cukor did direct several films identifiable in retrospect as part of the classic Hollywood noir cycle of the 1940s: *A Woman's Face* (1941), *Keeper of the Flame* (1942), *Gaslight* (1944), and *A Double Life* (1947). We can easily call these films noir, in part because the mood and style of such pictures dominated the era. Film noir "was an essential part of the 1940s outlook, a cinematic style forged in the fires of war, exile, and dissolution."[2] Although more attuned to the gothic and the noir melodrama than the hard-boiled crime flick or the heist film, the noir style of these four 1940s films shows much about how Cukor negotiated the Hollywood system and style during the World War II era.

One way to support the specific application of the noir label to the quartet of Cukor films on which this chapter focuses is through attention to popular and academic studies and the writing of Cukor biographers. Most superficially, for example, Wikipedia identifies *A Woman's Face*, *Gaslight*, and *A Double Life* as noir; while IMDb uses the noir label only for *A Double Life* and *Gaslight* and identifies *A Woman's Face* as a drama/thriller and *Keeper of the Flame* simply as a drama. Among Cukor critics, Emanuel Levy categorizes *Gaslight* as a "noir thriller," which he compares to Hitchcock's work in style—with reference to the films *Rebecca* (1940) and *Suspicion* (1941)—for its mood of paranoia and focus on duplicitous spouses.[3] Later, Levy adds to his assessment, comparing *Gaslight* to such noir staples as *The Spiral Staircase* (1946), *The Two Mrs. Carrolls* (1947), and *Sorry, Wrong Number* (1948). Together, Levy argues, these films create a mini noir "cycle" of its own that shares premise (particularly the evil husband), narrative structure, and "noir visual vocabulary."[4]

Like Levy, Patrick McGilligan links *Gaslight* with *A Double Life* and also compares these films with Hitchcock's *Suspicion*, referencing the "taut atmosphere," in particular.[5] Carlos Clarens uses noirish criteria when he describes *Gaslight* as a "relentless exercise in sado-masochism" and discusses the film together with *A Woman's Face* and *Keeper of the Flame* in his critical filmography.[6] By contrast, in *On Cukor*, Gavin Lambert links *Gaslight* with *Keeper of the Flame* for its melodrama and "strong atmosphere and detail," but he does not mention noir.[7]

Like Lambert, Gene D. Phillips refrains from using the term "noir" as he compares *Gaslight* to Hitchcock's work through the "principle of opting for prolonged suspense." He does use the term to describe *A Double Life*, however, which he calls part of a "trend" inspired by war-era disillusionment and uncertainty and "characterized by an air of grim, unvarnished realism." His criteria lead him to include *Keeper of the Flame* in this category. Idiosyncratically, Phillips also includes *A Life of Her Own* (1950) in his list. The film's best scenes, according to Phillips, are full of "grim realism," focused as they are on Ann Dvorak's secondary character, Mary, an aging model addicted to drink and drugs, who ultimately commits suicide.[8] However, the film's lead, Lily (played by Lana Turner), is a model who suddenly abandons her determination to make good on her career and instead unexpectedly and inexplicably falls for billionaire recluse Steve Harleigh (Ray Milland), a married man. The plot devolves into conventional melodrama, and we lose any vestige of the film's promise as a commentary on women's career struggles, especially in jobs, like modeling, that are based on powerful men's assessment of youth and beauty. Of course, this was lost even earlier in the film for anyone who watches and wonders how a small-town Kansas girl becomes a supermodel in six months. When we then meet Steve's angelic invalid wife, Norah (Margaret Phillips), all pretense at realism is gone. We know Lily will send the man she loves back to his paralyzed, self-sacrificing wife, and she does. Even as she walks off into the darkness of night at the end of the film with the implication that she is likely to kill herself as Mary did, the bleak mood is unearned. This does not mean the film does not have noir elements, but it is difficult not to agree with Cukor, who, when originally told the scenario, declared, "Oh, my God, they're not going to use *that* old chestnut again?"[9]

Only recently has a critic brought the four films together, as I do here. Christoph Huber identifies these pictures as those that defined the 1940s for Cukor, a decade in which we see him "branch out impressively toward noirish terrain."[10] That Cukor did direct noir in the 1940s should not be surprising, of course, given the proliferation of dark thrillers during this era. As Paul Schrader posits, "Most every dramatic Hollywood film from 1941 to 1953 contains some *noir* elements."[11]

While it can be called a genre, most critics emphasize noir as a style. For Raymond Borde and Étienne Chaumeton (1955), noir is a "cycle," linked to a specific group of 1940s films that were shared with French audiences in the summer of 1946, beginning with John Huston's *The Maltese Falcon* (1941) and including Otto Preminger's *Laura*, Edward Dmytryk's *Murder, My Sweet*, Billy Wilder's *Double Indemnity*, and Fritz Lang's *The Woman in the Window* (all 1944). In terms of genre, this list contains mysteries, thrillers, and melodramas; however, all share a characteristic dark, cynical mood and an identifiable style. As Janey Place and Lowell Peterson explain, "Nearly every attempt to define *film noir* has agreed that visual style is the consistent thread that unites the very diverse films that together comprise this phenomenon."[12] When we link visual style with mood, we can understand 1940s noir as actively figured, in the words of Raymond Durgnat, "against the rosy ground of Anglo-Saxon middle-class, and especially Hollywoodian, optimism and puritanism."[13]

Within the context of film noir studies and Cukor's emphases as a Hollywood director in the 1940s, we can explore Cukor's *A Woman's Face*, *Keeper of the Flame*, *Gaslight*, and *A Double Life* for a shared mood of paranoia and cynicism related to criminality within dramatic contexts that downplay physical violence in favor of psychological tension. These films also display characteristic noir visual style, including chiaroscuro lighting, oblique camera angles, night scenes, and ornate (gothic) settings. Beyond these qualities, Cukor's noir is identifiable for its lack of hard-boiled protagonists, part of the director's affinity for drama over action and his depiction of men who are, posits Richard Lippe, "less than committed to projecting a masculine male image and sensibility."[14] Such elements notably link Cukor less with American noir production and more with the work of European émigré directors primarily responsible for the development of Hollywood film noir (e.g., Fritz Lang, Otto Preminger, Robert Siodmak, Edgar G. Ulmer, and Billy Wilder). Such a context provides explanation for Quentin Crisp's identification of Cukor as European in his introduction to Boze Hadleigh's *Conversations with My Elders* (1986), a collection of six interviews with influential gay men. Although incorrect, Crisp's description reflects accurately Cukor's emphasis on what Lippe calls "qualities usually associated with a European sensibility, e.g. grace, charm and sophistication" and his "tendency to avoid genres—the gangster film, the Western, the war film—which archetypically define the American ethos and its particular concept of masculinity."[15]

Further links between Cukor and European style within a noir context appear related to his cultural and ethno-religious heritage. Vincent Brook argues in *Driven to Darkness: Jewish Émigré Directors and the Rise of Film Noir* that we must add "a Jewish factor" to the study of the European origins and style of film noir. Brook explores the backgrounds of noir's most prolific and creative auteurs to find that all are émigrés of Jewish heritage who fled Germany for freedom and safety and ended up—some sooner, some later—in Hollywood. These men share a directorial perspective, especially the "bleak worldview" that led them to emphasize the "stark exposure of society's underbelly, which had already characterized Weimar cinema and would permeate film noir."[16] Once in Hollywood, these directors were forced to meld their Western European artistic perspective with the business-oriented Eastern European producers for whom they worked. There were more than a few clashes related to the battle for creativity versus cash, and the émigré directors felt intellectually superior even as they were beholden to the powerful "moguls" for their ability to find work.

If it is true that dark, bleak themes "found greater, or at least more overdetermined, resonance among Jewish émigré directors than among their American-born (Jewish or non-Jewish) counterparts," resentment of the moguls by creative American-born directors was also widespread, argues Brook.[17] Certainly, Cukor could relate to this, as well as to their émigré secularism. While he prided himself on his ability to flourish within and despite the Hollywood emphasis on the bottom dollar, he also complained frequently of a lack of creative freedom, especially the restriction against controlling the final edits of his films. Although Cukor proved expert at compromising and holding his tongue when he felt it necessary, he was of middle-class, Western European heritage and shared the émigrés' desire for artistic control and class distance. Like the Jewish émigré directors, cinematographers, and composers, Cukor socialized primarily with those he considered his own set. For him, this meant Hollywood's theatrical elite—particularly the British, whose style of speech and spelling he would emulate.[18] The intellectualist émigrés, in comparison, generally spent time with one another.

When Cukor did turn to bleak, violent subjects, from murder to madness, he echoed the strategies Brook finds central to Jewish émigré noir. The émigré directors featured a significant number of female protagonists, for example.[19] In a proportion similar to that of his entire film output, three of four Cukor noirs center on resilient female leads portrayed by major Hollywood stars: Joan Crawford as Anna Holm in *A Woman's Face*, Katharine Hepburn as Christine Forrest in *Keeper of the Flame*, and Ingrid Bergman as Paula Alquist in *Gaslight*. Historical context further nuances such casting. Sheri Chinen Biesen reminds us that the male talent shortage of the war years led to increased opportunity for female stars. "A number of screen actresses gained prominence, ideally coming into their prime in the 1940s," she writes, and Cukor aided several of them in this pursuit.[20]

Cukor also shares with the Western European émigré directors a tendency to concentrate on the artist or intellectual over either the hard-boiled male or the femme fatale. Brook writes, "Heirs to a Jewish legacy and historical circumstance that privileged intellect over action, . . . Lang, Siodmak, Ulmer, and the others were preternaturally less disposed than their American cohorts toward the virile, gun-toting, tough-talking detective."[21] We can easily consider Cukor an exception to the American rule. Scarred blackmailer Anna Holm in *A Woman's Face*, for example, plays both piano and violin, is well read in music history, and claims to know all the love poetry of the greatest writers—not to mention having tried her own hand at writing and painting. Spencer Tracy's journalist Steven O'Malley in *Keeper of the Flame* and Ronald Colman's lauded Shakespearean actor Anthony John in *A Double Life* are men of brains over brawn. And even villain Charles Boyer's Gregory Anton in *Gaslight* has a suave cunning rather than a menacing physical presence.

Because German Expressionism was so central to émigré noir, we might note that Cukor was not immune to its emotive excesses. He argued that "the text dictates the whole style." Nonetheless, he could be critical of overuse of high style. For instance, Cukor felt the brilliance of Orson Welles's *Citizen Kane* was tainted by what he called "too much UFA," a reference to the major German film company that produced such key Expressionist films as Lang's *Metropolis* (1927), *M* (1931), and *The Testament of Dr. Mabuse* (1933).[22] Nonetheless, there is homage to Expressionism in Cukor's noir, particularly in the villain Torsten Barring in *A Woman's Face*. The character is portrayed with melodramatic verve by émigré Conrad Veidt; the actor fled the Nazis with his Jewish wife after achieving fame in early German film. He is celebrated for playing somnambulist Cesare in Weimar director Robert Wiene's influential Expressionist thriller *The Cabinet of Dr. Caligari* (1920), Gwynplaine in *The Man Who Laughs* (1928), and roles in dozens of other films before his emigration.

Veidt's performance in Cukor's *A Woman's Face* is highly emotional and malicious, almost cartoonishly evil; he even invokes fascist aims in his goals for world domination (a subject dealt with more fully in *Keeper of the Flame*, although the fascist figure himself never appears on-screen in that picture). While some critics described the character of Barring as overwrought, I read him as Expressionist homage, as does critic Carlos Clarens, who labels his casting and performance a "master touch of Expressionism" in the film. "Veidt has only to toast Satan to conjure up the whole miasmal world of the old German cinema," Clarens writes.[23]

Brook goes further in his analysis of the émigré directors' character typing, linking the preference for soft-boiled types to the directors' own feminization as Jews and products of the highly stylized Weimar cinema. Of the characters they created, he argues that "they were said, and perhaps sensed themselves, most to resemble: the woman." Brook uses the work of Sander Gilman to reference a European historical linkage between "Jewish masculinity and effeminacy and, by extension, homosexuality."[24] It is not difficult to see the relationship of such history to Cukor himself, particularly through the implications of being labeled a "woman's director." This, however, is not as persuasive a focus as the details of the films themselves.

The outstanding feature of Cukor's noirs is their engagement with the free-floating anxiety that defined the World War II era. We find in the four films anxieties related to gender, sexuality, and ethnicity/nationality displaced onto noir elements including female criminality (*A Woman's Face*), American fascism (*Keeper of the Flame*), madness (*Gaslight*), and murder (*A Double Life*). To explore how this displacement functions, we can productively apply facets of Kelly Oliver and Benigno Trigo's *Noir Anxiety* (2009) to Cukor's films. The authors read existential anxiety in noir as reflecting "concrete anxieties over arbitrary and blurred boundaries of racial, sexual, and national identity."[25] Rather than proceeding chronologically, the following paragraphs work from the most obvious to the subtlest examples of the "blurred boundaries" within this chapter's quartet of films.

A Double Life is chronologically the last of the films under discussion in this chapter, and it is also the most direct in its work with noir anxiety related to race and gender boundaries in 1940s America. It tells the tale of acclaimed actor Anthony "Tony" John, who invests himself too deeply in his theatrical performance of the intense title role of Shakespeare's *Othello* opposite his ex-wife, Brita (Signe Hasso), and goes mad. His jealousy over Brita's attention to their publicity agent, Bill Friend (Edmond O'Brien), translates into murder, but not of his ex-wife. Instead, Tony blurs reality with the text of Shakespeare's *Othello* and kills a young waitress, Pat Kroll (Shelley Winters), whom he takes as a lover and then strangles after he conflates her with both Brita and the character she plays, Desdemona. She must die once he determines (wrongly) that this composite woman has been unfaithful to him. When suspected by Bill late in the film, Tony chooses to stop his violence by ending his life. He stabs himself on stage in a truly lethal performance of Othello's suicide in the final scene of the play. The original screenplay for *A Double Life* is written by Garson Kanin and Ruth Gordon, the team who would become frequent Cukor collaborators and close friends in the years after this film. While original, the script echoes the murderous actor theme of French director Marcel Carné's *Les Enfants du Paradis* (1945) and is quite similar to the premise of Jewish émigré director Max Nosseck's *The Brighton Strangler* (1945).

As I have noted elsewhere, *A Double Life* does not use World War II as an overt referent, while *The Brighton Strangler* does.[26] In Nosseck's film, the British actor protagonist (John Loder) invests himself deeply in his current stage role as a serial murderer, the titular Brighton Strangler. When he receives a head injury during the London bombings, he believes himself to actually be the strangler. By contrast, the motive for Tony John's slip into psychosis is never explained beyond his jealousy over his ex-wife's engagement, his tendency to get quite involved in his roles, and the specific part of Shakespeare's barbarous Moor.

The psychosis that leads Tony to murder well exemplifies the existential anxiety of the postwar era of the film's release, in which graphic newsreels and the increasingly common sight of traumatized returning soldiers vied with fears over fascism that were quickly turning into anticommunist hysteria. The changing status of women as well as anti-immigrant and antisemitic perspectives all reflected and heightened the tensions of the day. The cultural Other was both without and within our borders, and this led to a popularity of texts that worked symbolically to address America's greatest fears. With these issues in mind, Oliver and Trigo read darkness as both literal and symbolic in noir. Although "noir" is translated as "dark" in studies of the film genre/style/cycle, the word literally means "black." This is echoed in the "'dark' style of noir [that] puts both protagonists and villains into the shadows, so much so that they appear visually black on the screen." Whereas the "Negro problem films" of the 1940s and 1950s fixate on blacks passing for white, the classic noir cycle of the same era "presents whites who look visually black." Oliver and Trigo thus conclude that "film noir, with its sharp black-and-white contrasts, conjures the specter of race like no other cinematic style."[27] We see this contention doubly echoed in the style and content of *A Double Life.* Unlike many a Cukor film, the cinematography is dark and moody in this film, even as it features a more typical Cukor emphasis on the theater and theatricality. As reviewer Robert F. Willson Jr. declares, "The setting for the stage murder looks as if it could be transferred with few changes to films like *Double Indemnity* and *The Killers*. Shadows hang heavily on the walls and actors; the floor approximates the black and white tiles of a chessboard; a chiaroscuro storm rages outside; and wind rustles the curtains and arrases. The play and film world merge suddenly in the thematic emphasis on man's dark, disturbed nature."[28]

Even more specifically, the film relies on the racial resonances of *Othello*, which arguably "conjures the specter of race like no other" of Shakespeare's works, making it the perfect choice as the textual catalyst for Tony John's madness. Sympathetic portrayals of Othello tend to rely on the Moor's status as a cultural outsider and his false presumption that high military status would translate into social and interpersonal respect. In Shakespeare's day, such sympathies were harder to come by, for the British of the era identified emotional volatility as a "racial" characteristic of non-European peoples.[29] A similarly racist reading dominates the spectacle of *A Double Life*, in which Tony's violence is directly linked to Othello's temperament and is made manifest in blackface. Though not of minstrelsy's burnt-cork variety, the racist cultural trace is present in the dark makeup Tony wears when he plays Othello.

To grasp the play's full symbolism, we must remember that "Othello *was* a *white* man" when he originally appeared onstage.[30] Shakespeare wrote a part for a white actor to portray a character of color developed from within the white racial imagination. Hence, any invocation of this black man written by a white man for the entertainment of white audiences necessarily invokes the anxiety of boundary crossing arguably central to noir. *A Double Life* portrays this connection directly, relying not only on chiaroscuro lighting and an emotive score by Hungarian Jewish émigré composer Miklós Rósza but also on the figure of a white British man disguised as a white-written North African figure identified with "dark" motives and intent.

Eric Lott's "The Whiteness of Film Noir" points to Cukor's *A Double Life* as one of many Hollywood noir "racialized dramas of interiority," in which "the troping of white darkness in noir has a racial source that is all the more insistent for seeming off to the side."[31] He concludes, "Film noir rescues with racial idioms the whites whose moral and social boundaries seem so much in doubt," absolving whites of "evil and moral ambiguity."[32] In short, the "injury" Tony John faces in *A Double Life* is not that of a bombing, like his predecessor in *The Brighton Strangler*, but that of racial indeterminacy.[33] "Racial ambiguity, not the fear of blackness," as Oliver and Trigo clarify, "is the real anxiety of noir."[34]

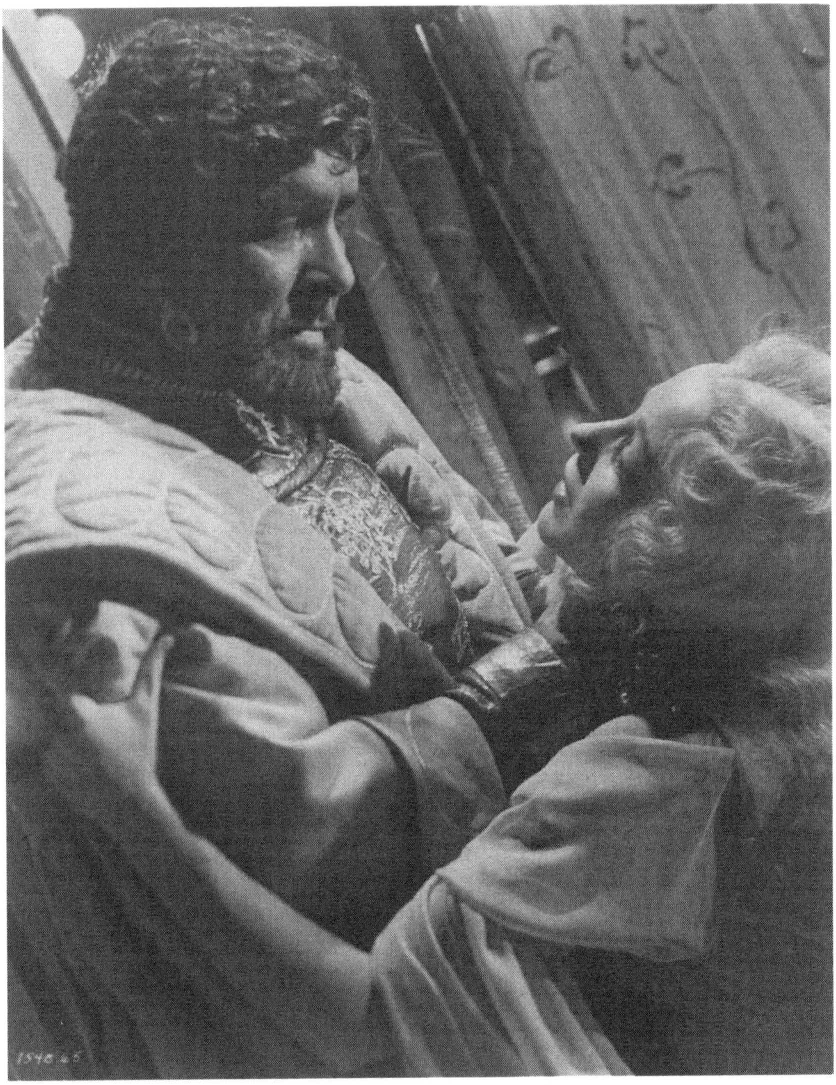

Ronald Colman in blackface as Othello, a performance that affects life offstage in the noir thriller *A Double Life* (1947).

Tony's particular choice of victim further delineates the concrete anxieties masked by noir symbolism. Most significantly absent from the film's work with the Othello myth is the villainous figure of Iago. Without this externalized foil, *A Double Life* becomes invested in "internalizing blackness as a deviant aspect of the white male psyche."[35] Tony-as-Othello punishes the sexualized white woman who breaks taboos against miscegenation with him and thereby becomes both victim and villain herself. While Pat Kroll, the doomed waitress who stands in for Brita/Desdemona, may seem important only in that her murder reveals the degree and racial implications of Tony's pathology, we may consider her against Oliver and Trigo's claim that "the most significant and telling aspects of film noir often appear as insignificant details or marginal figures."[36] In a film about doubling, we can read Pat as the "dark" alter ego of Tony's ex-wife, Brita. "Brita" (from the Latin, meaning "from England") highlights the whiteness in the film and the Anglophilia of its production context (to be discussed presently), particularly as her Desdemona wears a long, voluminous, platinum blonde wig.

Pat, in contrast to Brita, signifies ethnic otherness through her identifiably German surname, Kroll, and her uneducated, working-class sensibility. Tony, we learn early in the film, seeks success to escape his working-class British roots. Attraction to Pat symbolizes Tony's ineffective assimilation into white, upper-class American social norms, as does his willingness to take on the role of Othello in the first place. Such choices are set in contrast to the life and choices of the privileged Brita, whose foreign roots are not connected with the working class and who resists getting "mixed up in an *Othello* sort of thing" as dangerous for any sort of relationship with Tony.[37] Brita's forthright relationship with publicity director Bill (whose surname, "Friend," signifies his harmlessness) contrasts strongly with Pat's secretive and openly sexual relationship with Tony. The low-class female ethnic Other thus becomes the victim of the white man's "blackened" rage. The "racial underpinnings" of this crime are stressed, argues Lott, in Pat's response to Tony's raving about all the assumed nationalities he carries within him as an actor: "I got mixed blood too."[38]

In this context, both Pat (by murder) and Tony (at his own hand) must die to resolve the racialized and sexualized anxieties that the film invokes. As Oliver and Trigo explain, "One defense against this anxiety is ambivalence or the polarization of ambiguity into extremes that can easily be located and can help reestablish lost boundaries: black or white, masculine or feminine, familiar or foreign."[39] The white masculine figure destroys the sexually and ethnically corrupt feminine figure, but he then must destroy himself because his own identity is also racially ambiguous in that he has internalized (and externalized through blackface) the figure of the primitive, violent Moor, Othello.

Waitress Pat Kroll (Shelley Winters), the low, ethnic female of *A Double Life* (1947), flirts with racialized danger as she chats up unstable actor Tony John (Ronald Colman).

When interpreted broadly, in the context of its postwar production and relationship to the output of the Jewish émigré noir directors, we see in *A Double Life* how film noir serves a director like Cukor, a child of Western European Jewish parents who was quite aware of antisemitism within and beyond Hollywood. Although he did not experience Nazi Germany directly or visit it postwar, Cukor enlisted in the Army Signal Corps at forty-three and directed training and propaganda films, including *Winged Victory* (1944), a tale of five men preparing to become pilots, a joint production of Twentieth Century-Fox and the US Army Air Forces. The State Department's decision to bring a delegation of Hollywood executives—including such Jewish Americans as Jack Warner (Warner Bros. production head), Barney Balaban (Paramount president), and Harry Cohn (Columbia president)—to visit concentration camps and bear witness proved ultimately unproductive, for fears of antisemitic backlash increased rather than decreased thereafter.[40] Nonetheless, within a postwar context that revealed the evils of Nazi racial "science" and an

America that made little effort to welcome Jewish survivors and refugees, there might be appeal, conscious or unconscious, in the ways "film noir redefined race by undoing its 'natural' links to skin color or to blood."[41]

If *A Double Life* offers ample and overt evidence of the racial and gendered substructure of noir anxiety, then the earliest of Cukor's noir films, *A Woman's Face*, with screenplay by frequent Cukor collaborator David Ogden Stewart, provides substantiation through focus on disfigurement. Released the same year as the United States entered World War II, this noir melodrama features multiple lost boundaries and their reestablishment, both in its setting and within and between characters. Where the original 1938 Swedish film (*En kvinnas ansikte*) follows a chronological path, for example, Cukor's remake uses the framing device of Anna's trial for the murder of Torsten Barring (a typical noir structural convention). The courtroom can be read as borderland, a site where truth and falsehood must be divided by wise judges who sort through the various conflicting testimonies they hear. Strangely, in the Cukor film, the testimony is offered by a diverse group of actors/characters with wildly differing accents but Swedish names. This makes a kind of babel of the interrupted frame, deepening the murkiness of boundaries in the film. Several other settings add to this anxiety-producing atmosphere, especially the deep forest setting of the inn from which Anna and her blackmailing cohorts operate and in which we see a lesbian couple dancing as well as a man cavorting with a married woman (who turns out to be the wife of Melvyn Douglas's surgeon character, Dr. Gustaf Segert).

Gender is a central part of the lost boundaries that must be reestablished in *A Woman's Face*. Anna has two love interests, the corrupt Torsten Barring (Conrad Veidt) and, much later, the altruistic surgeon, Segert. Both men are fascinated by Anna's face, her scar in particular, a marker of difference that Torsten claims to identify with, stating, "We are both proud. We are both wretched." He will exploit her vulnerability to his manipulative affection. Meanwhile, Dr. Segert sees her as the potential subject of his greatest surgical triumph. In this triangle, Anna Holm represents the abject, the anxiety-producing borderline figure that is "both fascinating and terrifying."[42] Through Crawford's portrayal and the film's narrative, we find Julia Kristeva's perspective on the abject validated. Anna is "not, as we might ordinarily think, what is grotesque or unclean," even as she thinks this of herself. Instead, Anna is the abject as she "calls into question borders and threatens identity" in ways the film must repair to achieve its Hollywood happy ending.[43] Unlike *A Double Life*, however, *A Woman's Face* does not require the destruction of the menacingly ambiguous. Instead, Anna is transformed into a proper white feminine subject.

The twelve surgeries (only one in the original film) through which Dr. Segert puts Anna highlight her role as external threat. She must show strength, patience, and endurance if she wants to be healed or "reborn," as Anna herself puts it, into a world in which she can belong without (gendered) fear or shame. As the judge of her murder trial puts it, "You wanted to be like other women, not warped and twisted and bitter." The split self is manifest in Anna's before/after appearance as well as the trajectory of the film, which shifts in tone from noirish suspense to melodrama.[44]

The gender significance of Anna's split is shown in the impact the change has on her attitude and behavior. The doctor worries that, if his final operation is a success, he will have created "a monster: a beautiful face and no heart." Because proper femininity is linked both with external beauty and internal traits such as nurturance, gentleness, and affection, Anna's surgery will only be deemed successful if she fulfills both physical and emotional requirements. Anna rejects this dichotomy at first, validating the doctor's concerns through her awareness that beauty does not always come with a sympathetic nature. She has seen glamorous deceitfulness, after all, in the figure of the doctor's own philandering wife, whom she is in the process of blackmailing when she first meets the doctor. In response to his worry that outer beauty will mask a cold heart, she snaps, "In distinction, I suppose, to all other women with beautiful faces." This silences the doctor for the moment, but as the film moves toward melodramatic, heteronormative closure, Anna comes to buy into his perspective and the comforting world of clear binaries. This is echoed in Crawford's performance. As Emanuel Levy aptly describes, "As soon as she regains her looks, she becomes Joan Crawford. Viewers could actually see touches of the movie queen gradually sneak in: artificial eyelashes, lifted breasts."[45]

With her new face, Anna is at first eager to surprise Torsten and win not only his sympathy but his love. She agrees to become the governess of Lars-Erik (Richard Nichols), the heir to the Barring fortune, in the home of patriarch Magnus Barring (Albert Bassermann). She also agrees to kill the child to assist Torsten in his quest for inheritance by throwing the boy

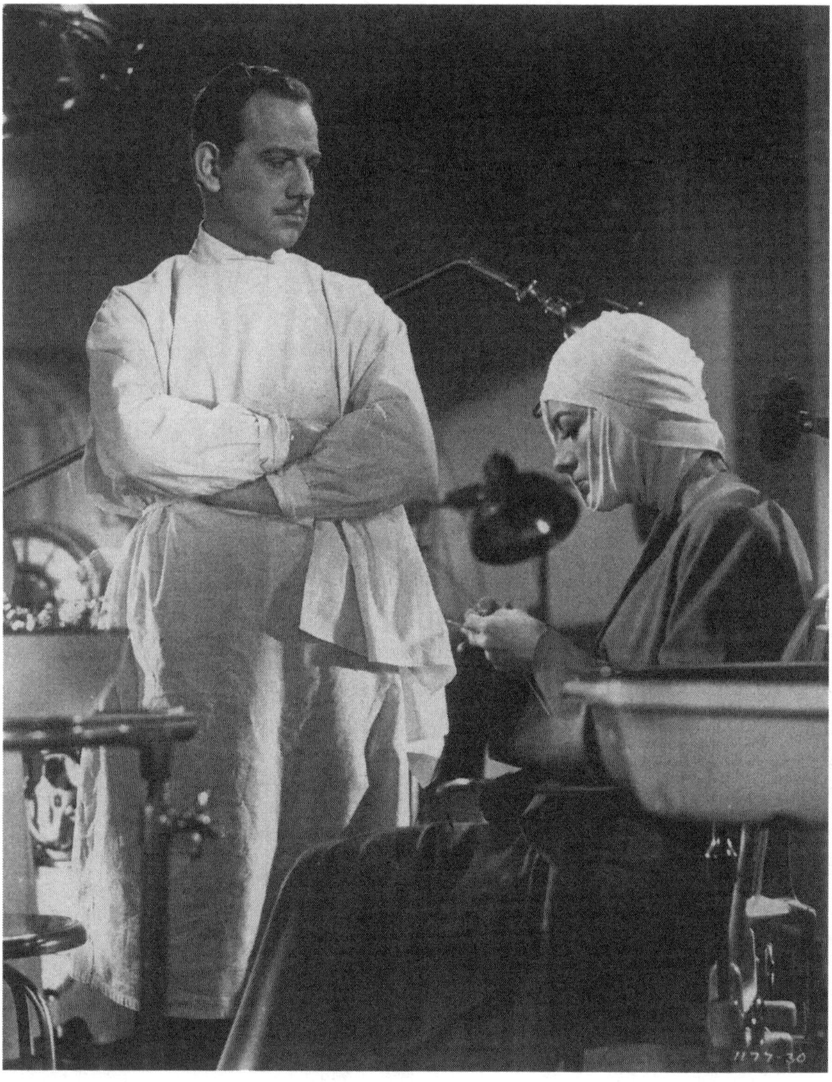

In *A Woman's Face* (1941), cynical, scarred Anna Holm (Joan Crawford) must suffer and humble herself before Dr. Segert (Melvyn Douglas) to achieve beauty and the heteronormative rewards of traditional femininity.

over the huge waterfall on Barring land—a particularly liminal, anxiety-producing locale. When Anna agrees, Torsten calls her "some kind deity's answer to my prayer." Anna responds that she is "the devil's answer," and Torsten smiles, toasting her with "Skål, Satan." Soon, however, Anna the "devil" is contrasted with her opposite, a "guardian angel," which Magnus calls her once she falls prey to Lars-Erik's charms, summed up in the boy's assertion upon meeting her, "You couldn't be mean, you're too pretty."

If Anna is angel and devil to the Barrings, she is Frankenstein's monster and Galatea to Segert. He identifies clearly his role as creator in both cases, with hope he will be the romantic Pygmalion and not the covetous Dr. Frankenstein. "Galatea" is the name popularly applied to the ivory statue Pygmalion brings to life in Greek mythology. Because the statue/woman's name means "she who is milk-white," we also see here a symbol of how the racialized black/white opposition of film noir links whiteness with proper femininity. As the film ends, with Torsten having drowned in the waterfall to which he was taking Lars-Erik when Anna balked, Segert can be Pygmalion, declaring his love for his Galatea, a reformed, beautiful Anna, rather than rejecting his monster. In melodramatic form, he affirms that her "true" self has a "hard, shining brightness." Before they kiss and walk back into the courtroom where Anna will be forgiven and released into Segert's loving embrace, she offers a declaration of submission and commitment to a proper, domesticated femininity that proves her worthy of her beautiful face and no longer an ambiguously gendered representation of the noir abject: "I want to get married. I've always wanted to get married. I want to have a home and children. I want to go to market and cheat the grocer and fight with the landlord. I want to belong to the human race. I want to belong." Any transgressions she commits now will be domesticated scuffles rather than dangerous crimes, and thus the film ends with all anxieties and ambiguities not only tempered but narratively and visually quashed. How different this is from the original Swedish film, in which Ingrid Bergman's Anna remains a more morally ambiguous character with only a daughterly affection for her surgeon. She ends the film on a boat to America, where she must begin her life anew and very much alone.

Gaslight, the most domestic of Cukor's trio of noir melodramas, shares with *A Woman's Face* the more typically Jewish émigré directorial emphasis on the female protagonist. With *A Double Life*, it shares focus on the intellectual over the physically powerful male. All three films as well as *Keeper of the Flame* also share emphasis on the psychological, especially on noirish unease related to identity. However, while the anxiety-producing borderline in *Gaslight* is less overtly about issues related to race than the two previously discussed films, the film does mobilize anxiety over nationality in ways similar to the jarring Swedish context of *A Woman's Face*. In addition, through its invocation of the thin line between sanity and insanity—evident in both obsessive Gregory Anton (Charles Boyer) and his victim, tortured wife Paula Alquist (Ingrid Bergman)—we see a film that exemplifies noir as set in a mad, melodramatic world.

Cukor's adaptation of the original 1938 stage play and 1940 British film version was longer (by 30 minutes), richly detailed, and arguably deeper in narrative and psychological depth.[46] The original film begins at the moment of the newly married couple's arrival in London, while the Cukor remake lets the plot unfold over a course of years, following the long-term plans of Gregory Anton and the life of his eventual wife, Paula Alquist, who is changed from the 1940 film into the niece of the woman Anton murders to attain her jewels. Paula is also stronger of mind than is her predecessor in the original. We watch her destroyed by Gregory slowly, purposefully. It is not difficult to read this interaction with reference to women's changing position within America of the 1940s, both during and after the war. Women's increasing presence in the public sphere offers a social explanation of the psychological power and terror of Cukor's *Gaslight*. Gender is divided into a familiar binary, Paula as the privileged-class virgin and maid Nancy (Angela Lansbury in her first Hollywood role at age seventeen) as the working-class whore; both are less empowered than the patriarch, Gregory. There is also proto-feminist critique through links to the literary theme of the abusive husband who drives his wife to madness (e.g., Charlotte Perkins Gilman's "The Yellow Wallpaper" or feminist readings of Rochester's relationship with his first wife, the madwoman in the attic in *Jane Eyre*). Such relatively familiar tropes, however, do not cause anxiety so much as relieve it. Critics commonly "interpret the sense of fate or doom in film noir as a response to white men's sense of a loss of control and authority, especially control and authority over women," and then read the resulting anxiety directly.[47] However, in addition to a free-floating anxiety and the specific anxieties produced by material conditions, noir frequently works through images and techniques that simultaneously hide and reveal the major social issues of the day.

If anxiety over 1940s gender relations is portrayed directly in *Gaslight*, I would argue that anxieties related to race and nationality are the issues dealt with through "displacement and condensation."[48] Most important in this context is that while the protagonist and antagonist are British in the original play and film, they are Swedish and French in Cukor's 1944 adaptation, despite the fact that the picture takes place in London. We can consider location and nationality through symbolism to interpret how the accents of the actors—both famous enough at the time to be known for their countries of origin—impact the film's meaning. Many locations have been given emblematic meanings and overtones in Hollywood films. There is the exoticism and dangerousness of Chinatown and east Asia generally, for example, while Mexico and Latin America often signify criminality and sexuality, especially in noir.[49] In keeping with such analysis but through focus on white foreigners, I posit that the Swedish and French accents of Bergman and Boyer, placed without explanation within the London setting in *Gaslight*, serve to displace fears of the ethnic and racial other.

I am not arguing that the cast was intended to actively invoke such fears any more than were the Swedish names and multinational cast of *A Woman's Face*. Nevertheless, we can view Cukor's films as reflections of their eras within the popular Hollywood cinema context. We can also read more biographically and psychologically, should we choose to. Cukor's Western European Jewish heritage, his homosexuality, and his attitude about both his ethnicity and sexuality may have (unconsciously) influenced his working relationships with actors.[50] For example, biographers note that Cukor both admired and feared Ingrid Bergman's directness and self-confidence. Levy goes so far as to say, "Bergman had him so spooked that when he had something important to say, he was afraid to."[51] Nonetheless, just as he admired British poise and etiquette, Cukor was also said to love Swedish women, finding them "extraordinary," as Signe Hasso quipped in the context of working with him on *A Double Life*, after he had already directed Greta Garbo in *Camille* (1936) and *Two-Faced Woman* (1941) and Bergman in *Gaslight*.[52]

Beyond interactions with Cukor, Bergman's accent let her be cast as women of various nationalities in the 1940s, including Norwegian

(*Casablanca*, 1941) and German (*Notorious*, 1946). Taken together, these diverse international portrayals suggest a general white/western Otherness during an era when both patriotism and national anxieties for Americans were high. Certainly, *Gaslight* is set more than fifty years before the war and our sympathies are aimed in support of the tormented ("gaslighted") Paula. Yet, we can see condensation and displacement of anxieties related to national boundaries in her fluid performance of the internationalized white woman. By contrast but with similar displacement, Boyer's criminal Frenchman may signify what Carlos Clarens identifies as "the sensuously corrupt and socially inferior foreigner."[53] In war-era terms, he might signal the treacherousness of Vichy France. In this reading, Paula would represent the more palatable outsider, that is, the neutral Swede or other innocent Western European civilian or refugee.

Because *Keeper of the Flame* offers the most overtly political and least psychologically invested script of the four films discussed in this chapter, its noirish displacements work differently, primarily as related to genre, critical response, and production context. The film centers on the character of Steve O'Malley (Spencer Tracy), a famous journalist who returns from war correspondence to write a biography of Robert Forrest, a wealthy businessman known and loved nationwide for his patriotism. Forrest has recently died in a car accident when a bridge collapsed near his estate, and the first half of the picture deals with Steve's attempt to get the dead man's widow, Christine Forrest (Katharine Hepburn), to talk with him. Soon, Steve and his fellow reporters begin to believe Forrest may have been murdered, and that Christine may be the guilty party. Eventually, however, we learn that Forrest's patriotic façade covered a seething, cynical fascism and plans to take over the country, and that Christine did her wifely and patriotic duty by allowing him to crash to his death (rather than warn him) when she saw the bridge was out.

Classic noir style accompanies the dark plot, especially early in the film. There are the rainy skies under which stand the public and a particularly ominous line of boys in military-style uniforms (who, as we later learn, are members of the Hitler Youth–like "Robert Forrest Boys Army") for the public funeral. There is also the sinister high barred gate that keeps the journalists out of the Forrest estate after the event. Long shadows and black/white contrast dominate the setting, too, when Steve first sees Christine after sneaking into her home: she is clad all in white and is holding white flowers while he hides in a dark recess observing her, only his eyes showing. The soundtrack, composed by Polish-Jewish émigré Bronislaw Kaper, echoes this dark mood.

As discussed above, American noir staples such as the hard-boiled detective and the femme fatale do not appear in Cukor's films. More in focus in *Keeper of the Flame* is the émigré-style complex female protagonist and a pessimistic commentary on the war's impact on America. Early in the film, Steve runs into his former colleagues Jane (Audrey Christie) and Freddie (Stephen McNally). Jane claims to barely recognize him:

> Jane: It's your eyes, that's what it is. You've seen an awful lot over there, haven't you, Stevie?
>
> Steve: Is it that bad?
>
> Jane: Were you in a concentration camp or with the Berlin Press Bureau?
>
> Steve: I'm still wondering, Jane.

Nonetheless, noir tropes are momentarily evoked as the film begins, enhancing suspense elements. As they speak, Freddie stands nearby with a copy of *Detective Magazine* in his hand, hinting at the potential for the plot to become hard-edged noir, with Tracy as the tough guy who will break the case and Hepburn as the black widow who killed a national hero. But these tropes ultimately prove misleading. Hepburn is no seductive murderer, and her husband was no "true" (i.e., patriotic) American. Thus, the film invokes anxiety related to genre both directly (as related to content) and indirectly (as related to Hollywood demands for the production of what it deemed entertainment rather than Leftist political propaganda).

The response of Cukor critics to the film is instructive in reflecting these anxieties. Gary Carey, for example, declares, "Whatever political viewpoint the film has is lost in the murky atmosphere of a gothic mystery complete with a fortress-like house and a long-suffering wife." He finds the film's message, moreover, "is probed with about the same depth as those one- or two-minute shorts the British made during World War II warning that the enemy lurked everywhere" with "nowhere near the same cleverness."[54] Such vitriol reveals anxiety in its attack on the film for both its lack of distinctness in genre and its overly distinct antifascist message. Clarens offers a somewhat similarly confounding response, arguing that the film is "at times treading on *Citizen Kane*'s territory" while being "ill-served by Gothic excess and patriotic sentiment."[55]

Beyond genre, anxiety related to gender boundaries also appears. Phillips identifies the picture as one of many Cukor films that addresses "the attempt of individuals to reconcile their cherished dreams with the sober realities of life." His reading of Christine Forrest is relatively unsympathetic, claiming that her death shows how she "pays the price for having tenaciously held on to her private illusions about her revered husband for far too long." Even as he blames Christine, he gives Tracy's Steve O'Malley too much credit, claiming that Steve suspected Forrest was a fascist although the film suggests no such thing.[56] When the film was first released, some reviewers were even harsher, such as Manny Farber in his 1943 *New Republic* review, who suggested that the fate of the nation hanging on Christine's "autocratic self-sufficiency" is as disturbing a suggestion as her husband's fascism.[57]

Martha Nochimson argues that the film offers a resolution to such anxieties, asserting that "Christine is more powerful as a dead saint than she might have been as a live heroine." "Instead of cautioning us that American Fascism is possible," Nochimson continues, the picture "soothes us with a fairy tale assurance that the good forces in the United States will never let that happen." She concludes, "A soporific happy ending was his [Cukor's] way because it was Hollywood's way."[58] I have no resistance to this interpretation, though Nochimson does have to twist the facts of the film a bit to get there. She argues that Clive Kerndon (Richard Whorf), Forrest's secretary, kills Christine "to keep Forrest's evil plans alive."[59] Christine herself tells Steve, by contrast, that the secretary knew nothing of her husband's fascism; more likely, given that Clive burns all of Forrest's plans, is simply that he feared Christine was not obeying the great man's orders to destroy his papers after his death. One way to read this contradiction in interpretation is to see the happy ending as an attempt to reduce the anxiety produced by the film regarding its commentary on home-grown fascism. As a viewer, I personally felt far less secure than Nochimson that American "forces" could always be counted on to save the day. Christine could easily have decided not to trust Steve, or Clive could have burned the papers she had kept and made Christine's testimony incredible for lack of physical evidence.

In addition to content and critical response, production context offers a further site for study of noir anxiety over the boundaries and borders that inflect Cukor's films. *Keeper of the Flame* is based on an unpublished work by white female writer I. A. R. Wylie; the manuscript was only subsequently published as a novel to coincide with the release of the film. David Ogden Stewart once again wrote the screenplay for Cukor, and he ultimately considered it his finest work for film. Stewart had been best known to this point for his adaptations of sophisticated comedies and melodramas. He had already collaborated with Cukor twice before, first on the pre-Code weepy *Tarnished Lady* (1931), a Tallulah Bankhead vehicle, and then on Phillip Barry's *The Philadelphia Story*, for which he was awarded the 1940 Oscar for Best Adapted Screenplay. During this time, Stewart was also an active member of the Hollywood Anti-Nazi League and the Communist Party USA. Although it was not until 1950 that Stewart was blacklisted, he long resented not being able to write film scripts that allowed him to articulate his Leftist politics. Thus, *Keeper of the Flame* was particularly special to him, even as it was used as evidence during his appearance before the House Un-American Activities Committee.[60]

By contrast, the film was far from being a favorite of Cukor's. With typical depoliticized language, he decried the implausible characters and scenario, particularly the second half, which featured arson and murder. Moreover, between Stewart and Cukor there was Katharine Hepburn, who pushed hard to have the film produced, finding it a compelling project for a pairing with Spencer Tracy, with whom she had recently begun an intimate relationship. She sought Cukor to direct, for she knew she worked well with him and suspected the "actor's director" would work well with Tracy, too. It was, however, Hepburn who proved difficult in the production of *Keeper of the Flame*. She argued for increased screen time and an enhancement of the romantic relationship between her character and Tracy's. When Stewart rejected the requests and Cukor remained silent, she went over their heads to producer Victor Saville, and when he backed Stewart, she went to the studio executives. Stewart was particularly incensed, writing to his wife that Hepburn had betrayed him and that Cukor had "turned yellow completely." He invoked gender (anxiety) as well, stating, "I created an intelligent male with action as his keynote. . . . Is it not interesting that Miss H., not being an active character in the story, is Goddamned if there will be an active male in the same story?"[61]

Within this production context we can see manifestations of anxieties over borders including and beyond those of genre and gender, including art/entertainment/politics and producer/director/actor. The interactions of the principal players reveal conflicting attempts to control definitions and their implications and also pose powerful and anxiety-producing questions, such as How political should a Hollywood film be? and Who controls a film production? For Cukor, such quandaries were best downplayed or avoided, which he generally achieved through the genres in which he primarily worked and through a friendly, collaborative process. It is not difficult in such a context to see why he began the project with pleasure in doing a favor for his friend David Ogden Stewart, but ultimately denounced the content and quality of *Keeper of the Flame*.

Taken together and read through their affinity to the work of Germany's Jewish émigré directors and their mobilization of existential anxiety related to boundaries of race, gender, and nationality, Cukor's noir melodramas illustrate his ability to work within the dominant style of the World War II era and its aftermath. The films' pleasures may differ in some ways from most of his best-known works, but they still adhere to the Hollywood filmmaking norms that ground them and led to many awards. *A Double Life* was nominated for four Academy Awards (including Best Director and Best Writing/Original Screenplay), and *Gaslight* was nominated for seven (including Best Picture, Best Writing/Screenplay, Best Cinematography/Black-and-White, Best Actor in a Leading Role, and Best Actress in a Supporting Role for screen newcomer and British immigrant Angela Lansbury). Both films won Oscars for one of their leads, Ronald Colman in the former and Ingrid Bergman in the latter. In addition, Miklós Rózsa won the Academy Award for Best Music (*A Double Life*) and Cedric Gibbons for Art Direction (*Gaslight*). Both *A Woman's Face* and *Keeper of the Flame* went without nominations, although Cukor felt that Crawford's work in his film helped her attain the Best Actress Oscar for *Mildred Pierce* several years later; and he went on to direct Hepburn and Tracy to great success in *Adam's Rib* (1949) and *Pat and Mike* (1952), for both of which Garson Kanin and Ruth Gordon received nominations for Best Writing, Story and Screenplay.[62]

9

Ethnic Assimilation and 1950s Hollywood

In *An Empire of Their Own: How the Jews Invented Hollywood*, Neal Gabler argues that the immigrant Jews who founded Hollywood (Carl Laemmle, Adolph Zukor, William Fox, Louis B. Mayer, and Benjamin Warner) created not only a powerful independent economic force but also an American mythology that refashioned the nation on-screen. Despite nativist bias and outright antisemitism, the Hollywood moguls succeeded in establishing a world where they could find respect and success while actively configuring the twentieth-century American Dream. For these ambitious, business-savvy men, a longing for upward mobility and social acceptance was matched by love for their adopted land and the opportunities it offered them. This combination resulted in what Gabler calls "a ferocious, even pathological, embrace of America" that required "assimilation so ruthless and complete that they cut their lives to the pattern of American respectability as they interpreted it."[1] Hence, "While they were mythologizing America on the screen, the Hollywood Jews also set about redesigning themselves."[2] Some divorced their old-world wives and married younger, blonder non-Jews, and many lived in enormous estates that echoed those of the East Coast WASP (white, Anglo-Saxon Protestant) elite. With the assistance of assimilationist Tin Pan Alley composers such as Irving Berlin, these assimilationist Jews could even find ways to celebrate Christmas and Easter. In Gabler's words, "Above all things, they wanted to be regarded as Americans, not Jews."[3]

The films these men produced offered a corresponding vision of American ideals. "By making a 'shadow' America, one which idealized every old glorifying bromide about the country, the Hollywood Jews created a powerful cluster of images and ideas—so powerful that, in a sense, they colonized the American imagination." Thus, these immigrants arguably "reinvented the country in the image of their fiction."[4] The motivations and methods that Gabler attributes to the first generation of Hollywood producers can be effectively applied to other Jewish Americans involved in the moviemaking business, including directors, screenwriters, and actors. By illustrating their links and the cinema they produced, we can learn a great deal about the immigrant Jewishness of classic Hollywood pleasures.

Of course, this control and impact did not last forever. As decades passed and the moguls lost power, assimilationist ideals shifted. The Hollywood-American Dream continued to thrive on-screen in the post–World War II period, but the 1950s came after a difficult era of adjustment that led to the end of the studio system and the beginning of the Cold War. On one hand there was the increased presence of women in the public sphere and early civil rights efforts. On the other, there was the House Un-American Activities Committee (HUAC), disproportionately aimed at attacking Hollywood for its alleged communist influence, an attack that was bound up with antisemitism. Eventually, the clash of progressive and regressive forces would produce a reevaluation of cultural understandings and interactions regarding gender, race, and ethnicity, including attitudes toward Jewishness. And Hollywood cinema reflected this directly.

Not until the late 1960s would American culture welcome visibly and audibly marked Jewishness, as found in such figures as Barbra Streisand and Woody Allen.[5] The 1950s, by contrast, were a contentious period for Jews in Hollywood, behind and on-screen. However much he might have downplayed his religious/ethnic identity, Cukor was enmeshed in this tension. To elucidate the era and its politics, this chapter will explore four of Cukor's 1950s films, considering the subject of assimilation within both production context and film content. First, I consider a pair of pictures dominated by three Jewish American voices: director George Cukor, writer Garson Kanin, and star Judy Holliday. In *Born Yesterday* (1950) and *It Should Happen to You* (1954), issues of ethnicity, class, and gender combine to illustrate the presence as well as the limits of an assimilationist American Dream that had recently been proven false and even harmful to Jews in the era of the films' creation. Next, I address the representation of biracial experience (as performed by white actors) as metaphor for hyphenated American identity (i.e., Jewish-American) in the Indian partition epic/romance *Bhowani Junction* (1956). Finally, I consider the melodrama *Wild Is the Wind* (1957), a film in which the immigrant experience and pressure to assimilate is explored through the lens of middle-class marriage norms. With his pleasure in working with the "difficult" Italian actress Anna Magnani and his distaste for the film's forced happy ending, Cukor can be seen here to decry the limits of the very assimilationist norms that governed much of his life and brought him such success as a studio director.

The stylistic feature that unifies these films is perhaps its most important element. Regardless of genre, all four pictures raise serious cultural issues and do so through location shooting and what we might call, after Lee Carruthers, "pseudo-documentary effects." Whether adapted from plays or written for the screen, the films include emphasis on external shots, including urban New York streets, massive Indian crowds, and wide Nevada vistas. As the subjects of self versus other and isolation versus belonging emerge in the narratives, the cinematic style enhances the films' efforts "to bridge the divide between reality and its idealized Hollywood reflection." The realist settings separate the films from much of Cukor's output and "heighten the affective force," enhancing pleasure in both the escapism from and the reality of 1950s America for spectators and Cukor himself.[6]

One popular way to interpret *Born Yesterday* is as a Cukor-style literacy narrative. Beyond the obviously Shavian *My Fair Lady* (1964) and the pedagogical elements of *Little Women* (1935), *Born Yesterday* celebrates the education of Judy Holliday's ex–chorus girl Billie Dawn under the tutelage of reporter Paul Verrall (William Holden). This instruction is begun at the request of Billie's crass crook of a boyfriend, Harry Brock (Broderick Crawford), who does not recognize his own ignorance or foresee that an education is not easily curtailed once started. Specifically, Harry wants Billie to fit in with the educated, privileged class of Washington, DC, including the congressman he plans to buy off to increase his wealth. But Paul leads Billie to do more than to mimic the educated; she also learns about the workings of the American judicial system and the high and low points of the capitalist democracy she lives in.

For Scott F. Stoddart, the success and depth of Billie's education emerges from Paul's treatment of her as an "equal" and his ability to instill confidence in her through his encouragement and attraction to her. If

In an example of location shooting in Cukor's films of the 1950s, ex–chorus girl Billie Dawn (Judy Holliday) and journalist Paul Verrall are dwarfed by the statue of Jefferson in the Washington, DC, of *Born Yesterday* (1950).

patriarchal norms have kept Billie ignorant (neither Harry nor his lawyer will explain anything about his business dealings), then Paul does offer a more benevolent guidance. Comparing Billie directly to *Pygmalion*'s Eliza Doolittle, Stoddart concludes that the primary subject of the film is the "symbolic re-birth of a socially fallen woman."[7] I posit that the message of *Born Yesterday* is more complex than this description suggests and is less about benevolent teachers than the changing politics of assimilation in the postwar era. First, Billie's open sexuality is scarcely resisted by Paul, who falls prey to her charms even more quickly than she gives in to the pleasures of book learning. And she does not yield her strength of personality or loud voice even as she acquiesces to, and comes to value, lessons on the Founding Fathers' ideals. But what precisely does she learn? Persuasive is Clarens's declaration that "by 1950 some of the more the more high-sounding talk about democracy and knowledge being freedom had fallen flat in the wake of the McCarthy witch-hunts." Billie learns only a few basic lessons in the course of the narrative, which makes the film's message in this area both trite and easy to champion: "one-third Shaw and two-thirds Damon Runyon."[8]

We must seek elsewhere to explain the film's power and longstanding popularity, evidenced by a 1993 film remake, a sixty-three-performance 2011 Schubert Organization restaging of the play at the Cort Theater, and numerous regional stage productions, such as that of the Wisconsin's American Players Theater in 2018. I find an explanation in the film's surprising critique of materialism. Like the Hollywood moguls, Billie is unquestionably drawn to upward mobility through marriage outside her class, but, unlike these men, she also learns to critique materialism. By the film's conclusion, Billie proposes to live in opposition to *both* working-class criminal louts like Harry and well-mannered criminal members of the class-privileged Washington set. Such a perspective reaches beyond patriotic platitudes to critique both the high and the low, and so does not privilege the adoption of upper-class mannerisms and perspectives. In fact, Billie's deconstruction of America reaches further than Cukor himself was willing to go as a director, during and beyond the era. Cukor shared Philip Barry's perspective on the wealthy, for example. When Gavin Lambert noted that "Barry really seems to think the rich are the most marvelous people on earth," Cukor responded, "Maybe so do I. Let's face it—don't you?"[9] Certainly, his massive estate and frequent elegant dinner parties illustrate well his preference for privilege. As one of the Hollywood elite, he certainly did not choose, as Billie does at the end of *Born Yesterday*, a dive into the middle class. Cukor also did all he could to sound educated and refined, enjoying but eschewing the New York Jewishness of Judy Holliday's famous voice. As lyricist Edward Eliscu declared, Cukor's speech "never showed a trace of New Yorkese."[10]

Within this context, the primary characters' trajectories deserve further analysis through readings of ethnicity, Jewishness in particular. Writer/director James Toback once claimed that, although not antisemitic, Cukor did call some Jews "kikes," but he did so only around other Jews. Toback stated that, for Cukor, "there was a sense of Jewishness as being something low," though Cukor never claimed such a perspective.[11] If we read both Billie and Harry as signifying Jewishness in *Born Yesterday*, we can see both validation of and reaction against Toback's declaration. When we first meet the film's central pair, they can easily be seen as exemplifying stereotypes of the loud, pushy personalities of Ashkenazi Jewish immigrants of the early twentieth-century New York ghetto. They yell out of windows to one another, do not mix with the general populace, and engage in ostentatious display rather than quiet WASP confidence. Like the Hollywood moguls who rose from positions as peddlers and salesmen—but not the middle-class Hungarian Cukors—Billie and Harry are shown to need refining through assimilation to the white, middle-class norms that make up the American Dream.

Gender is also central to this process. Harry is not only "too Jewish" but also too masculine. He is domineering and aggressive, demonstrating a stereotype of working-class manhood that relies on verbal and physical bullying to attain goals. Billie, by contrast, adheres to feminine norms centered in her sexuality, using her looks to seduce, giving or withholding to get what she wants. As Paul declares, however, such manipulation only works if she knows what she wants. Learning to change what she wants ultimately separates Billie from Harry, the assimilable from the unassimilable.

The differing paths of these two characters pivot on their relationship to Paul, who, in this reading, is the film's symbol of middle-class WASP ideals, the American Dream figure of the Hollywood imagination. Through the film's romantic comedy ending, we learn that Billie's path (assimilation and adherence to middle-class gender norms) will likely lead to happiness and connectedness, while Harry's path (refusal to assimilate and resistance to middle-class gender norms) leads to misery (i.e., prison time) and isolation. To nuance this opposition, however, we must note that Billie's assimilation is not complete in Hollywood melting-pot terms. She retains her open sexuality and, most notably, her strong, working-class (Jewish) voice. We can see Billie late in the film as teacher, arguably guiding Paul to value gendered ethnic and class difference, an exchange that would eventually come to identify the multiculturalist perspective of Hollywood in the later decades of the twentieth century, which turned Barbra Streisand, for example, from a 1960s gawky singer to a 1970s sexy superstar.[12]

But perhaps Billie does not need to teach Paul quite as much as it may seem if we read the character through Daniel Boyarin's concept of *Edelkayt*, as seen in my reading of the film in chapter 5. Casting certainly does not link William Holden to Jewishness as it does Judy Holliday. However, Paul can serve to exemplify a countertype to Harry's crude, hypermasculine cruelty through his sense of honor, education, antimaterialism, and shyness. If we interpret the film through this application of Boyarin's work, both Billie and Paul illustrate positive Jewish types, a decade or more before Woody Allen will give us the even more "unmanned" (yet sexualized) romantic comedy nebbish.

We can read 1954's *It Should Happen to You* as an extension of or postscript to *Born Yesterday*. Both films feature the same director, writer, and star; and both explore gender roles, ethnicity/Jewishness, and the dangers of cynical materialism. A link between the films was also actively drawn in the original trailer to the later picture, which identified leading lady Judy Holliday as "that 'Born Yesterday' girl." In terms of content, like Billie, protagonist Gladys Glover of *It Should Happen to You* exists within a Hollywood romantic-comedy world that emphasizes humor and a heteronormative happily-ever-after. And her choice of partner is not dissimilar to Billie's in *Born Yesterday*, even if the latter film's tone is more cynical. Gladys must select between an arrogant, wealthy soap company heir and a struggling documentary filmmaker. The leading men in both films feel they know what is right for Holliday's character and both texts clearly guide the viewer to feel the wealthy schemer must be rejected and the down-to-earth antimaterialist valued.

It Should Happen to You is the story of a young woman who seeks her fortune in New York but achieves only the level of girdle model. When she is fired from even this lowly enterprise, she feels defeated until she sees an empty billboard and decides to have her moment of fame by renting it and seeing her name in lights. When a soap company seeks possession of the well-placed advertising space she has paid for, Gladys is eventually given six other billboards in exchange for her one. Soon she actually becomes famous, a household name—though no one knows who she is. Wooed on the one hand by penniless Pete Sheppard (Jack Lemmon) and on the other by wealthy playboy Evan Adams III (Peter Lawford), Gladys must decide what is most important to her. In the film's terms, it is not only wealthy executive versus common man but also empty fame versus meaningful relationship. Yet, even after she chooses the latter and thereby fulfills the gendered norms of the Hollywood romantic comedy, the film ends with Gladys momentarily drawn to the sight of an empty billboard as she and her new filmmaker husband drive off together.

Because *It Should Happen to You* is intended as comedy and its male love interest is more neurotic everyman than *Born Yesterday*'s awkward intellectual, Gladys and Pete do not have a teacher/student relationship.

More persuasive, particularly in the McLuhanesque context of a film that emphasizes how the medium is the message, Pete can be described best as "lobbying" for a "credo," in the words of the Celluloid Liberation Front, an astute film blog, a credo that Gladys eventually adopts along with his name. And names are vital to the film. Pete Sheppard clearly "shepherds" Gladys from a desire for fame to his more unpretentious perspective, for example, and the original title of the film was "Making a Name for Herself." Cukor, Kanin, and every critic I have read, from the era of its release to the present, finds the original film title more appropriate, and for good reason. "Making a Name" is exactly what Gladys does, with the pointed humor directed at the fact that this is *all* she does. As our heroine becomes a household name—eventually selling soap and giving advice on talk shows—there is no substance or body of work behind her stardom. Here the film offers a prescient comment on contemporary notions of celebrity (as exemplified by reality TV, social media icons, and the 2016 US presidential election).

Beyond this, however, the idea of "making a name" has both gender and ethnic significance related to issues of assimilation. The phenomenon of Jews in Hollywood (and beyond) changing their names to seem more "American" is well known and still occurs today. The Cukor family was originally "Czukor," for example, and Judy Holliday was born Judith Tuvim. "Gladys Glover," by contrast, does not shout an ethnicity; it is a safe and pleasingly alliterative Anglo-American name, especially catchy for its matching trochees. But it is thus a doubly hollow name, first in the empty celebrity sense and second in its lack of cultural identification. When Gladys marries and becomes, in traditional fashion, "Mrs. Pete Sheppard," giving up her name is giving up nothing of substance.

Nonetheless, there is more to say about *It Should Happen to You* and assimilation than these conventional readings elucidate. The critique of the film only works if we agree with Pete that Gladys is naive and wrong in trying to seek "a name for herself" without substantial deeds to support her fame. Critics generally interpret the film in this way. Gene D. Phillips, for example, calls Gladys "obtuse" and "goofy," with "unrealistic expectations of what life holds in store for her."[13] Emanuel Levy identifies the role of Gladys as a "dumb blonde part."[14] Gary Carey calls her "one of those kind-hearted, upright, almost simple-minded characters."[15] Carlos Clarens references theorist Roland Barthes to describe Gladys as "a signifier without a signified, a mere denotation."[16] And, most recently,

Dominic Lennard calls her "air-headed" and "dull-witted," even as he develops a more sympathetic feminist reading of the film overall.[17]

Such descriptions miss the fact that Gladys is, in many ways, the film's most sympathetic character. Carey almost recognizes this when he acknowledges that "Holliday is intrinsically so sympathetic and plays with such infectious delight that one can't help responding."[18] The word "intrinsically," however, limits viewer identification to the actress rather than the character. Similarly, instead of arguing that the satire fails, he and other critics compare the film unfavorably to Ben Hecht's earlier script for the 1937 film *Nothing Sacred*, which Carey identifies as a better satire about "a freak celebrity."[19] While Lombard and Holliday are arguably both whimsical and a touch manic in their performances, this comparison misses the mark. Rather than a "good-natured lampoon" or a "satire without any teeth in its bite," I find *It Should Happen to You* most enjoyable and most powerful as a lamentation over a changing cultural landscape that offers particular insight into what the postwar era meant for women as well as for Hollywood Jews and their cinematic American Dream.[20]

First, the film presents Gladys as a "freak" only in the eyes of specific characters, all male, including the salesman who can't understand why Gladys wants to rent the sign (but approves as soon as she shows him the cash), the corporate yes-men of the soap company who laugh at the idea that anyone would just put a name up on a sign, and Pete, who is drawn to Gladys's warm, open personality but feels free to ridicule her dreams. The film adheres to classic Hollywood romantic comedy dictates in its sympathy to Pete's perspective that anonymity is what is best for Gladys, especially when Gladys chooses him over the executive who financially supports—even if he doesn't understand or appreciate—her ambitions.

When we take a closer look at dialogue between Pete and Gladys, as well as the way the camera displays his visible frustration and dismay, however, we have opportunity to consider Gladys's worldview in the film's style and content. Pete argues that seeking fame is not only empty but wrongheaded. "Everybody can't be above the crowd," he declares. "Everybody can try if they want to," replies Gladys, articulating in a few simple words the American Dream championed by the founders of Hollywood—not to mention Cukor, Kanin, and Holliday. Pete is momentarily silenced, but soon begins to despair, lamenting, "I can't seem to get you

In *It Should Happen to You* (1954), Pete (Jack Lemmon) looks on in disbelief as Gladys (Judy Holliday) basks in the attention of strangers at Macy's who recognize her name from the billboards she has rented.

down to earth." Once again, Gladys's witty rejoinder trumps his commentary: "What's so wonderful about earth?" Such exchanges do not show Pete either teaching Gladys or controlling her desire for success on her own terms. She flatly advises Pete not to be the one to "burst the bubble" of her fame. These are hardly the insights of a "dumb blonde."

Visual signs of Pete's dismay and Gladys's happiness also dominate their interactions. When her name is recognized at the Macy's store through whose windows her original sign can be seen, Gladys cheerfully signs autographs that truly make her feel visible and valuable in the vastness of New York City, a city to which she is a struggling newcomer, an urban immigrant. Pete, by contrast, fumes and snarls in the background. Someone in the growing crowd of autograph seekers eagerly asks, "Who is it?" and Pete barks back, "Nobody, believe me!" The line is played as comic exasperation, but it is delivered with bitterness and a grimace that reveals a petty jealousy and competitiveness that speak to gender roles. As

Dominic Lennard observes, in Gladys's efforts toward fame, we see that she "creates an idealized image that is both physically and morally 'above' the casual harassment and degradation she encounters every day," including the "haranguing that Pete inflicts." This appears as we see her reach "beyond the domestic passivity her suitor requires" to "'illegitimately' [eclipse] him in social standing."[21] Gladys achieves, at least temporarily, an identity beyond patriarchal control, and we see in the conflict between her and Pete evidence of its effect.

Katherine S. Woodward echoes this argument and extends it to actively address feminist perspectives on naming and coming to voice. She distinguishes two "stories" within the film, the first about "the emptiness of celebrity status and the exploitative fakery of the television and advertising industries" and the second relating "the desire of women to exercise the power of public naming or language and the concomitant male drive to thwart that desire and silence women." For Woodward, naming is giving power to a woman's gendered experience, so placing her name on a billboard is "a positive effort to express her authentic female voice."[22]

To achieve power as a woman, Gladys must resist silencing by men. In the opening scene of the film, she has just been fired from her job by male managers who judge her by appearance, specifically by a quarter of an inch in hip size. She is further disempowered by strangers in the park, men who tell her to shut up and misattribute her innocent desire to listen to a man's radio to attempting a pick-up.

In visual terms, we are directly in the realm of the male gaze. When Pete meets Gladys in the park, he does not just see and speak to her. Instead, he actively constructs his first sighting of Gladys by filming her. Here, we see a film representation of the classic Hollywood narrative style, with woman as image and man as bearer of the look. As Laura Mulvey originally conceptualized the male gaze, the objectification of woman in film derives from "a world ordered by sexual imbalance," in which "pleasure in looking has been split between active/male and passive/female." Women are on display, "coded for strong visual and erotic impact so that they can be said to connote *to-be-looked-at-ness*."[23] At the level of filmmaking, to play her role within a romantic comedy, actress Judy Holliday is styled in this fashion for the camera: her hair is bleached; she is heavily made up; and she is corseted into fashions of the era. Her image contrasts strongly with that of actor Jack Lemmon, whose appearance and body language are purposely rendered as plain and disheveled. Within the film diegesis, the camera that Lemmon's character Pete wields extends the male gaze, with Pete turning Gladys into a spectacle, a desirable object under his control.

When Gladys turns out to be less easy to control interpersonally than visually, the film addresses the opposing tactic for achieving male pleasure in looking, described by Mulvey as narrative sadism. If woman cannot be kept at the level of satisfying fetish object, then she must be controlled through the narrative, forced to change through "a battle of will and strength."[24] In such genres as the thriller, types such as the femme fatale may be sent to prison or killed. The most common resolution for the romantic comedy, by contrast, is marriage.

The battle between Gladys and Pete is primarily seen in their frequent bickering. Pete, despite his ultimate presentation in the film as a good choice for a husband, disallows Gladys's authority and even her own self-knowledge throughout the picture. After he turns off his camera and talks with her, she shares her recent experiences. She tells Pete her throat is dry because she is angry. He immediately reinterprets, attempting to shift blame from male mistreatment to eating too many peanuts. Next, when she shares her dreams of fame with him, he does not offer approval or even reply neutrally; instead, he dismisses her hopes and calls her "young." Thus, from their first encounter, Pete, unlike Paul in *Born Yesterday*, is neither partner nor teacher but authority figure, wielding the male gaze and supporting the patriarchal control of women begun by her former boss and the men in the park.

Gladys's ultimate goal is legitimation, and, despite the necessary struggles with patriarchal control, the film does illustrate her success. If the male gaze is invoked, the camera's attention to Gladys's gaze is also worth noting, as Woodward does, in compelling detail. She points to the six separate scenes that feature Gladys's face, shown with active excitement, admiring her own name on a billboard. She notes the soap company conference room, where instead of men silencing her, as addressed above, Gladys silences them, dominating "both the space and the conversation."[25] Moreover, she points to the break in realism that presents Gladys's subjective gaze instead of the male gaze: when Gladys wants the painters to complete her billboard quickly, they do so, in fast motion. Finally, Woodward points to the scene in which Adams drives her around Columbus Circle three times to see her billboard and Gladys's exhilaration "controls the visual and aural mise-en-scène."[26]

We can nuance this feminist reading with attention to ethnicity. As with characters in *Born Yesterday*, I find traces of the New York Jewish immigrant in Gladys's general struggle for success as well as in the loud bickering and door-slamming that goes on between Gladys and Pete in their tiny apartments on the same floor of a rundown tenement. This behavior defines the couple's growing affection as much as do their expressions of attraction and their quaint duet of the 1933 standard "Let's Fall in Love" (written by Jewish American cantor's son Harold Arlen). Through such details, the film hearkens back to the heyday of the Hollywood moguls and their desire for upward mobility through assimilation. Of course, the film is also inflected by the cynicism of the 1950s. Within the boundaries of classic Hollywood standards, we can see both gendered and ethnic parallels in the film's tensions and reconciliations. Affectionate tension between Gladys and Pete illustrates the male gaze and feminist resistance to it as well as Jewish American determination to retain an "authentic" ethnic voice versus assimilated decorum.

Although ultimately resolved, these tensions do threaten Gladys's happiness within the film. The more famous Gladys gets, the more disempowered Pete feels. He is placed in a more traditionally feminine role of follower, one who waits rather than leads in private and public spheres alike. While Gladys cooks for him, she also dominates their topics of conversation (billboards, of course). He must wait during her television appearances, must suffer as she cancels two dates, and is even pushed to the literal edge of the film frame when the crowd gathers around her at the department store. Ultimately, Pete states he will only marry Gladys if she relinquishes her female/ethnic public voice, and as a romantic comedy, we know this will occur. Such predictability makes the ending of the film feel even more sexist than the beginning, argues Woodward.[27] When she accepts Pete's patriarchal/assimilated perspective, we are encouraged to do the same as viewers.

I find the ending more ambiguous. Pete is insecure and infatuated with Gladys, and I suspect that she will find desire and methods to continue to subvert patriarchal and assimilated norms. My pleasure in the film is primarily in Gladys's negotiation of social rules. Attention to the ending as first scripted helps to extend the ambiguity. In the original screenplay, the final moment of the film shows the couple in a honeymoon hotel room. Pete points out of the room's window at a sign that reads "Mr. and Mrs. Pete Sheppard."[28] Patriarchy and assimilation are not overthrown by feminism and ethnic pride in this image, but there is compromise. Gladys arguably loses the battle as she is clearly muzzled by the absence of her name beyond the possessive "Mrs." of the billboard; yet she still finds public voice, however crass (i.e., ethnic) it may seem.

Writer Kanin very much disliked the filmed version of the ending, calling it "dangerously tepid."[29] From a feminist perspective, the peril is in the casual (and generically causal) reassertion of patriarchal dominance over Gladys, although Kanin was just as likely opining on the film's lost message about empty celebrity. Yet, even without the Mr.-and-Mrs. billboard announcement that Gladys is still actively asserting herself, viewers can still engage with and enjoy the identity struggles we have witnessed that the picture's ending cannot displace entirely.

As the 1950s progressed, so did tensions over gender, race, and ethnicity. Assimilated Jews and housewives alike began to suffer and share their unhappiness, as exemplified by Jewish second-wave feminist pioneer Betty Friedan, whose 1963 book *The Feminine Mystique* revealed the dangerous power of the media to reduce middle-class white women to objects in their own lives. In ways direct and indirect, I read *It Should Happen to You* as suggestive of "the problem that has no name," as Friedan named the anxiety faced by many women as postwar conservatism gave women damaging messages about leaving the public sphere for a new world of consumer goods and suburban isolation.[30]

Bhowani Junction contrasts sharply in tone, setting, and genre with the two Cukor/Kanin/Holliday productions. The film is epic drama rather than romantic comedy and is set in partition-era India, far from then-contemporary New York City. Moreover, the film is even more directly about issues of gender roles and assimilation. The three pictures do share a Hollywood-style focus on heteronormative romance that suits the conservatism of the 1950s, but the intercultural relationships and biracial protagonist of *Bhowani Junction* are unique in Cukor's oeuvre.

Although some critics identify the romance as the most Cukoresque element of *Bhowani Junction*, the director himself talked at length about how important the social elements of the film were to him, including the politics. "This picture took a great deal of effort," Cukor told Gavin Lambert, "a great deal of integrity and self-expression. . . . We did it on location, we were clearly involved with a condition of the world, and a political struggle."[31] He was upset that the Indian government would not allow him to film in India, for example, because one character condemns Gandhi with a crass insult. Cukor pointed out that the character was unsympathetic, but this did not sway those who made the final decision, so the film had to be shot in Lahore (Pakistan). Cukor took up a five-month residence to research and complete the picture, the only time in his life he lived outside the United States and the only foreign locale apart from London in which he ever shot a film.

McGilligan finds it surprising that the director would make *Bhowani Junction* at all, "that Cukor's first film under his renewed MGM contract was an improbable, exotic, anti-Communist potboiler of the type that proliferated in Hollywood in the 1950s." Cukor was deeply fearful of HUAC and of being blacklisted. He was never called to testify, but he also shied from controversial associations of the type that would get him called. For instance, while he did support Ingrid Bergman when she was attacked on moral grounds for her relationship with Rossellini, he actively neglected the exiled Donald Ogden Stewart when his former friend and frequent collaborator was formally blacklisted. "Mention of the word *blacklist* seemed to terrify Cukor," McGilligan asserts, "as if he was worried about being tinged with guilt by association." The biographer dismisses the seeming inconsistency in the context of Cukor's Indian epic, stating that "the politics and history lessons of *Bhowani Junction* are silly and simplistic."[32]

The belittling of the film by McGilligan and other critics comes primarily in response to the reduction of the British–Indian conflict to one biracial woman's struggle to find happiness within a setting of cultural upheaval. This, however, was not the film Cukor hoped to make. "The story is basically very serious and brutal, not romantic at all," the director declared, "and we had to lose so much of that because of censorship." For example, in one scene, British soldiers dump excrement onto Indian men who are lying on train tracks as an act of civil disobedience; excrement was changed to swill to please the censors.[33]

The most significant cuts and changes in the film do seem to relate most to the Victoria Jones (Ava Gardner) character and her race and sexuality. The film personalizes its tale of cultural conflict through Victoria, an Anglo-Indian British army nurse trying to make peace with herself even as the world around her cannot. Cukor hoped to mesh his epic scenes of the violence of the culture, such as the terrorist bombing of a train, with the internal and romantic life of Victoria. Here he was met with objections even more extreme than in the depictions of violence. In Lambert's words, "The leading character in the film is really India, and it's even more censored than Ava Gardner."[34] Excised was a moment in which Victoria, fresh out of the shower, dipped her lover's toothbrush in booze and then brushed her teeth with it. Entirely cut was the film's sole graphic sex scene, the first in Cukor's career, in which Victoria's biracial lover slides down her body and out of sight while the camera stays focused on Victoria's face, showing sexual pleasure in her expression. As McGilligan decries, "In this, the first Cukor film in which sex was foremost—almost *palpable*—all the erotic implications were trimmed back in order to adhere to 1950s conventions, and to accommodate fears about reaction in some foreign markets to a film concerning miscegenation."[35]

When the resulting product was previewed, audiences responded negatively, complaining the film was too long. They found Victoria unsympathetic for her promiscuity, despite the cuts. Cukor lamented the fact that viewers seemed to miss the point and purpose of the film. In response, MGM demanded the addition of a romantic happy ending. Against Cukor's wishes, Victoria is made to end up with her white British lover, Col. Rodney Savage (Stewart Granger). Cukor had already lost his request to star Trevor Howard in this role, arguing Granger was more superficial star than actor. Yet, even yielding to both substitute male lead and forced heteronormative closure did not ultimately satisfy the studio's concerns. To the altered, shortened film was then added first-person voice-over narration by Granger as Colonel Savage. This made for the most drastic change of all: shifting perspective from Victoria and India to Savage and England, from a biracial woman seeking an identity she can embrace to a white male symbol of dominance and western military might.

Cukor hated these changes, but Granger loved them. The actor fought with and badmouthed the director throughout the production and afterward, and the terms with which he condemned Cukor shared the racist, sexist tone of studio edits. Moreover, they were homophobic and antisemitic. Granger did not mind if Cukor gave line readings to women, for example, but he objected to a man telling a man how to act, and *Cukor* telling *him* how to act in particular. He barked, "But here he is, a little homosexual Jew from Brooklyn, and I'm playing an English colonel, and my father was a colonel in the Indian Army, and I was in the English Army, and he's telling me how to say the lines."[36] Ultimately, Granger took the studio's decision to add his voice-over narration as a personal triumph over the director and his vision.

The specifics of Granger's slur are worthy of additional attention as they relate to the issues of gender, sexuality, and ethnic difference tangled within the details of this film's production. Although Cukor downplayed details of his family background that he felt were irrelevant to his work (religion, ethnicity, and sexuality), he was sensitive to personal attacks. Nonetheless, he was proud of his efforts on *Bhowani Junction*, an international picture about political struggle. The film even offered Cukor the opportunity to explore a more personal identity politics. McGilligan explains, "On location, he would have an opportunity to observe firsthand and maybe collect some data on the Jews of India and west Pakistan—to tramp his ancestral ground, that part of the world where the Cukors, as a clan, were thought to have originated."[37]

With this production context in mind, Cukor's "data collection" can be read alongside Victoria's story, which remains vital to the film, however edited, censored, and framed. Victoria is half English and half Indian; the clash of cultures exists both within and around her. Externally, this is illustrated in costume; she often wears a sari wrapped around a more English skirt and blouse. We also see it in her three lovers—one bicultural, one Indian, one British—broadly symbolizing her struggle to find a livable identity that neither misrepresents nor reduces her.

First, Victoria chooses Patrick Taylor (Bill Travers), an Anglo-Indian like herself. But Patrick has no more of a strong, stable sense of self than she. Next, she commits to marrying an Indian nobleman, Ranjit Kasel (Francis Matthews). The wedding scene is the film's most artistically ornate, the most enmeshed in an exhibition of exoticism and artifice. As this conspicuous display of traditionalism threatens to overwhelm Victoria, she recalls the voices of others and flees, resisting adherence to the strictures of a noble Indian woman's lifestyle.

Enter Col. Rodney Savage, the winner of Victoria's heart. He has no confusion over his identity and can help her with confidence as Patrick cannot. And his white western masculinity is drawn to allow for at least superficial democracy regarding a woman's life. This is largely, of course, because it contrasts so broadly to Ranjit's Indian masculinity, depicted from a western perspective. Victoria can, with Rodney, remain a British army nurse, technically subordinate to but personally respected by her colonel. Yet, she does not yield to an entirely western perspective. Victoria demands the respect her complex identity demands, deciding that she will remain in India, her country by birth. She makes plain it can also be Savage's country if he will allow it, by adoption and love for her. Victoria's demand and Savage's acquiescence provide pleasure despite the forced romantic closure. However artificial, the film's position on gender, race, and cultural conflict is to champion compromise.

The limits of compromise for 1950s Hollywood center in notions of whiteness. Ultimately, Victoria tells Savage, "I belong here. Not as a phony Indian or a phony white, but as myself." The character's life choices can be interpreted to echo the credo "write Yiddish, cast British." This widely adopted prescription admonished those in Hollywood to make one's public persona as white as possible to attain success, even though one's ethnic background is the acknowledged source of creativity. The maxim was popular among Hollywood producers, particularly in the late 1950s and early 1960s, exemplified in the Yiddish style of humor and white, non-Jewish casting of television programs such as *The Dick Van Dyke Show* (1961–1966).[38] Although Cukor directed rather than wrote the film, we can see this motto underpinning the casting of *Bhowani Junction*, where Indian or mixed-race characters are played by white British and American actors. How much easier it is within a conservative, racist America to accept a biracial character when she is played by the famous, popular, and very obviously white Ava Gardner.

Cukor explained to Gavin Lambert that cross-racial casting was "necessary." Casting white actors as characters of color, he said, "*can* work and in this case it *had* to." He claimed to have looked for Indian actors to fill roles, but he felt their broad performance style made them unsuited to Hollywood film. This led the assimilated Cukor to conclude not that preferred acting style is culturally dictated, but that "Indian actors are not good." Of the racist implications of brownface, Cukor also defended and explained his choices: "If you know what you're doing you can get what you want. In a case like this the actor must have something right about him for starters. You can't take somebody blond and have him play an Indian, but if the coloring and the shape of the face and the manner seem right, then makeup and acting can bring it off. Otherwise, no amount of

Victoria (Ava Gardner) and her three suitors in *Bhowani Junction* (1956): one British (Stewart Granger), one "half-caste" like her (Bill Travers), and one Indian (Francis Matthews). All four characters are portrayed by white actors.

burnt cork is any good." The possibility that he may be wrong, however, does come through in his insecurity even in his own answer. He follows his conclusion with a question to Lambert: "But you never got the feeling of actors in burnt cork, did you?"[39]

Within the film narrative Victoria identifies with whiteness by bonding through romantic partnership with Colonel Savage and by her military career with the British, even as she remains embedded in the life of her native land. In such context, we can argue that Savage racially "misunderstands" Victoria's perspective. He ignores that she may be Indian (that she may feel "Yiddish") as she "acts British." His incomprehension extends to gender and sexuality as well, where Rodney proudly lays final claim to Victoria where other (nonwhite) men could not. And such perspectives may reach the production context, echoing how Granger the actor/man "misunderstands" Cukor's strategies even as his hypermasculine voice-over triumphs over Cukor's "little homosexual Jew[ish]" vision.

The final film considered in this chapter on gender, assimilation, and Hollywood in the 1950s is *Wild Is the Wind*. In *Bhowani Junction*, Cukor was fascinated with bringing acting legitimacy to capable and cooperative star Ava Gardner; now, a year later, he experienced an equal but nearly opposite fascination with Italy's Anna Magnani, who needed little direction but much careful handling. *Wild Is the Wind* was the last of Cukor's work as a contracted studio director and reflects his increasing concern that he was being used primarily as a last-minute replacement for directors who had to withdraw. Cukor wrote to friends and associates during this period that he might be getting too old to handle the crises that emerged in such cast-off productions.[40] This can serve to explain what McGilligan refers to as the "visual verve" of Cukor's 1950 productions, as seen in the New York location scenes of *It Should Happen to You*, the Indian crowd scenes in *Bhowani Junction*, and Nevada's wide-open spaces in *Wild Is the Wind*. Clarens also references the "vigour and open-air freshness" of the film.[41]

Both *Bhowani Junction* and *Wild Is the Wind* feature epic vistas, cultural conflict, and a textually forced narrowing to emphasis on romance and interpersonal relations dictated by Hollywood expectations. Both films are about a woman who seeks a livable bicultural identity and happiness within romantic compromise. Unique to the latter is its direct confrontation of issues of American assimilationism, even as such issues are painted with broad strokes and heavy-handed symbolism. The lack of subtlety in *Wild Is the Wind* can be explained by Cukor's growing fatigue and perception of himself as an afterthought to most producers. Picking up the momentum after John Sturges left the picture—because he disliked the love story (as McGilligan argues), because he was ill (as Levy posits), and/or because he was replacing Fred Zinnemann as director of *The Old Man and the Sea* (1958) (as Phillips maintains)—was exhausting.[42] Young playwright Arnold Schulman participated in the shoot and described Cukor in terms uncharacteristic of the director as most knew him: "The most he would say to an actor: 'a little lower, a little higher, a little more energy.' He was not any more interested in the psychology of the characters than he was in his own psychology."[43]

Such a reading is supported by the film's use of symbolism as shorthand for character development. Magnani plays Gioia, the sister-in-law of widowed Italian American sheep rancher Gino (Anthony Quinn). Gino brings

The mismatched family at the heart of Cukor's ethnic domestic drama *Wild Is the Wind* (1958): (from left) adopted son and love interest Bene (Anthony Franciosa), blustery husband Gino (Anthony Quinn), and "wild" second wife Gioia (Anna Magnani).

Gioia to America from Italy as a replacement for his dead wife, Rosanna, but she is the polar opposite of her sister. Where the former was domestic, obedient, and pretty, the latter is wild, opinionated, and unconcerned with her appearance. Gioia's resistance to feminine norms infuriates Gino, and the two battle loudly in every scene, complete with thick Italian accents, much like Magnani's Academy Award–winning performance in *The Rose Tattoo* (1955), though against a more formidable male character. As Gioia attempts to adapt to the world around her, she finds affinity with a pack of wild horses—which Carey perhaps justly identifies as "embarrassingly facile symbolism."[44] Above all, she does not want the horses tamed, especially after she sees Gino's adopted son Bene (Anthony Franciosa) rope and throw one to the ground for her viewing. Her extreme reaction to the restraint of the wild and free animal enflames young Bene's desire, and the two begin a torrid affair that is primarily a means of escape for Gioia.

If he does share her passionate temper, Gino does not understand Gioia's reaction to the wild horse. Nonetheless, he wants to prove himself a worthy husband, so he has the horse broken for her and bound to a cart. He gives her this domesticated gift on her birthday, with his many friends and neighbors watching. Gioia is horrified by the gesture, the final transgression that makes her decide the marriage is over. She will return to Italy and end the trauma for both of them. To create the film's ending, Schulman argued, they had to resist the cliché of having the adulterous woman die for her transgression; but for a classic Hollywood drama, however tense, they had to head for another cliché: romantic reunion.

Like the efforts to tame Judy Holliday's characters in *Born Yesterday* and *It Should Happen to You* but with a darker, more dramatic tone, the imagery and narrative trajectory of *Wild Is the Wind* is well explained through reference to gaze theory. Gino finds Gioia desirable, for she looks much like his deceased wife, her sister. But both character and actress resist passivity in every moment; this woman cannot be fixed for Gino or the viewer as the fetishized beauty, coded for *to-be-looked-at-ness*. Instead, narrative sadism must control her, particularly when her active role includes sexual transgression with young Bene. She must be punished narratively, therefore, to assure male ease. Return to stable marriage is the control mechanism 1950s Hollywood demands.

The punishment is tempered, however. With Cukor's support, Schulman created an ending in which Gino pleads for Gioia's forgiveness.

McGilligan is right to consider this a "revolutionary" gender reversal for the era.[45] To this interpretation, we can add ethnic considerations. In representing Gioia as a worthy immigrant woman who need not compromise herself completely for an American man, the film's conclusion offers a more overtly complex pleasure than *Born Yesterday* or *It Should Happen to You* but not unlike that of *Bhowani Junction*, in which the woman compromises but sets at least some of the ultimate terms of the relationship.

An additional factor for considering Gioia as the capstone figure of Cukor's 1950s films about assimilationist challenges is the immigrant character's display of assimilated competence even as she resists docility. Her ability to handle technology is placed on display, specifically through interactions with a coin-operated drink machine at the train station that delights but flummoxes her upon first encounter. She masters the machine that symbolizes America as she does her husband, the film suggests, and achieves a level of power and control hinted at but not as fully earned by her predecessors in this chapter.

Like Gladys in *It Should Happen to You*, most important to Gioia is to be recognized. She resists being conflated with both her dead sister and wild, beautiful animals. And this insistence is manifested by her assertion of her name throughout the film. She takes out no billboards, but she shouts frequently. When Gino mistakenly calls her by her sister's name, she demands, "My name is Gioia! *Gioia!* Go and make love to Rosanna in the cemetery!"

As for ethnicity and culture, the film's representation of Italian Americans rests almost entirely in stereotype. Like the fights between Billie and Harry or Gladys and Pete, Gioia and Gino bark and gesticulate, displaying class and ethnic identity as their accents fly. McGilligan decries the "shouting, screaming ethnic mismatch" between Magnani and Quinn as a "patented 'crude peasant' routine."[46] Nonetheless, both actors earned Oscar nominations for their performances, perhaps saying more about Hollywood preferences than the film itself, which earned little attention from critics or audiences at the time. Interestingly, Magnani did not in fact speak English fluently. She used what Cukor called her "marvelous ear" and accomplished skill to play English-speaking Gioia.[47]

To dig more deeply into the Hollywood-styled theme of assimilation as presented in *Wild Is the Wind*, production context is as important as text. The "difficult" Magnani fascinated Cukor; from such actresses he drew what he felt were particularly excellent performances. She was a gifted actress of Italian cinema, so he did not have to deepen or invigorate her work as he felt necessary with Ava Gardner in *Bhowani Junction*. Unlike the kind of Method acting he eschewed—which made his relationship with Method actor Tony Franciosa tense and full of mutual impatience—Magnani was a "natural." She had recently won the Academy Award for her performance in *The Rose Tattoo*, a role that she had come to America to play at Tennessee Williams's urging, after great success in Italian neorealist films and a violent severing of relations with Roberto Rossellini, who had left her for Ingrid Bergman. The US press hailed Magnani as the world's greatest actress, primarily because she was so entirely unlike Hollywood stars. She was a new phenomenon in America, in part because she was also unique in Italy "for the series of grittily realistic and unglamourized roles in which she portrayed the Italian archetype of the *popolana* (woman of the people)."[48]

Carefully choosing her roles, Magnani emphasized both an emotional realism (often read as naturalistic even when plots were melodramatic) and an ability to resist dichotomies into which women were often placed by both Hollywood and neorealist Italian cinema. For example, in *Roma cittá aperta* (*Rome Open City*, 1945), considered by many to be her greatest film, she portrays Pina, an Italian widow with a son, pregnant by a man to whom she is not married. She dies chasing her beloved—who was soon going to marry her and legitimize their baby—as he is taken away by Nazis. She is shot and falls hard, sprawled onto the ground, her stockings and underwear exposed. Then, the film heaps upon the dead Pina the cruel irony that her lover would soon be liberated by partisans. Her death is "a sacrilege and a sacrifice," and Magnani here exemplifies her facility with character types that break neat binaries between good and evil.[49]

As critic Parker Tyler explains, Magnani "has a quality none of the great glamour queens can claim: a basic womanhood that exists beyond conventional beauty of face and figure, no matter what kind of beauty be the standard. Her elegance is, in fact, without standard and of no social identity."[50] Another appeal of Magnani as concerns this chapter is that she was not seen as an outsider, as alien to American sensibilities. According to Tony Mitchell, she was "not stigmatized as 'other' in America and the English-speaking world since most male critics were at pains to demonstrate their presumed familiarity with Italian culture."[51] Moreover, she was put in immigrant roles, as seen in both *The Rose Tattoo* and *Wild Is the Wind*. Her characters are recognizable through melting-pot mythology as "white," and they share working-class American values and desires—from the need for love to the importance of freedom in spirit and body. Even if he was exhausted by the demands required to step in as an eleventh-hour replacement for Sturges, how could Cukor not be drawn to working with this powerful force, both unique and familiar, whom Arthur Knight in the New York *Saturday Review* in 1953 called "the Italian Bette Davis" and whom James Agee dubbed "the nearest thing to an absolute I have seen in films since the early Garbo movies"?[52]

This concept of an "absolute," with its mythic, universal suggestiveness, relates well to the archetype of the *popolana* that Magnani symbolized for Italian filmgoers. For her work in *The Rose Tattoo*, Magnani was even praised by *Newsweek* in terms of classical Greek tragedy, as a "Neapolitan Medusa" who "conjures up the dignity of Medea." Magnani was the symbol of Rome come to America, a land that had an enormous, successfully assimilated Italian American immigrant population and was proud to welcome her. At the same time, however, how were critics to distinguish between her effusive performance, robbed of the Roman dialect that was the "well-spring of her technique," and a "heightened form of over-acting" that rang of stereotype?[53] As Luigi Barzini Jr. stated in a piece for *Harper's Magazine* in 1957, the beloved character type Magnani adopted in America "verges on caricature and is saved only by her native genius."[54]

Taking this complex and contradictory portrait into historical context, we can see the birth of a new type of actress, as wild on-screen as she was resistant to traditional feminine norms offscreen, battling through Hollywood roles that ultimately trapped her in domesticity and the middle-class American Dream. It is not surprising that by the 1960s, Magnani's international stature had been obscured by that of Sophia Loren, against whom Magnani refused to play a mother role in either Italian or Hollywood versions of *Two Women* (the latter of which Cukor was hoping to direct after *Wild Is the Wind*). Instead, Loren, whom Cukor would soon direct in *Heller in Pink Tights* (see discussion in chapter 6), offered Hollywood a performer of "more conventional and optimistic beauty" who, along with Gina Lollobrigida, could be "more easily assimilated into stereotypes of Italian sensuality."[55] In gaze theory terms, with neither actress would the pleasures of fetishization need to yield to narrative control.

Like the tamed mustang and Gioia's return to the begging Gino at the conclusion of *Wild Is the Wind*, Magnani's later career exemplifies the compromises required by Hollywood, especially after the loss of her Italian stardom as the postwar neorealist era came to an end. In the Italian consciousness, she remains a historical icon, largely ignored by film critics. For Americans the "harshness, raucousness, and abrasiveness that made her an unconventional, problematic figure" led to a meteoric rise to stardom without clear comprehension of the context of her success.[56] Ultimately, Magnani struggled to adapt to Hollywood norms, even after the collapse of the studios. In working with this brilliant yet soon forgotten star, Cukor came as close to the unassimilable as he ever would without risking his own career. Thus, however "feminist" the ending of *Wild Is the Wind* is because Gino apologizes and offers to do better in future, the couple's reconciliation rests on gender and ethnic stereotypes that reflect almost too well the pressure to assimilate that Cukor mastered at a young age and Magnani never would.

Taken together, *Born Yesterday, It Should Happen to You*, *Bhowani Junction*, and *Wild Is the Wind* illustrate Cukor's negotiation of ethnic, race, and gender norms in Hollywood of the 1950s. Perhaps most uniquely, none of the films is a woman's film. Though the tone and style of these four pictures vary significantly—from black and white to Technicolor and from romantic comedy to epic drama—none is a "weepy." They provide pleasure in the ways they show that Cukor was invested in directing stories of (women's) self-empowerment and that, as Dan Callahan puts it, he "wasn't attracted to self-sacrifice. He subscribed to the religion of self-improvement."[57]

Conclusion

My pleasures in writing this book have been many. My approach emerged piecemeal, as I endeavored to bring diverse perspectives to Cukor's films. There are certainly some hard limits to what a critic might argue and why, but I greatly enjoyed matching multiple approaches to suggestive groups of films. I proceeded from the argument that Cukor aimed his talents at the creation of texts at the meeting point of art and entertainment, "without one drowning the other," as the director explained.[1] I have taken each film seriously as a creative endeavor that involved collaboration rather than as a simple product of a studio system over which the director had little or no control. Historical and production contexts are important, of course, and I attended to these as well. I worked by keeping in mind that Cukor did turn down films he found uninteresting (especially during the studio era), and he influenced his pictures in both overt and subtle ways.

I also enjoyed a preference for the application of diverse theoretical and critical perspectives, past and current. I do not consider film criticism (or any other form of textual or cultural criticism) to function as a one-way trajectory toward perfection in which we should dismiss the old and welcome only the new. This does not mean we do not advance as we develop new modes and methods of consideration that prove useful and exciting, both generally and within specific historical contexts. Instead, it means I find it important to utilize varied approaches in order to build and achieve readings I find engaging, convincing, and useful. So, while I worked from a generally intersectional feminist/queer approach to consider constellations of gender and sexuality inflected by race and ethnicity within the book, I endeavored to nuance this through application of gaze theory, images of women studies, masculinity studies, and celebrity studies methodologies, plus considerations of camp, drag, and gender performativity as well as queer reading strategies. To draw out my interests from within the richness of film studies, I worked with narrative studies, genre studies, formal studies, and audience studies. Thus, the reader can find within these pages thematic and narrative readings, as in chapters 1 and 9, reflecting an older and more traditional approach to film. Production context is emphasized in chapters 2 and 3. Genre studies contextualize several chapters of the book, although genre itself is not the centerpiece to any single chapter. Film style is most fully attended through my approach to film noir studies in chapter 8. And work with theories of gender performance and queerness in chapters 6 and 7 utilize recent perspectives on the pleasures that can be drawn from classical Hollywood form, style, and content.

Even within this context, of course, there are multiple films and different approaches this book has not taken up. Unlike the comprehensive scope of a collection like Pomerance and Palmer's *George Cukor: Hollywood Master*, for example, which discusses all of Cukor's films within chapters that are organized by various elements and themes, my choices are both gender-focused and personal. There is, clearly, much more to be explored. As I think about future work, I see how one might explore the relationship of Cukor and Garbo, for example, in comparison to his collaboration with Hepburn. Garbo was another "difficult" actress, and Cukor directed one of her most highly regarded performances in *Camille* (1936) and then her dreadfully disappointing final Hollywood venture only six years later, in *Two-Faced Woman* (1942). Cukor's strong opinions on the actress (e.g., that she actively chose never to formally retire, that she had enough money to live without Hollywood, that she was somewhat lazy) might be brought into the context of Hollywood actresses' voices and silences. Putting *Camille* alongside *Romeo and Juliet* (1935), by contrast, would bring potential for considering early sound-era adaptations of classic tragedies and the concept of eternal youthful beauty through female protagonists' deaths. To this pair one might add *Zaza* (1939), another tale of a transgressive woman in an ill-fated romance. Then, *Zaza* might further be explored in terms of theatricalized feminine excess when juxtaposed with the much later *Heller in Pink Tights.* The possibilities for building on what I present in this book are not infinite, but they are multiple.

In the end, I have endeavored in this volume to explore some of the many and sometimes even contradictory viewpoints from which spectators (including film and popular culture scholars) can approach and appreciate classic Hollywood cinema generally and the work of George Cukor in particular. If I have contributed in useful ways to the study of Cukor, Hollywood, cinema, ethnicity (particularly Jewishness), and/or gender and sexuality studies, I will feel this effort has been worthwhile. It has certainly been a pleasure.

Acknowledgments

Like a Cukor film, a scholarly book is in many ways a collaborative effort, even though it features a single attribution. While the ideas and the writing herein are mine, I owe much to many for the completion of this work.

Back in 2007, when I was just beginning to write about Cukor and to conceptualize an extended project on Cukor's films, I had a particularly outstanding graduate research assistant; so, after all these years: Thank you, Collin Olson. I am also grateful for the efforts of recent graduate assistant Lauren Blade. Beyond such active contributions, I have had the good fortune of an outstanding colleague in film studies, Dr. Linda Badley, who provided heartening support, always. More broadly, Middle Tennessee State University's Office of the Provost awarded me several competitive faculty research grants to support this research.

At the University Press of Kentucky, I am extremely thankful to have had editor Anne Dean Dotson in my corner. She was enthusiastic and encouraging from the very first query. Appreciation also goes to UPK's Natalie O'Neal, Ila McEntire, Janet Yoe, Pat Gonzales, and Hayward Wilkirson. Cheers, too, to R. Barton Palmer and the anonymous reviewer who offered constructive feedback and supportive words to an advanced draft of my manuscript.

On a personal level, I am entirely grateful to my encouraging, supportive family, from Chad and Lane who keep our home a loving and learning space in which to write to Dr. Helene Lawson (my mother the sociologist), who has encouraged my career from its earliest days and has always led by example. Victor Helford (my father the actor) died more than a decade ago, but we shared a love of movies, television, and theater that inspired me as a scholar, a performer, and a daughter. Dr. Larry Lawson (my stepfather the physicist and lay rabbi) also died before this volume could make it to print, but he always cheered me on. And Dr. Reid

Helford (my brother the Renaissance Man) is brilliant, kind, and never judgmental. Kate Aulbach may not be family by blood, but our close friendship from a young age has included a shared love of classic Hollywood, including several Cukor films, especially *Holiday.* I've lost count of how many times we've watched it together.

Finally, a toast to George Cukor, whose films and personal contradictions have inspired me to write, and whose family names are similar enough to mine to make this book feel like fate: his mother is Helen while mine is Helene; his father and mine are both Victor; and his sister, Elsie, has a name only a few letters away from your truly. I never got to meet him, but that's probably just as well. He might not share my interpretations of him and his work.

Notes

Introduction

Epigraph: Theodore Strauss, "Out of the Pigeonhole." *New York Times* (October 19, 1941). *George Cukor.* Reelclassics.com.

1. Gavin Lambert, *On Cukor* (New York: Putnam, 1972). See also Emanuel Levy, *George Cukor: Master of Elegance* (New York: Morrow, 1994).

2. Levy, *George Cukor: Master of Elegance*. Murray Pomerance and R. Barton Palmer, eds., introduction to *George Cukor: Hollywood Master* (Edinburgh: Edinburgh University Press, 2015).

3. Pomerance and Palmer, *George Cukor: Hollywood Master,* 9.

4. See Neal Gabler, *An Empire of Their Own: How the Jews Invented Hollywood* (New York: Random House, 1988).

5. Patrick McGilligan, *George Cukor: A Double Life* (New York: St. Martins, 1991), 8.

6. Ibid., 36.

7. Ibid., 78.

8. Ibid., 320.

9. Ibid., 120.

10. Ibid., 78.

1. The Woman's Director and Women's Friendships

1. Karen Hollinger, *In the Company of Women: Contemporary Female Friendship Films* (Minneapolis: University of Minnesota Press, 1998), 26.

2. Hollinger, *In the Company of Women,* 27.

3. Ibid., 41.

4. Molly Haskell, *From Reverence to Rape: The Treatment of Women in the Movies* (Chicago: University of Chicago Press, 1974); Jackie Stacey, *Star Gazing: Hollywood Cinema and Female Spectatorship* (New York: Routledge, 1994).

5. Laura Mulvey, "Visual Pleasure and Narrative Cinema," *Screen* 16, no. 3 (1975): 6–18; Mary Ann Doane, *The Desire to Desire: The Woman's Film of the 1940s* (Bloomington: Indiana University Press, 1987).

6. Hollinger, *In the Company of Women,* 41.

7. Levy, *George Cukor: Master of Elegance,* 68. See chapter 3 for an alternative perspective on the impact of tone softening in *The Women.*

8. Carlos Clarens, *George Cukor* (London: Secker and Warburg, 1976), 37.

9. Clarens, *George Cukor,* 37.

10. Maureen Turim, "Cukor's Tragicomedies of Marriage: *Dinner at Eight, No More Ladies, The Women,* and *The Marrying Kind,*" in *George Cukor: Hollywood Master,* ed. Murray Pomerance and R. Barton Palmer (Edinburgh: Edinburgh University Press, 2015), 18–19.

11. Turim, "Cukor's Tragicomedies of Marriage," 16.

12. James Morrison, "George Cukor's Late Style: *Justine, Travels with My Aunt,* and *Rich and Famous,*" in *George Cukor: Hollywood Master,* ed. Murray Pomerance and R. Barton Palmer (Edinburgh: Edinburgh University Press, 2015), 40.

13. See Susan J. Douglas, *Where the Girls Are: Growing Up Female with the Mass Media* (New York: Three Rivers Press, 1995), 221–224.

14. Douglas, *Where the Girls Are,* 225. Also quoted in Hollinger, *In the Company of Women,* 65.

15. Hollinger, *In the Company of Women,* 41.

16. Morrison, "George Cukor's Late Style," 40.

17. Hollinger, *In the Company of Women,* 253, n20.

18. Susan Faludi, *Backlash: The Undeclared War against American Women* (New York: Crown, 1991).

19. See Hollinger, *In the Company of Women,* 253, n20. Hollinger offers another possible reading: "Given Cukor's reputed homosexuality, the film can also be read as a disguised portrayal of gay male sexuality" (253, n21). There is danger in reading gay men as promiscuous and invested in casual sex, especially with the overtones of psychological illness, which Hollinger attributes to Liz (253, n20). Nonetheless, this reading does hint at the loss of the lightheartedness of *Girls About Town* and in the conclusion of *Our Betters,* with men as playthings. In *Rich and Famous,* more like *The Women,* men are figures to desperately cling to in order to block out the meaninglessness of single women's lives within the context of an era of antifeminist backlash.

20. Hollinger, *In the Company of Women,* 7.

21. Cukor knew this well, having had to cut parts of the scene in which Dennie Moore's flirtatious Maudie kisses Katherine Hepburn's Sylvester in 1935's *Sylvia Scarlett*; see chapter 6.

22. Alexander Doty, *Flaming Classics: Queering the Film Canon* (New York: Routledge, 2000), 89.

23. Bill Krohn, "Cukor Maudit: *Tarnished Lady, Girls About Town, Our Betters, Susan and God, Desire Me, Edward, My Son, The Model and the Marriage Broker, Let's Make Love,* and *The Chapman Report,*" in *George Cukor: Hollywood Master,* ed. Murray Pomerance and R. Barton Palmer (Edinburgh: Edinburgh University Press, 2015), 127.

24. Ibid.

25. See Krohn, "Cukor Maudit," 127.

26. Dan Callahan, "George Cukor," *Senses of Cinema* (online journal), 2004, http://sensesofcinema.com/2004/great-directors/cukor/.

27. Morrison, "George Cukor's Late Style," 42.

28. Pauline Kael, *Taking It All In* (New York: Holt, Rinehart, and Winston, 1984). Morrison, "George Cukor's Late Style," 41.

29. Morrison, "George Cukor's Late Style," 41–42.

30. Barbara Koenig Quart, "Friendship in Some Recent American Films," *Film Criticism* (December 1982): 56.

31. Postfeminism is perhaps best described as a reaction against second-wave feminism, in which individualism rather than group action determines women's place in society. The postfeminist requires neither radical social nor liberal legal action for gender equality; she just needs to demand equality on an individual basis, use her sexuality as a form of power, and/or argue that careers make women no happier than lives as housewives and mothers. Postfeminism is thus based upon access to certain cultural privileges, such as wealth, youth, and whiteness.

32. See Doty, *Flaming Classics,* 131–149, for a detailed and persuasive bisexual reading of the latter.

33. Krohn, "Cukor Maudit," 137.

34. Lambert, *On Cukor,* 140.

35. Gene D. Phillips, *George Cukor* (Boston: Twayne, 1982), 137.

2. Collaboration and Chastisement

1. Katharine Hepburn, *Me: Stories of My Life* (New York: Ballantine, 1991), 185.

2. See Dan Callahan, "George Cukor." For contrast, see Richard Lippe, "Authorship and George Cukor: A Reappraisal," *CineAction!* 21/22 (1990): 28.

3. Hepburn, *Me: Stories of My Life,* 185.

4. Sheridan Morley, *Katharine Hepburn: A Celebration* (New York: Applause Books, 1984), 41–42.

5. Morley, *Katharine Hepburn,* 42.

6. Ibid., 50.

7. For a more in-depth reading of *Sylvia Scarlett,* see chapter 6.

8. See Candace Mirza, "The Collective Spirit of Revolt: An Historical Reading of *Holiday,*" *Wide Angle* 12, no. 3 (1990): 98–116.

9. McGilligan, *George Cukor: A Double Life,* 160.

10. Quoted in ibid., 163.

11. Andrew Sarris, *You Ain't Heard Nothin' Yet: The American Talking Film, History and Memory, 1927–1949* (New York: Oxford University Press, 1998), 451.

12. Lambert, *On Cukor,* 124.

13. Haskell, *From Reverence to Rape,* 181.

14. Robert B. Ray, "The Cukor 'Problem': *David Copperfield, Holiday,* and *The Philadelphia Story,*" in *George Cukor: Hollywood Master,* ed. Murray Pomerance and R. Barton Palmer (Edinburgh: Edinburgh University Press, 2015), 74.

15. Lippe, "Authorship and George Cukor," 30.

16. Marty Roth, "Something Wild: The Fruits of Filmic Intoxication," *Dionysos* 7, no. 1 (1977): 26.

17. Ibid., 24.

18. Callahan, "George Cukor."

19. Haskell, *From Reverence to Rape,* 182.

20. Mimi Martinucci, *Feminism is Queer: The Intimate Connection between Queer and Feminist Theory* (London: Zed, 2010), 76–77.

21. Levy, *George Cukor: Master of Elegance,* 177–178.

22. Anita La Cruz, "Is 'Who Wears the Pants' an Empty Question?: Comedy and Marriage in *Adam's Rib,*" *Barcelona English Language and Literature Studies* 9 (1998): 136.

23. David Jarraway, "Cukor and Collaboration: Subjective Displacement in America's Postwar Years," *English Studies in Canada* 33, no. 3 (2007): 12.

24. La Cruz, "Is 'Who Wears the Pants' an Empty Question?" 134.

25. Clarens, *George Cukor,* 90.

26. Jarraway, "Cukor and Collaboration," 10.

27. Phillips, *George Cukor,* 89.

28. Clarens, *George Cukor,* 125–126.

3. Tone, Genre, and the Actor's Director

1. Levy, *George Cukor: Master of Elegance,* 138.

2. Ibid., 121.

3. Although the authorship of the book is shared with John Emerson (listed as lead writer), it is well known that Loos did most if not all of the writing. See Brooks E. Hefner, "'Any Chance to Be Unrefined': Film Narrative Modes in Anita Loos's Fiction," *PMLA* 125, no. 1 (2010): 118, n5.

4. John Emerson and Anita Loos, *How to Write Photoplays* (Studio City, CA: First Strike, 2015), E-book, loc. 1789.

5. Ellen Carol DuBois, "The Women, Then and Now: Remaking a Film and Recasting Roles," *Perspectives on History,* American Historical Association (March 1, 2009), n.p., https://www.historians.org/publications-and-directories/perspectives-on-history/march-2009/the-women-then-and-now-remaking-a-film-and-recasting-roles.

6. Lambert, *On Cukor,* 136–137.

7. Gary Carey, *Cukor & Co.: The Films of George Cukor and His Collaborators* (New York: Museum of Modern Art, 1971), 87.

8. See chapter 4 for more about alcoholism in Cukor's male characters.

9. Bosley Crowther, "The Capitol Presents Joan Crawford and Fredric March in 'Susan and God'—'A Bill of Divorcement' and 'Devil's Island' Are Also Seen," *New York Times* online, July 12, 1940, https://www.nytimes.com/1940/07/12/archives/the-screen-in-review-the-capitol-presents-joan-crawford-and-fredric.html.

10. See Levy, *George Cukor: Master of Elegance,* 131.

11. Bosley Crowther, "Spencer Tracy Star of 'Edward, My Son,' Based on the Play, at Radio City Music Hall," *New York Times* online, June 3, 1949, https://www.nytimes.com/1949/06/03/archives/spencer-tracy-star-of-edward-my-son-based-on-the-play-at-radio-city.html.

12. Ibid.

13. Carey, *Cukor & Co.*, 104.

14. Phillips, *George Cukor*, 80.

15. McGilligan, *George Cukor: A Double Life*, 198.

16. Ibid., 199. Perhaps the only other exception to this rule within Cukor's nearly fifty-film oeuvre is *A Bill of Divorcement* (1932), an early melodrama that served as a vehicle for John Barrymore, playing a mentally ill father. Today, the film is best remembered as Katharine Hepburn's screen debut in the role of Barrymore's devoted daughter.

17. Stella Bruzzi, *Bringing Up Daddy: Fatherhood and Masculinity in Postwar Hollywood* (London: BFI, 2005), 3.

18. *Keeper of the Flame* (1942), *Adam's Rib* (1949), *Edward, My Son* (1949), *Pat and Mike* (1952), and *The Actress* (1953).

19. Levy, *George Cukor: Master of Elegance*, 170.

20. Clarens, *George Cukor*, 82–83.

21. Ibid.

22. Krohn, "Cukor Maudit," 133.

23. Crowther, "Spencer Tracy Star of 'Edward, My Son.'"

24. Clarens, *George Cukor*, 82.

25. Bruzzi, *Bringing Up Daddy*, 1–4.

26. Ibid., 5.

27. Philip Wylie, *Generation of Vipers*, 2nd ed. (Champaign, IL; Dalkey Archive Press (1943, 1996).

28. Bruzzi, *Bringing Up Daddy*, 3.

29. Ibid., 4.

30. Raymond Borde and Étienne Chaumeton, "Towards a Definition of *Film Noir*," trans. Alain Silver, in *Film Noir Reader*, ed. Alain Silver and James Ursini (New York: Limelight, 1996), 19–24. A more complete investigation of the relevance of film noir to gender and the films of Cukor is conducted in chapter 8.

31. Charlie Keil, "George Cukor and the Case of an Actor's Director: Hepburn and/or Tracy in *Little Women*, *The Actress*, *Keeper of the Flame*, *Adam's Rib*, and *Pat and Mike*," in *George Cukor: Hollywood Master*, ed. Murray Pomerance and R. Barton Palmer (Edinburgh: Edinburgh University Press, 2015), 110–123.

32. Phillips, *George Cukor*, 80.

33. Crowther, "Spencer Tracy Star of 'Edward, My Son.'"

4. Masculinity and the Man Who Drinks

1. Roth, "Something Wild," 23.

2. Lambert, *On Cukor*, 120.

3. Roth, "Something Wild," 25.

4. Quoted in ibid.

5. An extratextual solution to the question of what cures Dexter appears in Gary L. Green's "The Author behind the Author: George Cukor and the Adaptation of *The Philadelphia Story*" in *Film and Literature: A Comparative Approach to Literature,* ed. Wendell Aycock and Michael Schoenecke (Lubbock: Texas Tech University Press, 1988), 71. Green posits that Dexter should be read, through David Ogden Stewart's screenplay of Philip Barry's play and Cukor's direction, as "the surrogate author-figure." He notes that Dexter "stays primarily in the wings or on the fringes of both the action and the actual film frame," establishing perspective and control that he carries throughout the film. In such a reading, Dexter's miraculous cure serves primarily to justify his fitness as master of ceremonies for this comedy of remarriage.

6. Callahan, "George Cukor."

7. Lambert, *On Cukor,* 118.

8. See chapter 3 for discussion of how this led to problem films, especially *Edward, My Son.*

9. Norman Denzin, *Hollywood Shot by Shot: Alcoholism in American Cinema* (New York: Aldine de Gruyter, 1991), 8.

10. Ibid., 14.

11. Ibid., 4.

12. See Ibid., 14.

13. See Ibid., 44. The author describes this type of figure, both within and beyond the Hollywood setting, as the "lonely, highly talented male," who "is seriously flawed by a compulsion to drink that interferes with his ability to work, or form lasting intimate relationships with women."

14. Lambert, *On Cukor,* 46.

15. See Phillips, *George Cukor,* 41.

16. Lambert, *On Cukor,* 49.

17. For more on the subject of naming in *A Star Is Born,* see chapter 6.

18. See Carey, *Cukor & Co.* See also Andrew Velez, introduction to *What Price Hollywood?* (New York: Frederick Ungar, 1984).

19. Carey, *Cukor & Co.,* 30.

20. Velez, introduction to *What Price Hollywood?*

21. Levy, *George Cukor: Master of Elegance,* 60.

22. McGilligan, *George Cukor: A Double Life,* 96.

23. Lambert, *On Cukor,* 53.

24. Denzin, *Hollywood Shot by Shot,* xvii n.1.

25. Clarens, *George Cukor,* 27.

26. Lambert, *On Cukor,* 47.

27. Denzin, *Hollywood Shot by Shot,* 43.

28. McGilligan, *George Cukor: A Double Life,* 96.

29. Carey, *Cukor & Co.,* 39. See also Clarens, *George Cukor,* 39, who finds the autobiographical portrayal "almost too close for comfort."

30. Lambert, *On Cukor,* 63, 65.

31. *The Men Who Made the Movies,* directed by Richard Schickel (New York: PBS, 1973). Richard Schickel, "George Cukor." In *The Men Who Made the Movies* (Chicago: Ivan R. Dee, 1975), 163–188.

32. Phillips, *George Cukor,* 41.

33. Gabler, *An Empire of Their Own.*

34. In retrospect, the reference is poignant, for Garbo herself would eschew the screen for the rest of her life after a final performance in Cukor's *Two-Faced Woman* (1941), a failed romantic comedy. Garbo spent much of her time behind the scenes fretting about aging, though she was only thirty-five at the time.

35. Denzin, *Hollywood Shot by Shot,* 48.

36. See Denzin, *Hollywood Shot by Shot,* 47.

37. Tim Armstrong, "Addiction, Electricity and Desire," in *Beyond the Pleasure Dome: Writing and Addiction from the Romantics* (Sheffield, England: Sheffield Academic Press, 1994), 141.

5. *Edelkayt*

1. See Denzin, *Hollywood Shot by Shot,* 21.

2. See Lambert, *On Cukor,* 122.

3. Clarens, *George Cukor,* 54.

4. Phillips, *George Cukor,* 72.

5. Ibid., 71.

6. Carey, *Cukor & Co.,* 73.

7. Denzin, *Hollywood Shot by Shot,* 15.

8. Thomas S. Weinberg, *Gay Men, Drinking, and Alcoholism* (Carbondale: Southern Illinois University Press, 1994), 2.

9. Roy Young, *Alcoholism and Addiction in Homosexuals: Etiology, Prevalence, and Treatment* (online article). 1995. http://www.royy.com/pap.html.

10. Mirza, "The Collective Spirit of Revolt," 99.

11. Daniel Boyarin, *Unheroic Conduct: The Rise of Heterosexuality and the Invention of the Jewish Man* (Berkeley: University of California Press, 1997), 3.

12. See Ibid., 2–6.

13. Quoted in Levy, *George Cukor: Master of Elegance,* 48.

14. Quoted in ibid., 48.

15. McGilligan, *George Cukor: A Double Life,* 72.

16. Ibid., 72.

17. Quoted in Levy, *George Cukor: Master of Elegance,* 48.

18. Ibid.

19. Elsewhere, I have explored Mike more thoroughly as a queer character, bisexually positioned between Tracy and Dexter as well as between Tracy and Liz. Elyce Rae Helford, "'A Queer Feeling When I Look at You': Gender and Sexuality in Three Films by George Cukor," *Journal of Bisexuality* 7, no. 1–2 (2007): 91–112.

20. Boyarin, *Unheroic Conduct,* 2.

6. The Theatricality of Gender and Drag Performance

This chapter is adapted from Elyce Rae Helford, "Theatricality and Female Drag in Three Films by George Cukor," *Feminist Media Studies* 14, no. 4 (2014): 593–607.

1. Judith Butler, *Gender Trouble: Feminism and the Subversion of Identity* (New York: Routledge, 1990).

2. See Elyce Rae Helford, "'A Queer Feeling When I Look at You': Gender and Sexuality in Three Films by George Cukor," *Journal of Bisexuality* 7, no. 1–2 (2007): 91–112.

3. Lesley Chow, "The Double Standard: The Twins of *Two-Faced Woman* and *Sylvia Scarlett*," *Bright Lights Film Journal* January 31, 2008, n.p., https://brightlightsfilm.com/the-double-standard-the-twins-of-two-faced-woman-and-sylvia-scarlett/#.XInGJS2ZON8.

4. Lambert, *On Cukor*, 92.

5. Haskell, *From Reverence to Rape*, 225.

6. Alexander Doty, *Making Things Perfectly Queer: Interpreting Mass Culture* (Minneapolis: University of Minnesota Press, 1993), 35.

7. Chow, "The Double Standard," n.p.

8. Compton MacKenzie, *Sylvia Scarlett* (New York: Harper and Brothers, 1918).

9. Boze Hadleigh. *Conversations with My Elders* (New York: St. Martins, 1987), 164.

10. Doty, *Making Things Perfectly Queer*, 37.

11. See chapter 9 for additional investigation the 1950s era and its impact on Cukor films with focus on issues of ethnic assimilation as they inflect gender roles and relations.

12. Richard Dyer, "*A Star Is Born* and the Construction of Authenticity," in *Stardom: Industry of Desire*, ed. Christine Gledhill (London: Routledge, 1991), 136.

13. Adrienne L. McLean, "Feeling and the Filmed Body: Judy Garland and the Kinesics of Suffering," *Film Quarterly* 55, no. 3 (2002): 7.

14. See Richard Dyer, *Heavenly Bodies: Film Stars and Society*. 2nd ed. (London: BFI, 1986). See also Adrienne L. McLean, "Feeling and the Filmed Body: Judy Garland and the Kinesics of Suffering," *Film Quarterly* 55, no. 3 (2002): 2–15.

15. Adrienne L. McLean, "Feeling and the Filmed Body: Judy Garland and the Kinesics of Suffering." *Film Quarterly* 55, no. 3 (2002): 9.

16. Brett Farmer, *Spectacular Passions: Cinema, Fantasy, Gay Male Spectatorships* (Durham, NC: Duke University Press, 2000), 86.

17. Richard Dyer, *Heavenly Bodies: Film Stars and Society*, 2nd ed. (London: BFI, 1986), 139.

18. Ibid., 168.

19. Brian Currid, "Judy Garland's American Drag," *Amerikastudien* (*American Studies*) 46, no. 1 (2001): 130–131.

20. John Gillett and David Robinson, "Conversation with George Cukor," in *George Cukor: Interviews,* ed. Robert Emmet Long (Jackson: University Press of Mississippi, 2001), 9–10.

21. Charles Higham and Joel Greenberg, "George Cukor," in *George Cukor: Interviews,* edited by Robert Emmet Long (Jackson: University Press of Mississippi, 2001), 60–61.

22. Dyer, *Heavenly Bodies,* 173.

23. McLean, "Feeling and the Filmed Body," 12–13.

24. Jane Feuer, *The Hollywood Musical,* 2nd ed. (Bloomington: Indiana University Press, 1993), 24.

25. Currid, "Judy Garland's American Drag," 131, n15.

26. Dyer, *Heavenly Bodies,* 138.

27. Richard Lippe, "Authorship and George Cukor: A Reappraisal," 33.

28. See Michael E. Grost, Review of *Heller in Pink Tights, Classic Film and Television,* MikeGrost.com. (n.d.), http://mikegrost.com/cukor.htm#Pink, and Stuart Galbraith, Review of *Heller in Pink Tights* (DVD), *DVDTalk.com.* (June 7, 2005), https://www.dvdtalk.com/reviews/16176/heller-in-pink-tights/.

29. See Levy, *George Cukor: Master of Elegance.*

30. Richard Lippe, "*Heller in Pink Tights,*" in *The Book of Westerns,* ed. Ian Cameron and Douglas Pye (New York: Continuum, 1996), 236–237.

31. For discussion of woman-as-threat in the Western, see Steve Neale, "Masculinity as Spectacle," *Screen* 24, no. 6 (1983): 2–16. Reprinted in *The Sexual Subject: A* Screen *Reader in Sexuality,* ed. M. Merck (New York: Routledge, 1992), 283–284.

32. Lambert, *On Cukor,* 236.

33. Lippe, "*Heller in Pink Tights,*" 240.

34. Levy, *George Cukor: Master of Elegance,* 251.

7. Queer Musical Excess

1. Richard Overstreet, "George Cukor," in *George Cukor: Interviews,* ed. Robert Emmet Long (Jackson, MI: University of Mississippi Press: 2001), 41.

2. Ibid.

3. Quoted in Steve Cohan, ed., *Hollywood Musicals: The* Film *Reader* (New York: Routledge, 2002), 2.

4. Overstreet, "George Cukor," 64.

5. Richard Dyer, *In the Space of a Song: The Uses of Song in Film* (New York: Routledge, 2012), 57.

6. Clarens, *George Cukor,* 104.

7. Dyer, *In the Space of a Song,* 89.

8. Robert Altman, *The American Film Musical* (Bloomington: Indiana University Press, 1987), 27.

9. Dyer, *In the Space of a Song,* 91, 94.

10. Ibid., 94. See discussion of *Adam's Rib* (1949) in chapter 2, for example, and the films discussed in chapter 9.

11. Susan Sontag, "Notes on Camp," in *A Susan Sontag Reader* (New York: Vintage, 1964, 1983), 105–120. Moe Meyer, "Reclaiming the Discourse of Camp," in *Queer Cinema: The* Film *Reader,* ed. Harry Benshoff and Sean Griffin (New York: Routledge, 2004), 141.

12. Dyer, *Heavenly Bodies,* 176.

13. Jack Babuscio, "Camp and the Gay Sensibility," in *Queer Cinema: The* Film *Reader,* ed. Harry Benshoff and Sean Griffin (New York: Routledge, 2004), 122.

14. Cohan, *Hollywood Musicals,* 103.

15. Babuscio, "Camp and the Gay Sensibility," 125.

16. Doty, *Flaming Classics,* 82.

17. Doty, *Flaming Classics,* 1–2.

18. Farmer, *Spectacular Passions,* 78–82.

19. Dyer, *In the Space of a Song,* 98–99.

20. See Levy, *George Cukor: Master of Elegance,* 241.

21. Susan Smith. *The Musical: Race, Gender and Performance* (London: Wallflower, 2005), 59.

22. Doty, *Flaming Classics,* 82.

23. Krohn, "Cukor Maudit," 134–135.

24. Ibid.

25. Doty, *Flaming Classics,* 4.

8. Race, Nation, and Gendered Noir Anxiety

1. Lambert, *On Cukor,* 186.

2. Tom Flinn, "Three Faces of Noir," in *Kings of the Bs: Working within the Hollywood System: An Anthology of Film History and Criticism,* ed. Todd McCarthy and Charles Flynn (New York: Dutton, 1973), 155.

3. Levy, *George Cukor: Master of Elegance,* 153.

4. Emanuel Levy, "Masterpieces of American Cinema: Gaslight Cukor's Superb Noir Thriller Starring Ingrid Bergman in her Oscar-Winning Role," emanuellevy.com, September 25, 2014.

5. McGilligan, *George Cukor: A Double Life,* 177.

6. Clarens, *George Cukor,* 79.

7. Lambert, *On Cukor,* 172.

8. Phillips, *George Cukor,* 49, 54.

9. Ibid., 116.

10. Christoph Huber, "George Cukor: A Master (of the) In-Between," *Cineaste* (Spring 2014): 16.

11. Paul Schrader, "Notes on *Film Noir,*" in *Film Noir Reader,* ed. Alain Silver and James Ursini (New York: Limelight, 1996), 53. A persuasive reason for the dominance of noir during this era is the war context. Sheri Chinen Biesen posits that

World War II "created a complex array of social, economic, cultural, political, technological, and creative circumstances and was, in effect, a catalyst for film noir." See Sheri Chinen Biesen, *Blackout: World War II and the Origins of Film Noir* (Baltimore, MD: Johns Hopkins University Press, 2005), 6.

12. Janey Place and Lowell Peterson, "Some Visual Motifs of *Film Noir*," in *Film Noir Reader*, ed. Alain Silver and James Ursini (New York: Limelight, 1996), 65.

13. Raymond Durgnat, "Paint It Black: The Family Tree of the *Film Noir*," in *Film Noir Reader*, ed. Alain Silver and James Ursini (New York: Limelight, 1996), 37.

14. Lippe, "Authorship and George Cukor: A Reappraisal," 32.

15. Ibid., 27.

16. Vincent Brook, *Driven to Darkness: Jewish Émigrée Directors and the Rise of Film Noir* (New Brunswick, NJ: Rutgers, 2009), 4–7.

17. Ibid., 4.

18. McGilligan, *George Cukor: A Double Life,* 6.

19. Brook, *Driven to Darkness,* 11.

20. Biesen, *Blackout,* 127.

21. Brook, *Driven to Darkness,* 14.

22. Lambert, *On Cukor,* 186.

23. Clarens, *George Cukor,* 74. Beyond Cukor's noir films, Biesen points to what she calls "an innovative pre-*noir* style" (which I would call Expressionism) in the suicide scene of *What Price Hollywood?* (1932). Biesen notes the "extreme skewed low angles, rapid cutting, slow motion, superimposed prison bars, and moody sound effects" that culminate in "a nightmare hallucination of shame and guilt as he pulls the trigger"; Biesen, *Blackout,* 19–20.

24. Brook, *Driven to Darkness,* 13, 12.

25. Kelly Oliver and Benigno Trigo, *Noir Anxiety* (Minneapolis: University of Minnesota Press, 2003), xv. Although Oliver and Trigo do not discuss Cukor's films, they do include Cukor's *A Double Life* and *Gaslight* in their noir filmography.

26. See Elyce Rae Helford, "Figuring Jewishness in George Cukor's *A Double Life*," *Jewish Film and New Media* 1 no. 2 (2013): 114–138.

27. Oliver and Trigo, *Noir Anxiety,* 1, 4.

28. Robert F. Willson Jr., "*A Double Life: Othello* as *Film Noir* Thriller," *Shakespeare on Film Newsletter* 11, no. 1 (1986): 3.

29. E. A. J. Honigmann, introduction to *Othello: The Arden Shakespeare,* 3rd ed. (London: Thompson, 2002), 20.

30. Dympna Callaghan, *Shakespeare without Women: Representing Gender and Race on the Renaissance Stage* (New York: Routledge, 2000), 76. Emphasis in original.

31. Eric Lott, "The Whiteness of Film Noir," *American Literary History* 9, no. 3 (1997): 545. Also referenced in in Oliver and Trigo, *Noir Anxiety,* 4.

32. Lott, "The Whiteness of Film Noir," 546; Oliver and Trigo, *Noir Anxiety,* 4.

33. For more on this subject and the relationship of Tony John's racial construction to Jewishness, see Helford "Figuring Jewishness in George Cukor's *A Double Life*."

34. Oliver and Trigo, *Noir Anxiety,* 5.

35. Marguerite Hailey Rippy, "All Our Othellos: Black Monsters and White Masks on the American Screen," in *Spectacular Shakespeare: Critical Theory and Popular Cinema,* ed. Courtney Lehmann and Lisa S. Starks (Madison, NJ: Fairleigh Dickinson University Press, 2002), 27.

36. Oliver and Trigo, *Noir Anxiety,* xv.

37. See Rippy, "All Our Othellos," 33.

38. Lott, "The Whiteness of Film Noir," 553. Additional discussion of Pat Kroll, particularly as related to the casting of Shelley Winters and issues of Jewishness, can be found in Helford, "Figuring Jewishness in George Cukor's *A Double Life.*"

39. Oliver and Trigo, *Noir Anxiety,* xxx.

40. See Gabler, *An Empire of Their Own.*

41. Oliver and Trigo, *Noir Anxiety,* 6.

42. Ibid., xxxi.

43. Ibid., xxx–xxxi.

44. See Lambert, *On Cukor,* 161; Levy, *George Cukor: Master of Elegance,* 143; and McGilligan, *George Cukor: A Double Life,* 164.

45. Levy, *George Cukor: Master of Elegance,* 143.

46. See, for example, Ibid., 152.

47. Oliver and Trigo, *Noir Anxiety,* xiii.

48. Ibid., xv.

49. See Oliver and Trigo, *Noir Anxiety,* xviii.

50. For more on this subject in terms of Cukor's work with Ronald Colman in *A Double Life,* see Helford, "Figuring Jewishness in George Cukor's *A Double Life.*"

51. Levy, *George Cukor: Master of Elegance,* 154.

52. Quoted in ibid., 163. William Rothman is persuasive and relevant in his description of Cukor's particular form of secularism: "If assimilating meant rejecting one set of strict rules [Orthodox Judaism], it also meant adhering to another: the rules of etiquette." William Rothman, "Hats Off for George Cukor!" in *Hollywood's Chosen People: The Jewish Experience in American Cinema,* ed. Daniel Bernardi, Murray Pomerance, and Hava Tirosh-Samuelson (Detroit, MI: Wayne State University Press, 2013), 91–110; quotation appears on 96.

53. Clarens, *George Cukor,* 80.

54. Carey, *Cukor & Co.,* 96.

55. Clarens, *George Cukor,* 77.

56. Phillips, *George Cukor,* 76.

57. Quoted in Clarens, *George Cukor,* 76.

58. Martha P. Nochimson, "George Cukor," in *Fifty Hollywood Directors,* ed. Yvonne Tasker and Susanne Leonard (New York: Routledge, 2015), 79.

59. Ibid.

60. Phillips, *George Cukor,* 77.

61. Quoted in McGilligan, *George Cukor: A Double Life,* 168.

62. Lambert, *On Cukor,* 151.

9. Ethnic Assimilation and 1950s Hollywood

1. Gabler, *An Empire of Their Own,* 15–16.

2. Ibid., 19.

3. Ibid., 12.

4. Ibid., 20, 21.

5. See Henry Bial, *Acting Jewish: Negotiating Ethnicity on the American Stage and Screen* (Ann Arbor: University of Michigan Press, 2005), 86–106.

6. Lee Carruthers, "Modulations of the Shot: The Quiet Film Style of George Cukor in *What Price Hollywood?, Born Yesterday, Sylvia Scarlett,* and *My Fair Lady,*" in *George Cukor: Hollywood Master,* ed. Murray Pomerance and R. Barton Palmer (Edinburgh: Edinburgh University Press, 2015), 81–82.

7. Scott F. Stoddart, "George Cukor's 'Take' on the Literacy Narrative: Hollywood Style," *CineAction* 50 (1990): 29, 28.

8. Clarens, *George Cukor*, 92.

9. Lambert, *On Cukor*, 124.

10. McGilligan, *George Cukor: A Double Life*, 4 n.1.

11. Ibid., 321.

12. See Henry Bial, *Acting Jewish,* 86–87, for this discussion, in which he references Streisand's appearance on the cover of *Playboy* in 1977 with the quotation "What's a nice Jewish girl like me doing on the cover of Playboy?" as signifier that she "has become a sex symbol *in spite* of her Jewishness," but that her Jewishness "somehow contributes to her sex appeal."

13. Phillips, *George Cukor,* 114.

14. Levy, *George Cukor: Master of Elegance,* 218.

15. Carey, *Cukor & Co.*, 123.

16. Clarens, *George Cukor,* 98.

17. Dominic Lennard, "Libel, Scandal, and Bad Big Names: *It Should Happen to You, Les Girls,* and *Romeo and Juliet,*" in *George Cukor: Hollywood Master,* ed. Murray Pomerance and R. Barton Palmer (Edinburgh: Edinburgh University Press, 2015), 44, 45.

18. Carey, *Cukor & Co.,* 122, 123.

19. Ibid., 122.

20. Ibid., 123.

21. Lennard, "Libel, Scandal, and Bad Big Names," 46, 47.

22. Katherine S. Woodward, "Female Naming: The Emergence of a Second Story in *It Should Happen to You,*" *Post Script: Essays in Film and the Humanities* 10, no. 2 (1991): 64, 66.

23. Mulvey, "Visual Pleasure and Narrative Cinema," 6–18. Reprinted in *Feminist Film Theory: A Reader,* ed. Sue Thornham (New York University Press, 1999), 62–63.

24. Ibid., 65.

25. Woodward, "Female Naming," 69.

26. Ibid.

27. Ibid., 71.
28. Levy, *George Cukor: Master of Elegance,* 219.
29. Ibid., 220.
30. Betty Friedan, *The Feminine Mystique* (New York: Norton), 1963.
31. Lambert, *On Cukor,* 225.
32. McGilligan, *George Cukor: A Double Life,* 242–243.
33. Lambert, *On Cukor,* 225.
34. Ibid.
35. McGilligan, *George Cukor: A Double Life,* 245.
36. Levy, *George Cukor: Master of Elegance,* 235.
37. McGilligan, *George Cukor: A Double Life,* 244.
38. See David Zurawik, *The Jews of Prime Time* (Lebanon, NH: Brandeis University Press/University Press of New England, 2003), 48–77.
39. Lambert, *On Cukor,* 226–227.
40. McGilligan, *George Cukor: A Double Life,* 253.
41. Clarens, *George Cukor,* 109.
42. McGilligan, *George Cukor: A Double Life,* 252; Levy, *George Cukor: Master of Elegance,* 247; Phillips, *George Cukor,* 121.
43. McGilligan, *George Cukor: A Double Life,* 253.
44. Carey, *Cukor & Co.,* 147.
45. McGilligan, *George Cukor: A Double Life,* 254.
46. Ibid.
47. Jeff Wise and Robert Smith, "An Interview with George Cukor," in *George Cukor: Interviews,* ed. Robert Emmet Long (Jackson: University of Mississippi Press, 2001), 90.
48. Tony Mitchell, "The Construction and Reception of Anna Magnani in Italy and the English-Speaking World, 1945–1988," *Film Criticism* 14, no. 1 (Fall 1989): 3.
49. Ibid., 4.
50. Quoted in ibid., 13.
51. Ibid., 9.
52. Quoted in ibid., 13, 9.
53. Ibid., 14.
54. Quoted in ibid., 15.
55. Ibid., 17.
56. Ibid., 18.
57. Callahan, "George Cukor."

Conclusion

1. Quoted in McGilligan, *George Cukor: A Double Life,* 11.

Selected Bibliography

Cukor Films Referenced in this Volume (directed by Cukor alone unless noted)

Adam's Rib. MGM, 1949.

Bhowani Junction. MGM, 1956.

A Bill of Divorcement. RKO, 1932.

The Blue Bird. Twentieth Century-Fox, 1976.

Born Yesterday. Columbia, 1950.

The Chapman Report. Darryl F. Zanuck Productions, 1962.

Dinner at Eight. MGM, 1933.

A Double Life. Universal, 1947.

Edward, My Son. MGM, 1949.

Gaslight. MGM, 1944.

Girls About Town. Paramount, 1931.

Heller in Pink Tights. Paramount, 1960.

Holiday. Columbia, 1938.

It Should Happen to You. Columbia, 1954.

Keeper of the Flame. MGM, 1942.

Les Girls. MGM, 1957.

Let's Make Love. Twentieth Century-Fox, 1960.

A Life of Her Own. MGM, 1950.

Little Women. RKO, 1935.

Love Among the Ruins. ABC, 1975.

My Fair Lady. Warner Brothers, 1964.

Our Betters. RKO, 1933.

The Philadelphia Story. MGM, 1940.

Rich and Famous. MGM, 1981.

Rockabye. RKO, 1932.

Royal Family of Broadway. Directed by George Cukor and Cyril Gardner. Paramount, 1930.

Something's Gotta Give. Unfinished. Twentieth Century-Fox, 1962.

A Star Is Born. Warner Brothers, 1954.

Susan and God. MGM, 1940.

Sylvia Scarlett. RKO, 1935.
Tarnished Lady. Paramount, 1931.
What Price Hollywood? RKO, 1932.
Wild Is the Wind. Paramount, 1957.
Winged Victory. Twentieth Century-Fox, 1944.
A Woman's Face. MGM, 1941.
The Women. MGM, 1939.
Zaza. Paramount, 1938.

Other Sources

Altman, Robert. *The American Film Musical.* Bloomington: Indiana University Press, 1987.

Armstrong, Tim. "Addiction, Electricity and Desire." In *Beyond the Pleasure Dome: Writing and Addiction from the Romantics,* 132–142. Sheffield, England: Sheffield Academic Press, 1994.

Babuscio, Jack. "Camp and the Gay Sensibility." In *Queer Cinema: The* Film *Reader.* Edited by Harry Benshoff and Sean Griffin. New York: Routledge, 2004.

Barthes, Roland. "The Death of the Author." In *Image/Music/Text,* 142–148. Edited and translated by Stephen Heath. New York: Hill and Wang, 1977.

Bélot, Sophie. "*Baise-Moi:* From a Political to a Social Female Friendship Film." *Studies in European Cinema* 1, no. 1 (2004): 7–17.

Bial, Henry. *Acting Jewish: Negotiating Ethnicity on the American Stage and Screen.* Ann Arbor: University of Michigan Press, 2005.

Biesen, Sheri Chinen. *Blackout: World War II and the Origins of Film Noir.* Baltimore, MD: Johns Hopkins University Press, 2005.

Borde, Raymond, and Étienne Chaumeton. "Towards a Definition of *Film Noir.*" Translated by Alain Silver. In *Film Noir Reader,* 17–25. Edited by Alain Silver and James Ursini. New York: Limelight, (1955) 1996.

Boyarin, Daniel. *Unheroic Conduct: The Rise of Heterosexuality and the Invention of the Jewish Man.* Berkeley: University of California Press, 1997.

Brook, Vincent. *Driven to Darkness: Jewish Émigré Directors and the Rise of Film Noir.* New Brunswick: Rutgers, 2009.

Bruzzi, Stella. *Bringing Up Daddy: Fatherhood and Masculinity in Postwar Hollywood.* London: BFI, 2005.

Butler, Judith. *Gender Trouble: Feminism and the Subversion of Identity.* New York: Routledge, 1990.

Callaghan, Dympna. *Shakespeare without Women: Representing Gender and Race on the Renaissance Stage.* New York: Routledge, 2000.

Callahan, Dan. "George Cukor." *Senses of Cinema* (online journal). 2004. http://sensesofcinema.com/2004/great-directors/cukor/.

Carey, Gary. *Cukor & Co.: The Films of George Cukor and His Collaborators.* New York: Museum of Modern Art, 1971.

Selected Bibliography

Carruthers, Lee. "Modulations of the Shot: The Quiet Film Style of George Cukor in *What Price Hollywood?*, *Born Yesterday*, *Sylvia Scarlett*, and *My Fair Lady*." In *George Cukor: Hollywood Master*. Edited by Murray Pomerance and R. Barton Palmer. Edinburgh: Edinburgh University Press, 2015.

Chow, Lesley. "The Double Standard: The Twins of *Two-Faced Woman* and *Sylvia Scarlett*." *Bright Lights Film Journal* (web). January 31, 2008. https://brightlightsfilm.com/the-double-standard-the-twins-of-two-faced-woman-and-sylvia-scarlett/#.XInGJS2ZON8.

Clarens, Carlos. *George Cukor*. London: Secker and Warburg, 1976.

Cohan, Steve, ed. *Hollywood Musicals: The* Film *Reader*. New York: Routledge, 2002.

Crowther, Bosley. "The Capitol Presents Joan Crawford and Fredric March in 'Susan and God'—'A Bill of Divorcement' and 'Devil's Island' Are Also Seen." *New York Times* online. July 12, 1940. https://www.nytimes.com/1940/07/12/archives/the-screen-in-review-the-capitol-presents-joan-crawford-and-fredric.html.

———. "Spencer Tracy Star of 'Edward, My Son,' Based on the Play, at Radio City Music Hall." *New York Times* online. June 3, 1949. https://www.nytimes.com/1949/06/03/archives/spencer-tracy-star-of-edward-my-son-based-on-the-play-at-radio-city.html.

Currid, Brian. "Judy Garland's American Drag." *Amerikastudien* (*American Studies*) 46, no. 1 (2001): 123–133.

Denzin, Norman. *Hollywood Shot by Shot: Alcoholism in American Cinema*. New York: Aldine de Gruyter, 1991.

Doane, Mary Ann. *The Desire to Desire: The Woman's Film of the 1940s*. Bloomington: Indiana University Press, 1987.

Doty, Alexander. *Making Things Perfectly Queer: Interpreting Mass Culture*. Minneapolis: University of Minnesota Press, 1993.

———. *Flaming Classics: Queering the Film Canon*. New York: Routledge, 2000.

Douglas, Susan J. *Where the Girls Are: Growing Up Female with the Mass Media*. New York: Three Rivers Press, 1995.

DuBois, Ellen Carol. "The Women, Then and Now: Remaking a Film and Recasting Roles." *Perspectives on History*. American Historical Association (March 1, 2009). https://www.historians.org/publications-and-directories/perspectives-on-history/march-2009/the-women-then-and-now-remaking-a-film-and-recasting-roles.

Durgnat, Raymond. "Paint It Black: The Family Tree of the *Film Noir*." In *Film Noir Reader*, 37–51. Edited by Alain Silver and James Ursini. New York: Limelight, (1970) 1996.

Dyer, Richard. *Heavenly Bodies: Film Stars and Society*. 2nd ed. London: BFI, 1986.

———. "*A Star Is Born* and the Construction of Authenticity." In *Stardom: Industry of Desire*, 132–139. Edited by Christine Gledhill. London: Routledge, 1991.

———. *In the Space of a Song: The Uses of Song in Film*. New York: Routledge, 2012.

Emerson, John, and Anita Loos. *How to Write Photoplays*. E-book. Studio City, CA: First Strike, 2015. First published 1920 by James A. McCann (New York).

Faludi, Susan. *Backlash: The Undeclared War against American Women.* New York: Crown, 1991.

Farmer, Brett. *Spectacular Passions: Cinema, Fantasy, Gay Male Spectatorships.* Durham, NC: Duke University Press, 2000.

Feuer, Jane. *The Hollywood Musical.* 2nd ed. Bloomington: Indiana University Press, 1993.

Fischer, Lucy. *Shot/Countershot: Film Tradition and Women's Cinema.* Princeton, NJ: Princeton University Press, 1989.

Flinn, Tom. "Three Faces of Noir." In *Kings of the Bs: Working within the Hollywood System: An Anthology of Film History and Criticism,* 155–164. Edited by Todd McCarthy and Charles Flynn. New York: Dutton, (1973) 1975.

Foster, Michael, and Barbara Foster. *A Dangerous Woman: The Life, Loves, and Scandals of Adah Isaacs Menken, 1835–1868, America's First Superstar.* Guilford, CT: Lyons, 2011.

Friedan, Betty. *The Feminine Mystique.* New York: Norton, 1963.

Gabler, Neal. *An Empire of Their Own: How the Jews Invented Hollywood.* New York: Random House, 1988.

Galbraith, Stuart. Review of *Heller in Pink Tights* (DVD). *DVDTalk.com,* June 7, 2005. https://www.dvdtalk.com/reviews/16176/heller-in-pink-tights/.

Gillett, John, and David Robinson. "Conversation with George Cukor." In *George Cukor Interviews,* 3–15. Edited by Robert Emmet Long. Jackson: University Press of Mississippi, 2001.

Green, Gary L. "The Author behind the Author: George Cukor and the Adaptation of *The Philadelphia Story.*" In *Film and Literature: A Comparative Approach to Literature,* 69–79. Edited by Wendell Aycock and Michael Schoenecke. Lubbock: Texas Tech University Press, 1988.

Grost, Michael E. Review of *Heller in Pink Tights. Classic Film and Television.* MikeGrost.com. (n.d.). http://mikegrost.com/cukor.htm#Pink.

Hadleigh, Boze. *Conversations with My Elders.* New York: St. Martins, 1987.

Haskell, Molly. *From Reverence to Rape: The Treatment of Women in the Movies.* Chicago: University of Chicago Press, 1974.

Hefner, Brooks E. "'Any Chance to Be Unrefined': Film Narrative Modes in Anita Loos's Fiction." *PMLA* 125, no. 1 (2010): 107–120.

Helford, Elyce Rae. "'A Queer Feeling When I Look at You': Gender and Sexuality in Three Films by George Cukor." *Journal of Bisexuality* 7, no. 1–2 (2007): 91–112.

———. "Figuring Jewishness in George Cukor's *A Double Life.*" *Jewish Film and New Media* 1 no. 2 (2013): 114–138.

———. "Theatricality and Female Drag in Three Films by George Cukor." *Feminist Media Studies* 14, no. 4 (2014): 593–607.

Hepburn, Katharine. *Me: Stories of My Life.* New York: Ballantine, 1991.

Higham, Charles, and Joel Greenberg. "George Cukor." In *George Cukor: Interviews,* 49–66. Edited by Robert Emmet Long. Jackson: University Press of Mississippi, 2001.

Hollinger, Karen. *In the Company of Women: Contemporary Female Friendship Films.* Minneapolis: University of Minnesota Press, 1998.

Honigmann, E. A. J. Introduction to *Othello: The Arden Shakespeare.* 3rd ed. London: Thompson, 2002.

Huber, Christoph. "George Cukor: A Master (of the) In-Between." *Cineaste* (Spring 2014): 14–20.

Jarraway, David. "Cukor and Collaboration: Subjective Displacement in America's Postwar Years." *English Studies in Canada* 33 no. 3 (2007): 31–65.

Kael, Pauline. *Taking It All In.* New York: Holt, Rinehart, and Winston, 1984.

Keil, Charlie. "George Cukor and the Case of an Actor's Director: Hepburn and/or Tracy in *Little Women, The Actress, Keeper of the Flame, Adam's Rib,* and *Pat and Mike.*" In *George Cukor: Hollywood Master,* 107–123. Edited by Murray Pomerance and R. Barton Palmer. Edinburgh: Edinburgh University Press, 2015.

Krohn, Bill. "Cukor Maudit: *Tarnished Lady, Girls About Town, Our Betters, Susan and God, Desire Me, Edward, My Son, The Model and the Marriage Broker, Let's Make Love,* and *The Chapman Report.*" In *George Cukor: Hollywood Master,* 124–138. Edited by Murray Pomerance and R. Barton Palmer. Edinburgh: Edinburgh University Press, 2015.

La Cruz, Anita. "Is 'Who Wears the Pants' an Empty Question?: Comedy and Marriage in *Adam's Rib.*" *Barcelona English Language and Literature Studies* 9 (1998): 133–142.

Lambert, Gavin. *On Cukor.* New York: Putnam, 1972.

Lennard, Dominic. "Libel, Scandal, and Bad Big Names: *It Should Happen to You, Les Girls,* and *Romeo and Juliet.*" In *George Cukor: Hollywood Master,* 43–59. Edited by Murray Pomerance and R. Barton Palmer. Edinburgh: Edinburgh University Press, 2015.

Levy, Emanuel. *George Cukor: Master of Elegance.* New York: Morrow, 1994.

———. "Masterpieces of American Cinema: Gaslight Cukor's Superb Noir Thriller Starring Ingrid Bergman in her Oscar-Winning Role." emanuellevy.com. September 25, 2014. https://emanuellevy.com/review/gaslight-6/.

Lippe, Richard. "Authorship and George Cukor: A Reappraisal." *CineAction!* 21/22 (1990): 21–34.

———. "*Heller in Pink Tights.*" In *The Book of Westerns,* 236–240. Edited by Ian Cameron and Douglas Pye. New York: Continuum, 1996.

Long, Robert Emmet, ed. *George Cukor: Interviews.* Jackson: University Press of Mississippi, 2001.

Loos, Anita. *Gentlemen Prefer Blondes.* New York: Liveright/Norton, 1998. First published in 1925 by Boni & Liveright (New York).

Lott, Eric. "The Whiteness of Film Noir." *American Literary History* 9, no. 3 (1997): 542–566.

Mackenzie, Compton. *Sylvia Scarlett.* New York: Harper and Brothers, 1918.

Martinucci, Mimi. *Feminism is Queer: The Intimate Connection between Queer and Feminist Theory.* London: Zed, 2010.

McGilligan, Patrick. *George Cukor: A Double Life.* New York: St. Martins, 1991.

McLean, Adrienne L. "Feeling and the Filmed Body: Judy Garland and the Kinesics of Suffering." *Film Quarterly* 55, no. 3 (2002): 2–15.

Meyer, Moe. "Reclaiming the Discourse of Camp." In *Queer Cinema: The* Film *Reader,* 137–150. Edited by Harry Benshoff and Sean Griffin. New York: Routledge, 2004.

Mirza, Candace. "The Collective Spirit of Revolt: An Historical Reading of *Holiday.*" *Wide Angle* 12, no. 3 (1990): 98–116.

Mitchell, Tony. "The Construction and Reception of Anna Magnani in Italy and the English-Speaking World, 1945–1988." *Film Criticism* 14, no. 1 (Fall 1989): 2–21.

Morley, Sheridan. *Katharine Hepburn: A Celebration.* New York: Applause Books, 1984.

Morrison, James. "George Cukor's Late Style: *Justine*, *Travels with My Aunt*, and *Rich and Famous.*" In *George Cukor: Hollywood Master.* Edited by Murray Pomerance and R. Barton Palmer. Edinburgh: Edinburgh University Press, 2015.

Mulvey, Laura. "Visual Pleasure and Narrative Cinema." *Screen* 16, no. 3 (1975): 6–18. Reprinted in *Feminist Film Theory: A Reader,* 58–69. Edited by Sue Thornham. New York: New York University Press, 1999.

Neale, Steve. "Masculinity as Spectacle." *Screen* 24, no. 6 (1983): 2–16. Reprinted in *The Sexual Subject: A* Screen *Reader in Sexuality,* 277–287. Edited by M. Merck. New York: Routledge, 1992.

Nochimson, Martha P. "George Cukor." In *Fifty Hollywood Directors,* 76–84. Edited by Yvonne Tasker and Susanne Leonard. New York: Routledge, 2015.

Oliver, Kelly, and Benigno Trigo. *Noir Anxiety.* Minneapolis: University of Minnesota Press, 2003.

Overstreet, Richard. "George Cukor." In *George Cukor: Interviews.* Edited by Robert Emmet Long. Jackson, MI: University of Mississippi Press, (1963) 2001.

Phillips, Gene D. *George Cukor.* Boston: Twayne, 1982.

Place, Janey, and Lowell Peterson. "Some Visual Motifs of *Film Noir.*" In *Film Noir Reader,* 65–76. Edited by Alain Silver and James Ursini. New York: Limelight, (1974) 1996.

Pomerance, Murray, and R. Barton Palmer. Introduction to *George Cukor: Hollywood Master,* 1–9. Edited by Murray Pomerance and R. Barton Palmer. Edinburgh: Edinburgh University Press, 2015.

Quart, Barbara Koenig. "Friendship in Some Recent American Films." *Film Criticism* (December 1982): 51–57.

Ray, Robert B. "The Cukor 'Problem': *David Copperfield*, *Holiday*, and *The Philadelphia Story.*" In *George Cukor: Hollywood Master.* Edited by Murray Pomerance and R. Barton Palmer. Edinburgh: Edinburgh University Press, 2015.

Rippy, Marguerite Hailey. "All Our Othellos: Black Monsters and White Masks on the American Screen." In *Spectacular Shakespeare: Critical Theory and Popular Cinema,* 25–46. Edited by Courtney Lehmann and Lisa S. Starks. Madison, NJ: Fairleigh Dickinson University Press, 2002.

Roth, Marty. "Something Wild: The Fruits of Filmic Intoxication." *Dionysos* 7, no. 1 (1977): 23–33.

Rothman, William. "Hats Off for George Cukor!" In *Hollywood's Chosen People: The Jewish Experience in American Cinema,* 91–110. Edited by Daniel Bernardi, Murray Pomerance, and Hava Tirosh-Samuelson. Detroit, MI: Wayne State University Press, 2013.

———. *You Ain't Heard Nothin' Yet: The American Talking Film, History and Memory, 1927–1949.* New York: Oxford University Press, 1998.

Schickel, Richard. "George Cukor." In *The Men Who Made the Movies,* 163–188. Chicago: Ivan R. Dee, 1975.

Schrader, Paul. "Notes on *Film Noir.*" In *Film Noir Reader,* 53–63. Edited by Alain Silver and James Ursini. New York: Limelight, (1972) 1996.

Smith, Susan. *The Musical: Race, Gender and Performance.* London: Wallflower, 2005.

Sontag, Susan. "Notes on Camp." In *A Susan Sontag Reader,* 105–120. New York: Vintage Books, (1964) 1983.

Stacey, Jackie. *Star Gazing: Hollywood Cinema and Female Spectatorship.* New York: Routledge, 1994.

Stoddart, Scott F. "George Cukor's 'Take' on the Literacy Narrative: Hollywood Style." *CineAction* 50 (1990): 24–31.

Strauss, Theodore. "Out of the Pigeonhole." *New York Times* (October 19, 1941). Reelclassics.com. http://www.reelclassics.com/Directors/Cukor/cukor-article.htm.

Turim, Maureen. "Cukor's Tragicomedies of Marriage: *Dinner at Eight*, *No More Ladies*, *The Women*, and *The Marrying Kind.*" In *George Cukor: Hollywood Master.* Edited by Murray Pomerance and R. Barton Palmer. Edinburgh: Edinburgh University Press, 2015.

Velez, Andrew. Introduction to *What Price Hollywood?* New York: Frederick Ungar, 1984.

Weinberg, Thomas S. *Gay Men, Drinking, and Alcoholism.* Carbondale: Southern Illinois University Press, 1994.

Willson, Robert F., Jr. "*A Double Life: Othello* as *Film Noir* Thriller." *Shakespeare on Film Newsletter* 11, no. 1 (1986): 3, 10.

Wise, Jeff, and Robert Smith. "An Interview with George Cukor." In *George Cukor: Interviews,* 81–91. Edited by Robert Emmet Long. Jackson: University of Mississippi Press, (1973) 2001.

Woodward, Katherine S. "Female Naming: The Emergence of a Second Story in *It Should Happen to You.*" *Post Script: Essays in Film and the Humanities* 10, no. 2 (1991): 64–76.

Wylie, Philip. *Generation of Vipers.* 2nd ed. Champaign, IL: Dalkey Archive Press, 1996. First published in 1943 by Farrar & Rinehart (New York).

Young, Roy. "Alcoholism and Addiction in Homosexuals: Etiology, Prevalence, and Treatment." (online article) 1995. http://www.royy.com/pap.html.

Zurawik, David. *The Jews of Prime Time.* Lebanon, NH: Brandeis University Press /University Press of New England, 2003.

Index

Page numbers in italics refer to illustrations.

Index

Index